CLASSIC TALES OF LIFE OUTDOORS

Michigan
Seasons

FEATURING STORIES AND ESSAYS BY:

Bob Butz

Tom Carney

Michael Delp

Jerry Dennis

Jack Driscoll

Ben East

Jim Enger

Dr. James W. Hall, III

Jim Harrison

Tom Huggler

Bob Linsenman

Nick Lyons

Norris McDowell

Thomas McGuane

Ann Miller

Steve Nevala

Kenneth Peterson

Ron Rau

Ernest Schwiebert

Glen Sheppard

Steve Smith

Doug Stanton

Kathleen Stocking

Matt Straw

Berrien Thorn

John Voelker

Jerry Warrington

CLASSIC TALES OF LIFE OUTDOORS

Michigan Seasons

Edited by
Ted J. Rulseh

Illustrated by
Christopher Smith

Jacket photography by
Richard T. Grost

The Cabin
Bookshelf

1234 Hickory Drive ■ Waukesha, WI 53186

MICHIGAN SEASONS
Classic Tales of Life Outdoors
Edited by Ted J. Rulseh

Publisher's Cataloging in Publication
(Prepared by Quality Books, Inc.)

Michigan seasons: classic tales of life outdoors/edited by Ted J.
    Rulseh; illustrated by Christopher Smith. — 1st ed.
    p. cm.
    ISBN: 0-9653381-3-4

    1. Hunting—Michigan—Anecdotes. 2. Fishing—Michigan—
Anecdotes. 3. Outdoor life—Michigan—Anecdotes. I. Rulseh,
Ted.

    SK33.M53 1997   799'.09774
                              QBI97-41071

Library of Congress Catalog Card Number: 97-69590

TABLE OF CONTENTS

CONTENTS, CONTINUED

FOREWORD

So, what's a Wisconsin publisher doing compiling and editing a Michigan outdoor writing anthology? Well, I can claim a bit of Michigan residency, having spent summer vacations as a kid at an Upper Peninsula lakefront cabin owned by a friend of my dad. It was a place of rustic grandeur: walls of varnished knotty pine; big screened porches front and back; a greatroom with vaulted ceiling, fieldstone fireplace and half a dozen twin and double beds lined up along one wall.

Best of all, it was five deep-woods miles from the closest town, a place where you drew ice-cold, iron-tasting water from a hand pump at the kitchen sink, where you did your bedtime reading by firelight or by the soft glow of wall-mounted kerosene lamps, where nights were so dark you could push out in a rowboat, sit on the floor, lie back against a boat cushion and watch the stars blaze.

I don't go there anymore because my dad's friend sold it — the new owner's first act was to bring in electricity, spoiling the place forever. But that was where I learned to love the outdoors, and where I encountered fine outdoor writing on the yellowing pages of sporting magazines kept on nightstands in the sitting area in front of the fireplace.

Ever since, I have admired well-told stories of hunting and fishing. A few years ago I assembled an anthology of such works by twenty-six writers from my native Wisconsin. That collection, *Harvest Moon* (Lost River Press, 1993) was a labor of love, but also a success as regional books go, and I soon began collecting more stories and essays for a second volume, and for similar books for Michigan and Minnesota. *Michigan Seasons* is the first of these to be published; the Wisconsin and Minnesota books are almost complete.

Since the three states are similar in many ways, and since hunting is hunting and fishing is fishing, you might think the three anthologies would be cookie-cutter copies, only the names and places changing. They aren't, and therein lies the magic, for me and, I hope, for readers. Each collection reflects its state's landscape and traditions and the unique styles and perspectives of more than two dozen writers.

While the variations are often subtle, a few distinguishing marks stand out. The Wisconsin anthology carries the influence of great conservationists Aldo Leopold and Frances Hammerstrom, and of national literary figures like Gordon MacQuarrie and Mel Ellis. Minnesota's collection reflects the wildness of the great expanse of Northwoods and the Boundary Waters Canoe Area, best personified by the incomparable Sigurd Olson.

Michigan's collection highlights the state's abundant trout water and people who write about trout and trout fishing with uncommon perception, beauty and wit. Michigan also has perhaps the most nationally known outdoor writers in the likes of Thomas McGuane, Jim Harrison, Ernest Schwiebert, Jerry Dennis, Tom Huggler and, of course, the late John Voelker and Ben East.

Some readers may want to argue over which state's writers are "better" than the others. If they do, they at least will have taken the time to get to know them all, and to explore each state through its outdoor literature, as I have had the abundant pleasure of doing these past three years. If work on these anthologies has taught me one thing, it is that I need to spend more time getting to know Minnesota and Michigan, and for that matter my home state. The release of these books, and the attendant marketing and promotion, may give me just the excuse I need.

Ted J. Rulseh
The Cabin Bookshelf
August 1997

Spring

"It is always a warm day
when the smelt run,
the kind of early spring day
when you hang your wash
on the line for the first
time, the kind of day when
there's not only that seagull
sound on the wind, but a
scent ... a tantalizing scent
that calls you outside
simply to sniff it."

KATHLEEN STOCKING
From "Listening for the
First Smelt Run"

GLEN SHEPPARD

Glen (Shep) Sheppard, a newspaperman for more than forty years, edits The North Woods Call, *a bi-weekly conservation journal that has covered northern Michigan since 1953. Glen worked for several newspapers before acquiring* The Call *in 1969. His passions are fly fishing, fly tying and upland bird hunting. He and Mary Lou hang out in the hardwoods on a drumlin just off Lake Michigan, between Traverse City and the Straits of Mackinac, with a bird dog and two retrievers. He is author of* Lure of the Lone Trail, *a collection of his "Ramblings" columns from* The Call, *in which the accompanying selection first appeared.*

NOT MUCH OF A CRICK

GLEN SHEPPARD

"*The little crick, which is the essence of life, gurgles, babbles and hums, challenging us to understand that we will never be as important, or as eternal, as it is, unless we contribute to its immortality.*"

You sure could say it isn't much of a crick. Where it starts in a big marshy puddle six or seven miles from Lake Michigan, a young man could leap across it here this late March afternoon. Breakup has come early. Usually in late March it is clutched by cold, snow stacked high and only beginning to churn down the banks of wood lots, cornfield and pastures. Today, it flows at mid-May levels. The snow is gone. Rain has been sparse.

Even at full breakup, or flood, it isn't a dramatic performer. There are a couple of places where it swirls down and around limestone, between cut banks. But not many people hike up from the lake's shore to discover them. Hundreds of thousands of people drive over it on US 31, intent on the bright lights of Condo City, never knowing this life exists, which is all the better.

Thousands see it loll into the big lake, just up from their campground in the state park. It looks, to city folks, kinda like a ditch there. Little do they know a person wading just off its mouth, casting flies, spoons or spinners, today could, probably, connect with a steelhead. We used to do it almost regularly, an old redbone hound and bird dog squatting on the sand bar, tails swishing as they watched us.

Back then, when salmon were new to these lakes, and before coyotes had pretty much run fox out of the country, this was one of the surest places to pick up a fox track in early winter, when they were scrounging dead salmon that littered the little crick's banks. Things change so much, in only a quarter-century. Now hundred-thousand-dollar homes dominate drumlins that drain into this waterway. Then they knew only the woodsmoke from farmhouse chimneys. Now, roads that didn't see a car or plow from first snow to mid-April are plowed and graded all winter.

And things get better, too. At steelhead time back then, in the 1960s, the banks of this fragile little creature would be trampled by people packing spears and guns. Today, a persistent fish cop has convinced them it isn't worth it. It is a challenge, breaking people of generations of bad habits. But Roger Bush has done it. Much of it by focusing on their kids, teaching them good habits, respect for their heritage. Poppa has a tough time violating that heritage if the kids hold it in high esteem. That's real law enforcement. It doesn't get your name in the paper or produce a lot of tickets. Just a lot more steelhead and a lot fewer trampled banks. It is the kind of law enforcement you can put in the bank and earn interest on for generations.

Nails, the bird dog, is back from snuffing up mice when the grouse starts clattering down in the cedar swale, toward the lake and Fisherman's Island. Rusty perks up. The big Lab probably thinks it is Kenny starting his tractor. It is a good sound. Nails squats and nods her head, the square snout straining to snort out the direction of the sound. She turns toward me, maybe asking for confirmation that a bird still survives. Sure. More than we've seen in years. Not many. But more. Why? Don't ask us, or the experts. None of us know.

We've stopped here to watch a fanned area of the crick bottom. The gravel is almost white. A steelhead has washed it clear of debris with its tail, intent on spawning. But with two busy dogs nearby there is little chance the trout will venture from under the banks to its redd. Yet, we gotta be entranced. Also gotta, sorta, wish only brook trout and lake trout still haunted these environs.

A male rose-breasted grosbeak begins his love song in the hardwoods, the first we've heard this spring. It is a wondrous melody. We're reminded of Mary Lou's threat to disinherit daughter Sherry. Sherry called to say she heard spring peepers last night, way down in Midland. Rusty Gates saw his first mayfly hatch (blue-winged olives) on the Au Sable last week.

Robins have been back for two weeks. Mary Lou spotted her first red-winged blackbirds more than a week ago. No one has reported bluebirds or swallows in these precincts, but we suspect they are scouting the nesting boxes. Mourning doves are cooing in the maples and beeches, playing cozy in the corn under the deck where turkey gobblers have been fanning their tails.

The little crick that ain't much of a crick, but is the essence of life, gurgles, babbles and hums, challenging us to understand that we will never be as important, or as eternal, as it is, unless we contribute to its immortality. We can do that only by preventing others of our breed from making it less of a crick.

Think about it. Cricks are pretty darned important to what you want to be and what you want your kids and grandkids to be. And to what you want them to remember you as having been. That includes all the cricks that ain't much as creeks go.

KATHLEEN STOCKING

Kathleen Stocking grew up in the lumber camps of the 1950s, the daughter of Leelanau lumberman Pierce Stocking. She is the author of two books of critically acclaimed essays: Lake Country, *and* Letters from the Leelanau: Essays of People and Place, *in which the accompanying selection appeared. Ms. Stocking, the single mother of three grown children, lives in Lake Leelanau, where she was recently three-year artist-in-residence under a major grant from the state arts council. She is a member of Michigan Creative Writers in the School and teaches at-risk children in the Traverse Bay Area Intermediate School District. She is the recipient of a 1997 Individual Creative Artist Award from the Arts Foundation of Michigan. She is at work on a book of millennial essays,* When All the White Horses Are in Bed.

*

From *Letters from the Leelanau*, by Kathleen Stocking, © 1990, The University of Michigan Press. Reprinted by permission.

LISTENING FOR THE FIRST SMELT RUN

KATHLEEN STOCKING

"*The smelt run is one of the first signs of spring in the north. People are glad, after a long winter, to have a sign like this. Word of the fish is spread quickly, from grocery store to bar to hardware store to post office to gas station.*"

What sixth sense lets fish know when it's time to spawn? This is the thought that crosses my mind as I think I hear the first faint sounds that tell me the smelt might be running. Not that I can actually hear the fish, for I imagine they are fairly soundless in their swimming, but I can hear the seagulls circling over Houdek's Creek, hear those cat-cry, lady-lovemaking, seagull mewling noises carried on the wind up Lake Leelanau to my house.

It is always a warm day when the smelt run, the kind of early spring day when you hang your wash on the line for the first time, the kind of day when there's not only that seagull sound on the wind, but a scent, a slightly sweet smell, of sap, of pungent old leaves, of woods relieved of a winter's worth of snow, a tantalizing scent that calls you outside to simply sniff it.

To get a feeling for the kind of day I mean, first try to picture the Leelanau Peninsula, a narrow wedge of land jutting into Lake Michigan two hundred eighty miles north of Chicago. Picture that peninsula's middle, where I live; then picture Houdek's Creek inlet, about three miles northwest of my place on inland Lake Leelanau. Then imagine a high wind, about tree level, carrying that sound.

Last year when I heard the sound of seagulls carried on the wind up the lake, I didn't know what it was. I got on my bike and followed the sound around to the other side of the lake where all the seagulls were congregated over Houdek's Creek inlet. The banks of Lake Leelanau are high and rocky here, more like places along Lake Michigan than an inland lake, and white gravel and sand lead steeply to a narrow shore. On this particular day the wind was whipping across from the west, almost visible. Whitecaps the size of chickens were scudding across Lake Leelanau's ice, blue-green waters. The seagulls were as thick as the whitecaps, only slightly smaller and in the air.

A boy was coming along the road, a boy with a baseball cap pulled down level with his eyes. Surely, I thought to myself, a boy like this would know why the seagulls were circling over Houdek's Creek inlet. As soon as the question was out of my mouth, I'd guessed the answer. The boy apparently thought the question was so dumb it wasn't worth raising his baseball cap visor to look at me. "Because the smelt are running?" I asked. The wind blew the words back at me.

"Yeah," he said then, raising his eyes just enough so he could see me but I still couldn't see him, "but probably not 'til tonight."

I knew enough not to ask how the seagulls knew the smelt were running, before they ran. I knew enough not to ask why smelt ran at night, or if the sound of the seagulls had brought him, too, to check out Houdek's Creek. I rode home with the wind at my back. Vaguely, I recalled hearing that smelt spawned in three-year cycles, swimming the Great Lakes until they returned to the same gravelly creek beds where they'd been spawned. Something about the changing water temperature in the spring or the lengthening daylight brought them back after the ice went out on the big lakes. But from there on, it was any-body's guess. They ran at different creeks at different times, any-where from late March to early May, depending on something only the smelt knew.

I remembered smelt dipping as a small child, further south on the peninsula, down near what is now a condominium complex called the Homestead near Glen Arbor but what was then just Art Huey's place. I recalled a night on the Crystal River when the smelt were running by the millions; I stood with skinny ten-year-old's legs in the slippery swarm of fish and dipped with a maca-roni strainer. That night when my husband came home from work I told him smelt were running at Houdek's Creek.

My husband and I have returned to the northern Michigan of our childhoods, after nearly thirty years away for him and half that for me. He has come back from Chicago and Indianapolis. I have come back from Ann Arbor and Manhattan. We came back because we missed the seasons, the sense of place, the people. My husband's ancestors, Ottawa Indians, had been from Harbor Springs — further north on Lake Michigan — longer than it had been Harbor Springs. He, too, remembered the annual spring smelt-dipping ritual, with people and fish thick in the cold Lake Michigan inlets.

The smelt run is one of the first signs of spring in the north. People are glad, after a long winter, to have a sign like this. Word of the fish is spread quickly, from grocery store to bar to hardware store to post office to gas station. Did the smelt wonder how we knew? I guess someone who lived close to a creek off Lake Michigan would see a few stragglers come up and then tell everyone.

And so one night, soon after the smelt ran at Houdek's Creek, they ran at Belanger's Creek. My husband went, leaving me and a sleeping baby at 2 a.m., to go stand in a cold creek. I didn't know he had gone until about 4 a.m. when I awoke to find his side of the bed cold and got up to put wood on the fire.

Belanger's Creek wasn't much, he said when he came home at gray light. A lot of so-called sports fishermen drinking and making the usual remarks about Indians at Peshawbestown a half-mile north. It was dark. He guessed they couldn't see he was Indian. He went on down to Weaver's Creek. "There was no one there but me," he said. "I looked at the lights over at Traverse City at the end of the bay. I wondered how many years it would be before the lights, I guess I mean the people, would be out as far as Weaver's Creek."

As we cleaned the fish, I wondered what I was doing taking the lives of little creatures who only hours before had been looking forward to spawning on the clean gravel. I remembered a story my sister had told me about reading a *National Geographic* to a little Inuit boy up at Frobisher Bay in Canada. "Bang," he said when they got to a picture of a baby seal. My sister had been shocked, first at him, then at herself. Of course, she realized, it was natural for him to see the seal as food and clothing and lamplight. But was it natural for me to be participating in the death of these fish? Did I need them? Or was I indulging a romantic fantasy of what I only imagined to be one of the natural rhythms of people on the planet? I was too intellectual, by far, I could see that.

"Is this milt or roe?" I asked my husband.

He looked a little piqued. He'd already told me that in his family the women (meaning his mother and four sisters) cleaned the fish, while the men (meaning him and his father) caught them. He'd gotten used to women's lib, but he hadn't bargained for cleaning fish.

"I think the yellow is the eggs," he said in the stiff voice he used to hide his feelings, "and the grayish stuff is the milt. I'm just guessing."

I didn't tell him I had found a recipe in a fancy French cookbook for raw smelt with roe dressing. I felt a little squeamish myself. It seemed to take forever to clean a pail of smelt. I couldn't imagine wanting to cook that many, let alone eat them.

The smelt were little and reminded me of goldfish. As I rolled one first in egg and then in cornmeal and fried it in hot bacon grease, my enthusiasm for smelt dipping waned. I began to wish each gutted fish was miraculously whole again and swimming in the creek. Yet I was not ready to let on about my disappointment.

"The kitchen is hot and greasy," I said with a wave of my arm at the imaginary cooking odors. "Let's eat at the picnic table outside."

We ate in the backyard under maple trees that I could imagine, but that were not, in red bud. We wore our down coats, eating the rapidly cooling smelt in blinding spring sunlight. I was aware of eating the same fish I had just cleaned. I wondered if their families were still in the creek. Somehow the whole experience of smelt dipping wasn't the way I'd remembered it. I'd remembered the excitement of the catch, the mounds of hot, delicious smelt my mother had cooked. Was it always on a Sunday? We would eat until noon.

Certainly the smelt had not changed. Rather it was I who had changed. I now saw the smelt as nuclear families. I had anthropomorphized the fish in a way that never would have occurred to my child's mind.

As I sat in the cold sunlight, it was with a sense of sadness that I realized I had been away too long, a sense of sadness perhaps my husband had felt all along. I had lived in cities too long, been away from fish too long. Perhaps the old instincts will return; the desire to dash down a cold creek in the middle of the night because the smelt might be running will seep back into my personality in the slow, imperceptible way it seeped out. I don't know. What I do know is that on a cold, sunny day in early spring last year I found out that the exploration of atavistic urges sometimes brings us up against the hard wall of our own so-called sophistication so we discover not our "roots," but the experiences that separate us from them.

ERNEST SCHWIEBERT

Ernest Schwiebert, regarded by many as one of the world's finest trout fisherman, is also a widely published fishing writer. He became a serious fisherman at age five when his first cast into a Michigan creek yielded a twelve-inch book trout. Before he was thirty, he had become a top trout angler. Since then, he has fished streams all over the world, in the process gathering material for numerous books and magazine articles. His first book, Matching the Hatch, *is considered a classic in the literature of American angling. His books of essays include* Remembrances of Rivers Past *(1972),* A River for Christmas *(1988) and* Death of a River Keeper *(1980) in which the accompanying selection first appeared. He now lives in Princeton, New Jersey.*

*

THOUGHTS IN
COLTSFOOT TIME

ERNEST SCHWIEBERT

" ometimes the lake was covered with fog, and I heard my father collect the oars and fishing tackle from the porch. Sometimes he simply disappeared into the mist, carrying his equipment down toward the dock."

It is still raining softly this morning, after several days of false spring that started the coltsfoot blooming in the sheltered places. Deer are browsing through the oaks and beeches behind the house, their coats still the somber color of winter leaves, although the snow is finally gone. Grouse are drumming in the overgrown orchard, and it is almost time for fishing.

Coltsfoot is a spare, dandelionlike flower, and as with many other wild flowers, history tells us that the coltsfoot is an alien species. It traveled across the Atlantic with our colonial forefathers, since its tiny hoof-shaped leaves were burned like incense to treat asthma and colds. Coltsfoot is found on the sheltered slopes and ravines that capture the late-winter sun, although only its bright blossoms are visible above the carpet of winter leaves this morning. Its flowers signal the weakening of winter, in spite of the bitter April weather, and in my library in these Appalachian foothills my thoughts are filled with boyhood summers in Michigan.

My first memories of fishing are there, in a simple cedar-shingle cottage among the hardwoods and pines, fifty yards above a lake that shimmered in the August sun. Lily pads filled its shallows, turning over lazily and drifting in the hot wind that smelled of orchards and cornfields farther south. Red-winged blackbirds called restlessly in the marsh. The lily pads were like the rowboats moored at the rotting dock, shifting and swinging in the wind until their stems stretched and pulled them back like anchor lines. The hot wind rose and stirred each morning, offering no relief from the weather.

The boats were poorly maintained, with peeling paint and rusting oarlocks and eyebolts. Their wrinkled seams desperately needed caulking. Moss-colored water surrounded a half-drowned bailing can in the boat that went with the cottage. The other rowboat was filled with water. Its wainscot bottom rested on the mud in the planking shadows of the pier. Its middle seat sheltered a small colony of tadpoles hiding in its anchor cord.

The hot wind dropped and died. Locusts started their harshly strident cadenzas in the trees, and the little lake was a tepid mirror at midday, its still surface marred only by the restless hunting of its clear-winged dragonflies.

My mother was sleeping in the bedroom upstairs. Our family had rented the cottage for the month, and my father planned to complete a textbook he was writing, but the fishing interrupted his daily schedule. The staccato of his typewriter on the screened porch filled our afternoon silences, and I dozed fitfully in the summer grass, thinking about the ice cream the farmer's wife made across the lake.

One morning when we went for eggs and milk, I watched the farmer's wife working with her tubs and cracked ice and salt in the springhouse. While she stopped to wipe her face, she let me wrestle with the crank of her ice cream maker.

It was a summer of sweet corn and ripe watermelon and cherries, mixed with fishing for bluegills and yellow perch and bass. But it was also a summer of poverty and poor crops, when the wheat farmers were driven from their homesteads in the high-plains states, and the dust storms soon followed. During those tragic years, my father and other college teachers were still employed. Small businessmen and major corporations and banks failed, and many factories and mills stood ominously silent. Many families in southern Michigan lost their orchards and house mortgages and farms, but that boyhood summer beside a lily-pad lake was strangely filled with riches.

It was perhaps the simple rhythms of our lives that sustained us through those Depression years, and the bass fishing was a critical part of our family rituals that summer.

My father usually awakened just before daylight, while mother still lay sleeping under the quilts, and climbed stealthily down the narrow stairs to the kitchen. Cooking smells of scrambled eggs and crumb-batter perch and sausages drifted through the cottage, and in spite of his efforts to let us sleep, there was always the grating scrape of the skillet on the wood-burning stove, mixed with the muffled clatter of cups and plates. The rich aroma of coffee lingered in the cottage long after his breakfast was finished.

Sometimes the lake was covered with fog, and I heard him collect the oars and fishing tackle from the porch. Sometimes he simply disappeared into the mist, carrying his equipment down toward the dock. It was delicious to lie there, only partially awake under the patchwork quilting listening to the familiar sounds and rituals of his embarkation. Planking creaked when he reached the pier, the lures in his tackle box rattled when he placed it into the boat, its padlock chain rattled across the eyebolts and piling and the oarlock rhythms marked his passage through the lily pads.

His fishing was a liturgy that I was still too young to share that summer, although sometimes he took me along to sample its secrets, and on those mornings I waited restlessly through breakfast with delicious shivers of anticipation.

We caught nothing those mornings, but I clearly remember the flashing handles of his reel, surrendering line as his lure arched out toward sheltering pockets in the tules and pickerelweed and lilies. Once there was a wild splash that engulfed his red-and-white plug, but the largemouth bass was not hooked, and when the summer ended it had been our only strike together. It was usually getting hot when we rowed back across the lake, and I sat happily in the boat, trailing my fingers in the water and listening to his strokes.

Textbook manuscript occupied the hours after lunch, and the rattle of his typewriter echoed across the lake. His work progressed well that summer, except for the brief disaster on the screened porch when a sudden storm scattered his pages across the wet floor. Late in the afternoons, his interest in history waned and his preoccupations ebbed, and we knew that he was thinking about the evening's sport when he started to sort through his tackle.

It was time to clean and lubricate his prized Pfleuger reel, its components lovingly collected in a saucer and sorted on the oil-cloth-covered table. The weedless spoons and tiny spinner blades and wobble plates on his lures were carefully polished. Port frogs and fresh pork-rind strips were cut with his fishing knife on a cheese board, and he patiently sharpened the nickel-plated trebles.

Supper was always early that summer, and when the shadows lengthened across the boat-pier shallows, it was time for fishing. My father gathered his equipment and loaded his boat, rowed out through the lily-pad channel, and began casting along the weedy shoreline. His fishing had its mixture of rhythms and rituals, and he seldom returned before nightfall. Sometimes it was completely dark when we heard his rowing, and I usually met him at the dock, waiting in the darkness while he secured its padlock. It was always exciting when he reached down to lift a dripping stringer of fish. There were usually two or three bass, and once we returned proudly along the path to the cottage while I held a flashlight on a six-pound largemouth.

It remains a special summer in my mind, rich with memories of swimming and bass fishing and sleeping on the porch, with the crickets and whip-poor-wills filling the night. It was a bucolic summer when my parents were still young, and mixed with such memories is a brief episode that took place on a grocery trip to Baldwin.

Our route to town crossed a trout stream, and my mother stopped the Oldsmobile just beyond the bridge when a solitary fisherman caught my eye. The little river flowed swiftly, tumbling past the timbers of the bridge, and there were mayflies dancing in the sunlight. Its riffles seemed alive over its pale bottom, where the cedar sweepers and deadfalls intercepted its glittering currents. The counterpoint of its river music filled the morning, its lyric images as sharply focused as yesterday after forty years.

The trout stream was utterly unlike the lukewarm shallows of the lake, tumbling clear and cold from the springheads in its cedar-swamp headwaters. Watercress thrived in the seepage places below the bridge, and the passage of the river only briefly touched the sunlight. Its ephemeral moments in the sun were quickly lost again in its sheltering cedars and willows. Its bright currents seemed startlingly alive there, collecting its rich palette of foliage and sunlight in its swiftly changing prisms, until their lyric threnodies seemed to promise a world of half-understood secrets.

The most pervasive memory of that summer remains the solitary fisherman working patiently upstream, the swift shallows tumbling between his legs, while the silk fly line worked its lazy rhythms in the brightness of that August morning.

It was the genesis of a lifelong odyssey in search of trout and salmon, a pilgrimage that started in Michigan, and has since carried me into the remote corners of the world. There are many happy echoes of those travels, memories embracing rivers and river people and the richly colored fish themselves, and with a cold rain misting through the black-trunked trees, thoughts of fishing and the butter-colored coltsfoot in the sheltered places help pass this season of discontent.

MATT STRAW

As a boy, Matt Straw traveled with his father to "every nook and cranny in Michigan, mostly in Ford Thunderbirds," exploring virgin forests, remote waterfalls, quaint villages and miles of sand dunes. He worked his way through night school and lunch-hour classes at the University of Michigan. He has been a teacher, editor of two college literary magazines, and a full-time reporter with a weekly in Grand Rapids. He is now an editor of The In-Fisherman *magazine and also appears on television and in radio spots for In-Fisherman and other outdoor programs. "I love nothing more than the feel of a good pair of waders and the promise of solitude on a steelhead stream, or the company of my old, battered canoe on a remote stretch of smallmouth water," he says. Matt lives in Brainerd, Minnesota, with wife Catherine Easter, son Clifton and daughter Chelsea (twins, age 11). But his heart remains "somewhere along the beaches and tributaries of Lake Michigan, which I return to and wander along at some point every year."*

RIVER OF TWO HEARTS

MATT STRAW

"$\mathcal{I}$ sat down amid the foliage hanging over the bank, my heart pounding, my hands shaking too badly to tie another knot. I was 19 going on 80, and that was my first face-to-face encounter with the wildest thing that swims. So that, I marveled, is a steelhead."

In the morning, the sun was up and the tent was starting to get hot. Nick crawled under the mosquito netting stretched across the mouth of the tent to look at the morning. The grass was wet on his hands as he came out. The sun was just up over the hill. There was the meadow, the river, and the swamp. There were birch trees in the green of the swamp.

From "Big Two-Hearted River" by Ernest Hemingway

It was early June 1974, the morning of my first acquaintance with the Two Hearted River near Newberry. It rolls north and east at a jogger's pace through a wilderness the natives call God's Country. They call it that, they say, because no one else will live there. I soon discovered why.

Fearful of what I might find outside the tent that morning, I fumbled for the zipper on the door. It had to be snowing, or worse. All night the wind had howled across Lake Superior and raged through the tiny campground like a wailing banshee. Wet snowflakes occasionally rattled my nylon shelter. My water temperature gauge, which starts at thirty-two degrees, failed to register.

Maybe this wasn't such a good call. Twelve hours earlier I was on my way to Canada. In three days, four friends would meet me at Ted Fenlon's fishing camp north of Wawa, Ontario. As I child I read Hemingway's famous Nick Adams stories, and here I was an hour away from the Two Hearted River. Suddenly, tracing Nick's footsteps along a wilderness trout stream sounded like the thing to do. And, since no one was there to defuse the starry whims of a 19-year-old, I turned west on M-28.

For the final sixteen miles, my trusty '69 Impala made its way along roads of pure sand, and through darkening tunnels of overhanging pine and oak boughs. I arrived late and set up camp in the darkness under a huge white pine. The cold kept me awake. My indulgence seemed certain to freeze me to death. Waiting restlessly for dawn, listening to my teeth rattle, I thought about Fenlon's cabins, each with its own little wood stove.

The ugly rattle of the travel alarm forced me, reluctantly, to survey my surroundings. The sun had yet to rise and it was still cold in the gray light. Freezing mists hung over the river like drapery, and fog formed a solid wall at Superior's edge.

Nick would have made flapjacks, but I didn't have the patience. I hoarded all the dry fruit and trail mix my pockets would hold, ate a quick, cold breakfast, and gathered my fishing gear. Others in the campground were still asleep, their campers and tents dark and silent, huddled little obelisks in the shadows of the towering trees. I slipped quietly out of camp and crossed the footbridge called Little Lac. Murmuring through the mist, the Two Hearted River swirled beneath me, her water dark as tea. A chill spider walked my spine.

Once across, I ascended the huge dunes that separate Superior and the Two Hearted along the last half-mile of its course. Here the world looks suspiciously like the eastern rim of Lake Michigan, denying allegiance to the surrounding Newberry moraine, with its long procession of lowlands, swamps, marshes and bogs. I rested momentarily at the top. Invisible breakers slapped at the dune's feet in the obscurity of the fog far below. Away to the south and east, gray light began sketching an outline of the landscape where the river ambled sedately through forests of hardwood and pine, skirting vast fog banks that marked the lay of the cedar swamps and wetlands. Dawn revealed a distant bend in the river, and I struck out in that direction.

The first rays of sun to penetrate the shadow-laden woodland found me several miles upstream. I pieced together a medium-light six-foot spinning rod, anxiously threaded Royal Bonnyl through the guides, and tied on a tiny snap swivel. Pushing the clip open stung the frozen tips of my fingers. I slipped the wire clip through the split ring on a small silver/gold Doctor Spoon, then unraveled waders from my pack and pulled them on, keeping one eye on the stream. Rise forms dimpled the surface in all directions.

I stepped softly into the river and kept my head low to avoid spooking any trout nearby. The tannic stain enveloped my feet and legs. The darkness of the water gave it an eerie, mysterious quality. Was this how Nick (Hemingway) felt when the cold hands of the river first clasped his ankles? Several small brookies came to hand in short order. I remembered Nick's advice: Wet your hand before touching them. Dry fingers remove the slimy membranes that shield trout against fungus and other infections. I could unhook smaller trout without touching them, simply by grabbing the spoon and twisting it under water.

As the sun began to checker the water with shadow and light, I waded up onto a sand bar on the inside of a crook in the river's course. On the downstream side, the sand bar trailed off into a deep, straight run that extended for over a hundred feet. Across the river a tangle of logs broke the current, forming an eddy at the top of the run. Beyond that a deep hardwood forest stood hushed and solemn. A kingfisher dived from his perch and skirted the surface of the river, following its course upstream. High above, an osprey circled through dissipating mists.

There was a long tug. Nick struck, and the rod came alive and bent double ... in a heavy, dangerous, steady pull.

Wading down the tail of the sand bar, I stopped with the water at my waist. I quarter cast cross-stream toward the logs, and the current carried the spoon fluttering near the bottom in a long, natural sweep. When the lure reached a point directly downstream of me, I could feel the rod tip thrum from the increased vibration as the spoon resisted the force of the current. If I held the rod out at a forty-five-degree angle, the spoon hovered just off the bottom, somewhere out in that deep run.

I raised the rod tip, then lowered it again, letting the spoon flutter back into place. I repeated the motion over and over, picturing the little spoon imitating a minnow rising with increased vibration toward the surface to feed, then dropping back into the security of the shadows near the bottom. My little trout stick snapped into an abrupt crescent, coming to life in my hands. The drag was too tight, but the line somehow held through long moments of amazement and thrashing, bucking graphite.

The thrashing stopped. Slowly, inexorably, the tension decreased. The fish was swimming toward me in a deliberate fashion, entirely uncharacteristic of a trout. A hooked trout tends to act like a canary released from a cage, bouncing off walls and crashing into windows until it tires or knocks itself silly. Not this fish. A sudden fear gripped me. It's coming after me, I thought. I backed nervously up the sand bar, staring at the spot where my line entered the tea-colored flow. My fear abated, if not my apprehension, when I spotted the wide-open maw of a huge steelhead moving slowly toward me. It passed within three feet of my legs, moving in slow motion, undulating its muscled peduncle and wide tail with just enough surge to beat the current as it swam past. It seemed to be sizing me up with an air of complete confidence.

Puzzled, I followed it up the sand bar, cautiously maintaining pressure on the line. Was he finished? Or did he just want a good look before taking me to the cleaners? Could I just beach him? Was he tired from some other struggle, or a long foray out of Lake Superior? And what was he doing here, so silver and bright, on the doorstep of June?

When I reached knee-deep water I began turning him toward shore. Between where I stood and the bank swam a thing of consummate beauty. In the glow from a beam of sunlight, his dark green and mottled back, his metallic pink lateral band and the bright silver sheen of his sides stood out against the creamy background of sand. The image wavered in opalescent swirls tumbling over the bar. The scene seemed plucked from a dreamscape. In fact, the entire struggle to that point held more elements of dream than reality. The water around him was less than two feet deep, and my spirit soared as I contemplated an easy victory over such a formidable adversary. Like a sleepwalker lost in reverie, I tried to beach that still-fresh cargo of muscle ripe from the freedom of Lake Superior.

With a ferocity and suddenness that nearly toppled me over backwards, the big rainbow jumped straight up, threw its massive head from side to side, and snapped my line like so much cobweb hanging from its jaw.

His mouth dry, his heart down, Nick reeled in. He had never seen so huge a trout. Nick's hand was shaky. The thrill had been too much. He felt vaguely, a little sick, as though it would be better to sit down. There was a heaviness, a power, not to be held.

I sat down amid the foliage hanging over the bank, my heart pounding, my hands shaking too badly to tie another knot. I was 19 going on 80, and that was my first face-to-face encounter with the wildest thing that swims. So that, I marveled, is a steelhead.

It was quite some time before I managed to tie on another spoon. At least the deep run had time to settle by the time I had gathered myself for another attempt. Funny how the teenage mind expects some sign of acknowledgment, but the world around me behaved, of course, as if nothing had happened. The hardwoods still stood, solemn and hushed. The river murmured. Occasional bird song lilted through the dense cover.

What would Nick expect? Nothing, I supposed. Rather than go home, he came here, fresh from the horrors of war, with only these woods to judge him. No guns to face. No stories to tell. Just solitude, the healing sigh of water and wood, and an occasional fish. That was all he might have expected, though we may find somewhat more than that in the pages of his story.

I made another cross-stream cast to the face of the log jam, and a decent brookie smacked the little Doctor. I led it over the sand, smiled at the sight of bright blue opalescent aureoles, twisted the hook free, and placed another cast against the wood. This time, the lure passed uneventfully through the jumble of pine logs and I let it drift, following its progress with my rod tip. At the end of the drift the lure stopped. I felt the pulse of the river beating through the flutter of that little spoon, and my own pulse began to race. Again I brought the rod tip up, then slowly dropped it, letting the spoon flutter back into place. Again. And again.

An eternity seemed to pass, marked by the mournful songs of doves. But it finally came, the strike burying my rod tip in the flow. I leaned back hard, and the little rod ached and pulsed. I'm ready, I thought, and no way is this one getting off.

The trout jumped and I changed my mind. The sight of its broad silver sides hovering in the spray of that leap is frozen forever in my mind. Memory is a funny thing, but having seen a few twenty-pound steelhead come to net by now, I have yet to see one appear so awesome, so ultimately uncatchable. It probably was not a twenty, but it might as well have been a forty. It raced downriver and my heart sank at the sound of the reel being strained to its limits. I tightened the drag. I pressed line against the blank until my fingers burned. The fish never slowed.

Finally the running stopped. There was a steady pull, then nothing. He had wrapped up on a snag and broken free. At the rate he was going, he probably reached Ontario before I collected my scattered wits and wallowed ashore. Feeling magnificently dejected, I started at my once-beloved trout stick, thinking I might as well chase sharks with a cane pole. Stouter rods were waiting in the trunk of my Impala, so I slowly flapped my way back toward camp. The alder thickets seemed harder to penetrate on this trip. So rare, I thought, to find no foot trails along such a beautiful river.

Back at camp, friendly people were eating breakfast around cozy fires. It seemed as if they all knew one another, as if the campground were the site of one big reunion. Such, I have since learned, is life in certain campgrounds. They had flapjacks, and they pried me for a story. So I ate and talked big.

For the rest of that day and all of the following, I caught only a few pan-sized trout, which served to condemn me as a liar all over the campground. My friends up in Canada never believed me, either, but I didn't care. It also didn't matter when I discovered later that Hemingway's title was largely symbolic, and perhaps purposely misleading. Nick jumped off the train at Seney, you see, which is on the Fox River, about twenty-four miles south and east of the Two Hearted.

None of it mattered, because I had been to the Two Heart, and had felt her cold embrace around my legs. Hemingway came here, too, but enjoyed better fishing on the Fox. I've visited that stream, too, camped along its shadowy course, and allowed coyotes to yelp me to sleep. Government folks, I am told, once ripped out much of the natural cover there for years so canoeists could make their way through, but later stopped to let the wild have its way with the river again. In my day, as a young man Nick's age, the Two Hearted seemed wilder. She had her own story to tell. And through many subsequent visits I have yet to hear the end of the tale.

On the morning of my departure, snaking along the trails Luce County called roads, trying to avoid getting stuck in the deeper sand, I stopped by a small bridge. The branches of oaks and maples closed together, forming a canopy over the road. A red-tailed hawk cried, and a soft breeze whispered through the jackpines. I walked out onto the bridge and looked down into the Two Heart. My eyes traced her course downstream, where the river finally bent away into the forest, out of sight. Catching a glimpse of diamond glitter on some far-off riffle, I knew that somewhere around that bend the river ran out of its natural course, into a second, parallel path, flowing deep into a realm of imagination, beating softly through meadows that haunt winter dreams.

THOMAS McGUANE

Thomas McGuane, novelist, essayist and screenwriter, lives on a ranch in Montana. His novels include Keep the Change, The Bushwacked Piano *and the National Book Award nominee* Ninety-Two in the Shade, *for which he also wrote a screenplay. His screenwriting credits also include* Rancho Deluxe *and* The Missouri Breaks. *His collection,* An Outside Chance: Classic & New Essays on Sport, *in which the accompanying selection appears, is a personal account of adventures from the Florida Keys to the Plains of Montana, and from the streams of his native Michigan to British Columbia.*

SMALL STREAMS IN MICHIGAN

THOMAS McGUANE

"*Years of casting and retrieving made it difficult to slackline a tumbling nymph — the forms of manipulation in trout fishing are always so remote — but I realized that fishing a nymph invisible under the pools and runs on a tensionless line was not inferior in magic to the dry fly.*"

The first fly rod I ever owned was eight feet of carpet beater made by a company whose cork grips were supplied by my father. My father worked for a Portuguese cork company whose owners swam at Estoril and supplied our family with innumerable objects of cork, including cork shoes, cork boxes, cork purses, and unidentified flying cork objects that my brother and I threw at each other. In our living room we had large cut-glass decanters of Burgundy, long soured; and my brother and I would have a couple of hits of that vinegar and head for the cellar to throw cork.

Everyone in our family had a huge brown fly rod with a Portuguese cork handle and identical Pflueger Medalist reels of the size used for Atlantic salmon. As I look back, I am touched by my father's attempts to bring us to sport, *en famille*.

I remember when he and my mother canoed the Pere Marquette in that early phase. Passing underneath the branches of streamside trees, my mother seized one of them in terror. The branch flexed, the canoe turned sideways in the current and began to go under. My father bellowed to let go of the branch; my mother did. The branch shot across the canoe like a longbow, taking my father across the chest and knocking him overboard.

With his weight gone, one end of the canoe rose four feet out of the water and my mother twirled downstream until my father contrived to race along a footpath and make the rescue.

When it was done, two rods with Portuguese grips were gone. The canoe was saved until the time my brother and I could use it for a toboggan in snow-filled streambeds and beat the bottom out of it.

At that time, we lived down on Lake Erie, where I conducted a mixed-bag sporting life, catching perch and rock bass on worms, some pike on daredevils, some bass on a silver spoon. In the winter, I wandered around the lake on the ice and shot crows.

But when we went up north with our Portguese cork handle fly rods, I knew the trout were there. And so I spurned worms, had a fly box and espoused purist attitudes, which, in their more mature form, nauseate folks all over.

There was a lake near the cabin, and I would paddle out upon it trailing all my fly line and a Mickey Finn streamer. Then I would paddle around the lake, trolling that fly until I caught a trout. This is about the minimum, fly-wise. But I do remember, with a certain finality, what those trout looked like lying between the canoe's varnished ribs, and how in the evening it felt to put the trout and jackknife on the dock, pull the canoe up on the beach, and clean my catch.

I don't doubt that for many fine anglers the picture of what could be, in fishing, begins with visions of worm gobs lying in dark underwater holes, the perfect booby trap. The casters I used to see, throwing surface plugs in flat arcs up under the brushy banks, made that kind of fishing seem a myth. And I even once could see the point of fishing with outriggers. But now trout seem to be everything that is smart and perfect in fish, and their taking of a floating fly or free-drifting nymph is a culmination in sport to be compared to anything. But what interests me is how I came to believe that.

I recall grouse hunting near the Pere Marquette when I was very young. It had just snowed, and I had killed one bird, which bulged warm in the back of my coat. I kicked out a few more birds in a forgotten orchard and couldn't get a shot; then walked down a hill that ended in a very small stream, perhaps two feet wide, but cut rather deeply in mossy ground. A short distance above where I stood, the stream made a pool, clear and round as a lens. In the middle of that pool, a nice brook trout held in the cold current. With a precision that still impresses me, it moved from one side to the other to intercept nymphs, always perfectly returning to its holding position in the little pool.

Not long after that, during trout season, I waded the Pere Marquette one hot day on which not a single fish was to be found. I plodded along, flicking wan, pointless casts along the bank.

The river at one point broke into channels, and one channel bulged up against a logjam, producing a kind of pool. I had always approached this place with care because trout often soared around its upper parts and if a cast could be placed very quietly on the slick bulge of water, a take often was the result. I crept up, but no trout grazed under its surface waiting for my Lady Beaverkill to parachute in.

But salvation was around the corner. The deep shadowy color of the pool seemed to hold a new glint. I stood erect. There was nothing near the top of the pool for me to spook, but clearly trout were deep in the pool, moving about enough to send their glints up.

I remembered the brookie in the minute fissure of stream when I had been grouse shooting, and I recalled how steadily he had held except to intercept a free-swimming nymph in the icy water. It occurred to me that something like that sudden lateral movement and return must be what was sending these messages to me from this large pool in the Pere Marquette.

I tied on an indeterminately colored nymph and shot a cast up to the head of the pool. The nymph dropped and sank, and the point of my floating line began its retreat back toward me at current speed. About a third of the way back, the line point stopped. I lifted and felt the weight. A couple of minutes later, I trapped a nice brown trout against the gravel at the foot of the pool with my trembling hands.

This was before I had learned the thrill of the release, of a trout darting from your open hands, or resting its weight very slightly in your palms underwater, then easing off. So three nice trout went from the pool into my creel and then, after a decent interval, into my mouth.

Anyway, the connection was complete. And even if I couldn't always put it together, I saw how it was with nymphs. Years of casting and retrieving made it difficult to slackline a tumbling nymph — the forms of manipulation in trout fishing are always so remote — but I realized that fishing a nymph invisible under the pools and runs on a tensionless line was not inferior in magic to the dry fly.

It was after that we found a long beaver pond covering many acres of ground in the dense mixed forest of pine and conifer. There were, I had heard, good-sized brook trout in the pond which had migrated down from the stream itself.

Beaver ponds are a mixed blessing, having only a few years of good fishing. Then the standing water turns sour and the size of the average fish gets smaller as his head grows proportionately larger. But this pond was only a couple of years old, with a soft bottom covered with drowned leaves.

I had some trouble locating the pond but ended up tracking its source through the cedars. It was almost evening when I got there, and huge columns of light came down through the forest. There was a good hatch of mayflies in progress along the stream, with small trout rising to them and cedar waxwings overhead hovering in the swarm.

The pond was perfect. Some dead trees stood ghostly in its middle, and the pond itself inundated small bays around the water-tolerant cedars. Best of all, big easy rises were in numerous places, slow takes that produced an actual sucking noise.

I cautiously waded for position. The pond was so smooth that I anxiously anticipated the fall of line on its surface. I had a piece of inner tube in my shirt and I used it to thoroughly straighten my leader.

Every time I moved on the soft bottom, a huge cloud of mud arose, carried behind me, and then filtered down through the beaver dam. It was a cool summer evening and I wore a flannel shirt; I shivered a little and tried to keep from looking up when one of the big rises opened on the pond.

I tied my favorite fly, the Adams, a pattern that exemplifies my indecisive nature. The Adams looks a little like all bugs. It's gray and funky and a great salesman. My fly box is mainly Adamses in about eight different sizes. In the future, I mean to be a fine streamside entomologist. I'm going to start on that when I am much too old to do any of the two thousand things I can think of that are more fun than screening insects in cold, running water.

You have a problem making a first cast on delicate water. You haven't warmed up, and it may be your most important cast. I had the advantage on this glassy pond of being able to see a number of widely separated rises, and I felt that, at worst, I could blow off one fish and still keep my act alive for one or two more.

I looked around, trying to find a place for my backcast, stripped some line and false-cast carefully until the instant a rise began to open on the surface. I threw and dropped the fly very much closer than I deserved. I poised myself not to break the light tippet on the strike, held that attitude up to the descending moment I realized the fish wasn't going to take. Another fish rose and I covered him, waited, and got no take.

I let the line lie on the water and tried to calm down. My loop was turning over clean and quiet; the leader was popping out straight. And the Adams sat cheerily on its good hackle points. I refused to believe the fish were that selective. Then I hung up a cast behind me, trying to cover a fish at too new an angle, and a lull set in.

You never know about lulls. You ask, Is it my fault? Do the trout know I'm here? Have they heard or felt my size-twelve tread on this boggy ground? Is my casting course inaccurate? Where can I buy a drink at this hour?

It was getting dark. I didn't have a fish. The rises kept appearing. I kept casting, and I never got a take. There is a metallic loss of light one feels when it is all over. You press to the end but it's kaput. I left in blackness. A warm wind came up and gave the mosquitoes new hope. I lit a cigar to keep them out of my face and trudged through the forms of the big cedars along the stream, trying not to fall. I snagged my suspenders on a bramble and snapped myself. The moon was full and I was thinking about the TV.

The next evening I was back earlier. This time I crawled to the edge of the pond with the light at my back and had a good look. The first thing I saw was the rises, as many as the night before. I remembered how they had failed to materialize and checked my excitement. As I watched, I caught a rise at the moment it opened, and saw the fish drop beneath the ring and continue cruising until it was beyond my view. The next rise I caught, I saw another cruiser, moving immediately away from the place of the rise and looking for another insect. I began to realize my error of the night before. These were cruising fish, waiting for something to pass through their observation lane. There were a good number of them traveling about the pond, hunting for food.

I retreated from my place beside the pond, circled around below the dam, and waded into my position of the night before. I tried on another Adams, but this time a rather large one. I cast it straight out into the middle of the pond and let it lie.

Rises continued to happen, picking up a little as evening advanced and as the cedar waxwings returned to wait, like me, for the hatch. My Adams floated in its same place, clearly visible to me. I could see the curves of my leader in the surface skin of the water and I waited for a trying length of time. I had to see my theory through because, like many a simple-minded sportsman, I see myself as a problem solver.

The fly dropped out of sight. I didn't respond until the ring had already started to spread, and I lifted the rod and felt the fish. The trout darted off in a half-dozen chugging didos in the dark water over drowned leaves. I landed him a moment later, a brook trout of a solid pound. I studied him a moment and thought what a bright, lissome, perfect fish this little American char is.

Brook trout are cheerfully colored in deep reds, grays and blues, with ivory leading edges and deep, moony spots on their fins. They are called squaretails elsewhere, after the clear graphics of the profile. I reached in for my Adams and felt the small teeth roughen the first knuckles of my thumb and forefinger. Then I let him go. He sank to the leaves at my feet, thought for a minute, and made off.

I rinsed the fly carefully. That long float required a well-dried fly. Then I false-cast the fly a moment to dry it, applied some Mucilin dressing, which I kept smeared on the back of my left hand, and cast again. This time I stared at the fly for ten or fifteen minutes, long enough to notice the Adams changing its waterline. But then it sank suddenly and I had another fish.

Since casting was nearly eliminated from this episode, the fishing did not seem fast. But at the end of a couple of hours, I had taken seven fish. The takes were all solid, confident and deep. I released all the fish, and by the time I had hiked out of the boggy forest that night, I could feel glory all around me.

It would be one thing to say pragmatically that in still or nearly still waters, feeding trout cruise, and that in streams and rivers they tend to take a feeding lane and watch a panel of moving water overhead, elevating to eat when something passes, and that the repeated rises of a holding trout in a stream are as unlike the disparate rises of my beaver pond as they are unlike the deep glintings of nymphing trout. But the fact is, these episodes are remembered as complete dramatic entities, whose real function, finally, is to be savored. It is fine, of course, to escalate them toward further successes, but in the end, angling has nothing whatsoever to do with success.

Nevertheless, by the time the aforementioned had been met and dealt with, I had come to think of myself as a pretty smart fisherman. I had a six-cylinder black Ford, a mahogany tackle box, two split cane rods and Adamses in eight sizes. I had cheap, clean lodgings within quick reach of the Pigeon, Black and Sturgeon rivers, where you ate decently prepared food with the owner, one or two other fishermen, and perhaps a young salesman with a line of practical shoes and perhaps a Ford like mine.

From here, I'd pick a stretch of the Pigeon or Black for the early fishing, and wade the oxbow between the railroad bridges on the Sturgeon in the afternoon. Then in the evening I'd head for a wooden bridge over the Sturgeon near Wolverine.

Below the bridge was a large pool deeply surrounded by brush and inhabited by nocturnal brown trout. A sandy bottom shelved off into the undercut banks and it was a rarity to find a feeding fish here in the daytime. But shortly after dinnertime in the summer, when the hatches seemed to come, the trout would venture out into the open pool and feed with greater boldness.

I stood on the bridge itself and rigged my rod with a relatively short, heavy leader; the fish were not leader-shy this late. And I tied on a fly known locally as a "caddis," though it was anything but an actual caddis. This was a huge, four-winged fly with a crosshatched deer-hair body. Lying in your open hand, it covered the palm, and when you cast it, the wings made a turbulent noise like a bat passing your ear.

The trout liked it real well.

What I appreciated was that I could fish from this wooden bridge in the black of night without fear of falling in a hole, filling my waders and passing on. I'd cast that big baby until two or three in the morning, guessing at the rate at which I should retrieve to keep up with the fly backing down on the current toward me. I had to strike by sound every rise I heard. Five out of six rises I struck would just snatch the fly and line into a heap at my feet. But that one out of six would be solid to a trout, and some of those trout were big by small-stream standards.

Finally, something would end the fishing, an especially baleful frog in the swamp, a screech owl or a train a couple of miles away, and I'd reel up for the evening. I'd take my trout and lay them in the headlights of the Ford and think how sweet it was. Then I'd clean them with my pocketknife, slitting them to the vent, separating the gills at the point of the jaw, and shucking those fastidious entrails; I'd run out the black blood along the spine with my thumbnail so it wouldn't change their flavor, restack them in the creel, and head back to my lodgings.

———————————

The first time I met my wife's grandfather I was twenty and a full-blown trout snob. Pomp, as he was called, was a gifted bait fisherman, and he took the position that I fly-fished because I didn't want to get worms on my hands.

Pomp and his wife lived near Kaleva, Michigan, which is one of the numerous Finnish communities in the state. They had a cabin overlooking Bear Creek on a small piece of ground next to a gradually approaching gravel pit. And they lived a through-the-looking-glass life, to which we all tried to annex ourselves.

My wife had a better line on the situation than I. She had simmered in a jungle hammock with her grandparents, helped bake pies for the raccoons, been accidentally locked in the sauna of the neighbor's farm, now abandoned, with nothing inside but a moth-eaten Korean War infantry uniform.

Moreover, she could report to me the kind of trout fishing Pomp was capable of — upstream bait fishing, the deadliest in the right hands. He had great hands. Secondly, he belonged to that category of sportsmen who will stop at nothing.

Bear Creek ran through a large corrugated culvert under a country road. Pomp had located a very large trout living there, a spotted brute that finned forward in the evening to feed in the pool at the upstream end of the culvert. How he knew about that trout, I can't say, but for sure he knew about it by indirection. He had great instincts about trout, much envied by the locals. Pomp was from farther south in Michigan; and even among the old-timers, there was competition about who was from farther north than who. Now it has become a perfect frenzy as the footloose Michigander wages the war of roots with fellow cottage builders.

Anyway, he crept up and hooked the thing and quickly discovered it was bigger than he suspected. The trout fought its way down the culvert. At the far end it would be a lost cause; the line would be cut through by the culvert itself. I was a fly-fisherman, new to Pomp's world, when I first heard this story; and I confess that I reached this point in the narrative without beginning to see how I would have landed the fish. But Pomp had a solution.

He had his wife lie across the far end of the culvert. He fought the fish to a standstill inside the pipe and landed it. As I say, this was early in our experience together; and the reader will remember that it was his opinion that I fished with flies in order to keep from touching worms.

Heretofore, I had hoped to outfish him in our already burgeoning, if covert, competition. But his emplacement of his wife at the far end of the culvert in order to beat that trout — well, it showed me what I was up against.

And, in fact, as a bit of pleasant foreshortening, I ought to say that he consistently outfished me, all along, right through the year of his death, the news of which came as usual in some pointless city, by telephone.

I had accumulated some ways of taking trout, above and below the surface. We would start at dawn with shots of bourbon from the refrigerator, cold to take away its edge in the morning. Then trout, potatoes and eggs for breakfast, during which Pomp would describe to me and my fly-fishing brother-in-law the hopelessness of our plight and the cleanliness of worms.

Then on into the day, fishing, principally, the Betsie, the Bear and the Little Manistee rivers. Usually, we ended on the Bear, below the cabin, and it was then, during the evening hatch, that I hoped to even my morbidly reduced score.

The day I'm thinking of was in August, when the trout were down deep where only Pomp could reason with them. I dutifully cast my flies up into the brilliant light hour after hour and had, for my pains, a few small fish. Pomp had a lot more. And his were bigger, having sent their smaller, more gullible friends to the surface for my flies.

But, by late afternoon, summer rain clouds had begun to build, higher and blacker, and finally startling cracks of thunder commenced. We were scattered along the banks of the Bear, and as the storm built, I knew Pomp would head for the cabin. I started that way, too, but as I passed the lower bridge pool, I saw trout rising everywhere. I stopped to make a cast and promptly caught a trout. By the time I'd landed it, the trees were bowing and surging, and casting was simply a question of rolling the line downwind onto the pool. The lightning was literally blasting into the forest, and I was suddenly cold from the wind-driven rain. But the trout were rising with still more intensity.

When I was a child, I heard that a man was killed by lightning that ran down the drainspout of a bus station. And ever since then, lightning has had a primordial power to scare me. I kept casting, struck, misstruck, and landed trout, while the electric demon raced around those Michigan woods.

I knew Pomp was in the cabin. Probably had a cigar and was watching the water stream from the corner of the roof. Something would be baking. But I meant to hang in there until I limited out. Well, I didn't. The storm stopped abruptly and the universe was full of ozone and new light and I was ready for the cabin.

Outside the cabin, there was a wooden table next to a continuously flowing well, where we cleaned our trout. The overflow ran down the hill to the Bear, and when we cleaned the trout, we chucked the insides down the hill for the raccoons. I laid my trout on the table and went in to get Pomp.

Pomp came out and said, "What do you know about that?"

NICK LYONS

Nick Lyons began to fish "before memory," at his grandfather's hotel in a remote corner of the Catskill Mountains. Though he has lived mostly in cities, fishing has remained the center of his life. While studying for his Ph. D. in English literature at the University of Michigan in Ann Arbor, he took a number of trips to the Au Sable River, and there lost his heart to fly fishing. Nick heads Lyons & Burford Publishers, New York, N.Y., specializing in fly fishing, outdoors, nature and sports books. He has written eighteen books of his own, mostly on fly fishing, but also "one on Sony Corporation, one on an obscure New England poet, and several others on this and that." His column has appeared on the last page of Fly Fisherman *magazine for twenty-five years, and his essays and articles have appeared in* Field & Stream, Outdoor Life, Harper's, The New York Times, The Michigan Quarterly Review, *and widely elsewhere. He recently wrote an article on the* Fox River *in Michigan's Upper Peninsula for* National Geographic. *Nick is married to the painter Mari Lyons, who has done cover paintings for his last four books. His four children, now grown, "are writers and teachers, with one literary agent thrown in to look after the others."*

From *A Flyfisher's World* by Nick Lyons, copyright © 1996 by Nick Lyons. Used by permission of Grove/Atlantic, Inc.

AU SABLE APOCALYPSE

NICK LYONS

"My eye picked up the yellow fly the other angler had cast, and I watched it float a dozen feet, smoothly, pertly bounding up and down on the surface. Then, dramatically, it disappeared ..."

Soon after we were married, my wife and I moved to Michigan; I to start graduate studies in Ann Arbor, Mari to study at the Cranbook Academy. We first lived in Pontiac — in the kitchen area of a huge, decaying mansion where it got so cold that first winter that a cup of coffee left on the table overnight froze solid. When our first son was born, we moved to Ann Arbor. Marrying, fathering and studying were each full-time occupations, and for more than a year I fished not at all. Soon afterward, we had a second child, and for a while I was so preoccupied that I even stopped *thinking* about fishing.

But you cannot hide fire in the straw. When I passed my oral exams, I begged for a rest and we all headed upcountry to the Au Sable River. I owned a white glass fly rod then and knew just enough about using it to avoid threading the line through the keeper ring. I had practiced casting on basketball courts and ponds, and I had caught bluegills — though never a trout — on a fly. I had to face it: I was lousy with a fly rod and didn't think I could catch a fish with one. Mostly, I used a Mitchell spinning reel and a C.P. Swing, the ultimate in simplicity and killing power, for all occasions.

We found a cheap motel near Grayling, had a noisy family dinner, and in the morning I sneaked out at about 5 a.m. and fished with my spinning outfit. It was late in April and quite cold. The water was a bit discolored, but clearing. I cast my spinner in against the famous "sweepers," into the heads of big bend pools, and by 8 a.m. had taken five or six good browns. It had been a very pleasant morning and I'd enjoyed this new river very much, and it felt terrific being on the water again.

We had a leisurely breakfast, and I asked Mari what she would like to do. I'd taken some fish and wasn't in any particular fever to fish again, at least not for a few more hours. I could be generous.

There really wasn't much to do on a drizzly late-April day in Grayling with two infants, so we ended up taking a drive. It ended (as have so many since) on a bridge over a beautiful river. It was still chilly, so Mari stayed in the car with the kids. I said I'd be back in a few minutes. The water had cleared a bit. It was a gorgeous stream, with deadfalls, overhanging willows, bright runs and riffles. You could see the bottom now, and I even thought I saw several auburn shapes upstream by a large boulder. I can't swear to it, though. I often imagine fish.

Farther upstream, a fly fisher was wading out from the right bank, stripping line from his reel, watching the route of the current along the far bank. He had on a large streamer, and moments later he was casting it with great authority against the bank and fishing it downstream toward me. It was a pleasant, rhythmic sight, and I must have lost my sense of time before I heard Mari call out from our parked car beyond the bridge.

I thought she might be upset, but when I got to the car, she laughed and said I'd looked as if I was enjoying myself, the children were asleep, and she'd gotten into a good book, so why didn't I take out my rod and fish, which is what we'd come upstate to do. In the trunk of the car, I saw the white fly rod lying to one side without a case, its Pflueger Medalist reel fastened to the handle. And I knew I had a plastic box full of flies in my canvas tackle bag. Why not? I'd caught some trout, the angler above the bridge looked as though he knew what he was doing, and the sight of water already had made me itchy to get into my hip boots. So I rigged up, kissed Mari goodbye, skipped to the bridge to watch the fly fisher for a moment, then headed downstream a hundred yards.

For a half-hour, I flailed away crudely, slapping the water behind me, ending my casts with big, flopping loops halfway to where I wanted them to be. Though I waded upstream, I remember casting across the downstream with a streamer, imitating the spin fishing techniques I knew so well. But my casts were hopelessly short, and the harder I cast, the shorter they fell. The movements of the current that I had exploited well with my spinning rod now perplexed me as it ramrodded the bulky fly line and sent my fly scuttling in odd directions. I did not feel my fly was any threat whatsoever to trout.

Above me, I saw the fly fisher take two trout and release them. Then, at the bridge, he changed the spool on his reel, tied on a new fly, and began to fish upstream. I now was close enough to see that his fly floated. And I also was observant enough to notice there were now some pale, yellowish flies coming up out of the water, a few fluttering just above it while others rode the current downstream.

I felt my hands tremble.

Clipping off my streamer, I rummaged through my fly box for a yellow fly. The best I could find was a battered Lady Beaverkill with a gray and yellow egg sac. I tied this onto the heavy leader I had been using. Leaving the river, I climbed back onto the bridge just in time to witness an event I had not seen before: a trout take a dry fly. My eye picked up the yellow fly the other angler had cast, and I watched it float a dozen feet, smoothly, pertly bounding up and down on the surface. Then, dramatically, it disappeared in a boil much like bluegills made when they took my flies. It was a decent brown, about thirteen inches, and soon he had it in his net, then returned it to the river.

Now my whole body started to tremble. Is that all there was to it? I fiercely wanted to try this, and when the angler waved to me that he was leaving the river, I scooted down the bank, took up a position near where he had been, and again began flailing away. Nothing. My casts slapped the water, and the fly dragged as soon as it landed. It was hopeless, and worse, frustrating beyond measure.

Finally, I breathed deeply, brought in my line and decided simply to watch. There were still a few flies floating about and an occasional rise. A bit below me and near the bank, a series of rises caught my attention. They always were within a four-foot circle, and when I inched downriver, I could see a big brown lolling just beneath the surface.

There had been some sun, but it now was gone and the drizzle had started again. I was tempted to go back to the car and get my spinning rod, which would make short work of this trout, but instead I kept inching downstream until I was parallel to the fish. Then I crept toward it as far as I dared, then a little more, and cold water came over the tops of my hip boots. That didn't matter. I looked at the bedraggled Lady Beaverkill and my thick leader and decided I needed a lighter connection. I found some four-pound-test spinning line and tied it on with three or four overhand knots, since that knot and the clinch knot were all I knew.

On my fourth cast, the fish came a foot upstream and took the fly at the surface in a rush. I struck, and the knot broke. It was a remarkable moment — electric, vivid, unforgettable — and eventually it changed my life. I fished for an hour after that, using the heavy leader, fishing myself into a fast and hopeless frenzy. Of course, I raised nothing. By this time, the rain was quite hard, the water roiled, and after I had seen no flies or rises for ten minutes, I headed back to the car, soaked and shivering.

"You should have seen that fish come up," I started to say as I neared the car. Then I stopped. The children were howling, and Mari — who had been alone with them in the car for hours — was crying bitterly.

It rained throughout our four-hour trip back to Ann Arbor, which was one of stony silences punctuated by muffled crying and the howls of infants, who could feel the tension. I had visions of a marriage slipping pertly downstream. I also kept seeing that trout rising and taking my Lady Beaverkill, and I dreamed of other trout in a world of which I had been given the briefest glimpse.

We soon moved back East and never again lived in places where coffee froze at night, or near enough, in my mind, to rivers. But now, thirty years later, I have the same wife, and we've made our fish truces, and four children, who have grown and mostly do not fish, and I am still trying to get a full look at that world I glimpsed one rainy day on the Au Sable when a trout rose — with astonishing power and grace — to my fly, and changed my life forever.

DOUG STANTON

Journalist and author Doug Stanton lives in Lake Ann, Michigan, with his wife Anne Stanton, a son and a daughter. Anne Stanton is a reporter, "who can expertly read a magazine and paddle a canoe at the same time, which is how we met; she paddled and read, I fished." Doug writes profiles, political and travel pieces and essays, and his work has taken him to Tierra Del Fuego, the Bahamas, Costa Rica, Chaipas, Mexico and Central Park. "I've had more fun lately bass fishing with my son in a tiny lake near our defunct farm in northern Michigan than I did in Costa Rica or Argentina." He holds a Master of Fine Arts degree from the Iowa Writers Workshop, and his work has been translated and reprinted in anthologies. He writes regularly for Esquire, Outside *and* Men's Journal *and is a contributing editor for* Sports Afield.

❧

SMILE OF THE LIVING

DOUG STANTON

"*Everywhere you look around this town there are things you know, places you fished or hunted, and where your grandparents fished and hunted, and now these are places you take your young son with your wife.*"

Where I lived in Louisiana, you could crash your golf cart into a magnolia tree and run across the street and rip a window off your buddy's ex-wife's house and use it to sieve the glass chunks from your Thermos bottle of gin and tonics broken in the crash. That kind of thing. It was no place to raise a family, unless you wore a helmet. It was the last stop on a ten-year parade which also ran through Massachusetts, Vermont, New York, Oregon, Maine and Iowa, places I lived because of jobs, school or the exhilarating, wind-in-your-mouth feeling of being young and not knowing who you are.

So I moved back here to Traverse City where I'd grown up, where, in the back of my mind, I always thought I was living, a ghost life, during the ten years' absence. It was strange. A country road at noon on a summer day with the smell of sandy hills blowing in, and the popple trees shimmering like green fountains flowing upward from the ground — that image, in the back of my mind always, like fruit sitting in the sun, untouched, seen only as a shadow.

Before Louisiana, it had been Iowa, mornings spent pheasant hunting before heading to the university. When I pulled up to the house I rented outside Iowa City, Dick, my landlord, was usually sitting on a Pepsi crate and wearing snowmobile boots, even though it was summer, and he'd be looking at the empty barnyard after a day's work. Sit down and let's chat a minute. He had a boxer's chest, thin legs, and maybe a pig had died that day in the heat and now he had to get it out of there before the other pigs ate it. I helped him. A man had once cut the rest of his wrist off, he said, with a pen knife because it was getting dark, and if he didn't get his arm free of the grain auger, he'd be dead before morning in the snow. And down the road, he pointed past the barn, were two African lions living in a mobile home, the male resting the broad mop of his chin on the windowsill and looking dully through the chain link at the cornfields. True.

Stories. Dick had quite a few. He was without guile or avarice, kind. He reminded me of relatives I hadn't known. After ten years on the road, I was human Velcro, with heavy traffic on Fifth Avenue and the thousand-pound fish leaping off Cape Cod stuck to me like animated fuzz. I wanted a place where I knew things, so I could write things down.

Everywhere you look around this town there are things you know, places you fished or hunted, and where your grandparents fished and hunted, and now these are places you take your young son with your wife, beaches and woods, the ghosts of the dead standing in the twilight, well back into the 19th Century — the terrifying comfort is the collision of the past with the present, as if you, your flesh, were the intersection of all the dead borne into the future.

See, you could go downtown at night and eat at Stacey's and make your own change in the register afterwards, and you knew it would take seven, eight hours to get out of the state, and when you were seven that seemed like a long time, and there seemed to be no other thing to be doing except walking out the door of Stacey's when you were older, and all this, the smell of your mother's White Shoulders as she walked beside you, would be only memory.

After supper came the warm, smoky smell of the applesauce factory, the Morgan McCool plant, the smell dropping down through the air like warm, golden felt, hushing everything, everyone, as if the air were a secret being told as night fell, and the air grew cool and then it was dark. During the day we made spears and snorkeled under the buckled concrete of the McCool boat dock, threading ourselves back through the caverns, looking for fish, popping up for air in the caverns, gasping, finally swimming almost all the way to Front Street, and treading for moments in the chill dark while traffic buzzed overhead.

In the spring I followed the swinging lantern in my dad's hand out onto the docks, the outbuildings from another time, the days of ships, very dark and beaten and smelling like dirt. My dad and I stood before them, blackness behind us, while he cast out in the lantern's bloom and let the bait drift down. Someone was drinking Schnapps and threw the bottle against the outbuildings and went home. And then it began to rain, gouts of it, and thunder like grand pianos shoved off the fantails of great ships far out at sea, and dad said, "Well, let's get it together," and driving home, he said he loved thunderstorms, loved them since he was a kid, and at home he put the fishing poles away and sat on the carport in a lawn chair, staring through the rain at some vanishing point in his life...

I am the age now that he was then, or close to it; there is that feeling now, in the air, this afternoon — warm and threatening to rain — of mortality, of home, of floating permanence, the detritus of this reality, the traffic outside, birds in the garden, the sand, the creek I saw yesterday near Mayfield, all bombarding the bloodstream, entering...

Home is where the mundane is beautiful by virtue of its patina of history. The trick is not to live a mundane life, but to realize that at any one moment another life is possible, if only you could slip through the keyhole of imagination into the unknown.

Yesterday, my wife and I and my dad were looking for morels, and my dad was carrying my three-month-old son John, who was crying — Dad stepping quickly over the mat of dead leaves stained like horsehide in the sun, trillium here, there, John yowling like a circus monkey over dad's shoulder, and dad running through the woods trying to quiet him, pointing and saying, "There's one. And there's one, John. A morel! Mushroom!"

As he bent to pick it, John's eyes widened, peering down now like a small owl's at the mushroom, and he laughed again, heartily, hard, like a tiny Jackie Gleason. Who could have imagined that pleasure would narrow to such a private moment?

The sweet pressure of that moment bleeds into this present. On the drive home, dad said again, twenty years later, "I always did love a thunderstorm," craning to look up through the windshield. "Yes, it might rain. Always did love to watch it rain," and those twenty years, the ten of my absence, accordioned into one moment, the giddy feeling of eternity pouring like tap water through the sun roof.

So, whatever I've said here is dedicated to this sweetness, and to the memory of the dead, the smile of the living who surround me here, now. Because, after all this, these words, I just realized that perhaps I live here not by conscious choice — say, the way you would move to Seattle — but by some other reckoning having to do with blood and history that maybe I will outgrow.

Loving a place is like falling in love with her, the horizon stretches before you as she did, and it takes years to understand its nuances, the refractions of sounds in the trees — one day it seems you could reach out through the sunlit, carbonated air of the clearing and touch that tree a hundred yards away, a feeling of inexplicable beauty too heartbreaking to bear up under alone. You can live in a hundred places, but die in just one. Home used to be a feeling always mixed with loss and the smell of gasoline and the roads dusty. No more.

Summer

"Behind me the sun was sliding beyond the tops of the cedars, turning a line of mare's tails an outrageous pink ... All over the north, on clear lakes and rivers, from cottage porches, from atop the dunes along Lake Michigan, the pace slows as people stop to watch the dramatically colored tendrils sweep high into the sky."

JIM ENGER
From "Getting Out of Dodge"

JOHN VOELKER

John Voelker (1903-91) needs no introduction in Michigan or anyplace else where fine outdoor writing is appreciated. Formerly known by the pen name Robert Traver, he wrote eleven books, including Trout Magic, Trout Madness, Danny and the Boys, Laughing Whitefish *and* Small Town D.A. *His book* Anatomy of a Murder, *besides being a national best seller, became a movie starring the late James Stewart and Lee Remick, George C. Scott and Eve Arden. His "Testament of a Fisherman," which appeared in* Trout Madness, *is possibly the most quoted passage anywhere on the love of the sport of angling. Born in Ishpeming, Michigan, Voelker worked his way through the University of Michigan Law School as a waiter. After graduating, he married Grace Taylor, with whom he raised three daughters. He worked three years for a Chicago law firm, then returned to Michigan. In 1934 he was elected Marquette County Prosecutor, and he served fourteen years. He served as a Michigan Supreme Court justice from 1957-59, resigning to devote himself to writing. Any number of Voelker's stories could fit admirably in a Michigan outdoor writing anthology. The accompanying selection is fitting because it provides insights into the Upper Peninsula hideaway Voelker called Frenchman's Pond.*

GAMBLING AT FRENCHMAN'S

JOHN D. VOELKER

"*The big lure of Frenchman's was its wild brook trout, mermaid-plump trout almost spectral in their taunting elusiveness, ghostly trout we could so rarely lure or ever land when we did. Yet scarcely a day passed when we failed to behold one of their wave-rippling rises — ker-plonk — and scarcely a week when one of us wasn't left blinking by being abruptly cleaned out — ping — surely two of the most exciting sounds in all fishing.*"

Show me a fly fisherman who's still out there flailing away — after all, a few fainthearted ones occasionally do go back to golf — and I'll show you one of the biggest gamblers outside Las Vegas. And one just as heedless of the odds against him. For who but a real compulsive gambler could continue to stand for hours, often up to his whizzle string in ice water, pelting out a series of bent pins adorned with bits of fluff and tinsel, all in the wistful hope that some hungry fish might finally mistake one of them for something good to eat?

My fishing pals and I know quite a bit about all this, for not only do we pursue one of the wariest creatures in all fishdom, the wild brook trout, but we do so in one of the toughest spots we've run across in the whole Lake Superior area of the rugged Upper Peninsula of Michigan, good old Frenchman's Pond, simply Frenchman's to the sturdy crew that regularly haunts the place, of which I am a charter member.

Just to list a few of the odds against fishing Frenchman's is enough to drive the average fisherman back to his golf cart, if not up one of the spruces and tamaracks that line the rear margins of its boggy banks. First of all it really isn't a true pond at all — which are quite tough enough to fish anyway, heaven knows — but rather a shallow, crystal-clear and long-abandoned old beaver dam, which, with the aid of our annual patching jobs, still backs up its chilly waters for nearly a mile.

The moods of this pixilated pond are as variable as its width and winding course — both as eccentric as a midwinter rabbit trail through a cedar swamp — here but an easy fly cast to reach a riser on the other side, there often needing both luck and prayer to accompany the final heave.

Wading is out because of the generations of accumulated silt, which must date clear back to the last glacier. Canoeing we quit when it early swept over us that in all that clear, shallow water any half-decent trout promptly spooked and went into a sulk at the first dip of the paddle. Floating in an inflated tube we put on probation for a spell, despite the accompanying clouds of churned-up silt, till the day we flatly banned the tube when a nodding Hal had to be lassoed and towed ashore still diapered in one, where it took most of a bottle of bourbon to start him cussing again.

"Wee touch of hypothermia from all those cold underwater springs," Doctor Lou diagnosed as he administered still another belt of bourbon to his shivering patient.

"Whatever in hell I've got, Doc, the treatment's too damned expensive," Hal finally croaked. "Imagine flooring nearly a bottle of *that* and not even knowing it."

Short of fly-casting from a balloon, an idea we periodically dallied with, this left us only the pond's boggy banks from which to fish. These ran virtually the length of the pond on both sides, and while there was generally room enough to cast a fly without snagging one of those rearguard spruces or tamaracks, the big feat was to work oneself successfully into position to make the attempt.

For both shorelines are composed almost entirely of countless wobbly hummocks rearing their grassy heads out of a hidden multitude of lurking mudholes, still further disguised by blankets of low matted bushes, each tentacled branch endowed with a passion for snapping off artificial flies or weaving eccentric spider web patterns out of fragile leaders and tippets.

Lloyd summed it up the day we finished building our log cabin on a bare granite knoll overlooking the pond, a cabin complete with an old school bell that would tell even the farthest-wandering fisherman that the late-afternoon cocktail hour had arrived. "Fellas," Lloyd said, pointing pondward during a between-drink lull, "trying to cast a decent fly out there is tougher than playing an old kid's game of rubbing your belly while patting your noggin."

Still we persisted, and the sight of all six of us engaged in our fishing devotionals at the same time moved some of our nonfishing cronies to occasional bursts of poetry.

"Know what you guys look like?" one of them one day suddenly cupped his hand and hollered from the open camp doorway.

"No!" one of our struggling band hollered back. "I've often wondered."

"Like a herd of stampeding water buffalo."

"Dead wrong," Hal hollered back. "More like a bunch of drunks on a trampoline."

Why would a crew of canny old fishermen continue to haunt such a crazy place, let alone build a camp there? It would be nice to say we were continually drawn back by its sheer rugged beauty, peeking up like a glittering jewel out of those low wooded serpentine hills with their occasional reddish gleams of ancient granite; by the continued ignoring by the choosy trout of not only our favorite flies but of our years of accumulated lore; yes, by the very dare and difficulty of the place — wups, I almost said challenge, a close call.

All this was indeed part of its charm, no doubt, for one likes to think there's still a touch of Thoreau in every fisherman. But the big lure of Frenchman's was something else — its wild brook trout, mermaid-plump trout we'd known all along were there, trout almost spectral in their taunting elusiveness, ghostly trout we could so rarely lure or ever land when we did. Yet scarcely a day passed when we failed to behold one of their wave-rippling rises — *ker-plonk* — and scarcely a week when one of us wasn't left blinking by being abruptly cleaned out — *ping* — surely two of the most exciting sounds in all fishing.

The presence of these magazine-cover trout in our pond was contrary to all the sacred precepts of fishing we'd picked up at out fathers' knees, of course. For hadn't every savvy fisherman learned from boyhood that few wild brook trout in our northern bailiwick ever grew to be more than twelve inches long? Especially when confined to living in old shallow beaver dams where they were so constantly vulnerable to their many natural enemies? And especially those haunting forsaken old beaver dams fed by dozens of bubbling underwater springs pumping gallons of ice water which, as everybody knew, sharply lowered a trout's metabolism, and therefore his appetite, and therefore the growth of any poor stunted creature forced to dwell there? To all of which certified scrolls of fisherman's wisdom Frenchman's continued to have but one teasing response: *ker-plonk!*

As for our prevalence of pings, these with true fisherman resourcefulness we managed to blame on everything but ourselves: the difficulty of ever luring a really big trout in all that stereopticon-clear water; the companion difficulty of successfully playing and landing one with all those hidden logs and ancient beaver cuttings and miscellaneous snags and roots and weeds and gobs of tenacious algae lurking in all that silt and along those snaggy-bushed shores, especially when fished from a swaying trampoline; the weirdness and unpredictability of the pond's natural fly hatches and the consequent difficulty of ever consistently matching them. On and on our excuses ran. Finally there was our almost helpless tendency, so common to prideful action-hungry fishermen — especially when the fishing is lousy — to keep tying on still more fragile tippets, so that we generally wound up being chronically underleadered.

This fine-leader syndrome that afflicts so many fishermen is not quite as sporting as it sounds. For the longer an angler fishes the stronger he's apt to feel that the finer his leader the more follows and hits he's likely to get, probably because so few flies in nature come tethered to nylon tails upwards of umpteen feet long. By and by it sweeps over him that his leader might be one of the weakest weapons in the whole fly-fishing arsenal; that, alas, the sad truth is that as yet there are no perfect leaders — that is, both perfectly invisible and unbreakable (though he nightly prays that Dan Bailey or someone out yonder is working on them) — and that any leader he uses is an inevitable compromise between attracting more fish and the increasing risk of losing those he attracts.

Good old Hal put it more tersely. "While there's no damn question that our hawser-leadered buddies stand a far better chance of landing a slob once they're on to it," he one day declaimed, "there's also no question that the fine-leadered boys who prefer action over avoirdupois will get on to far more biggies in the first place." He raised his glass. "Maybe the old poet fellow said a mouthful when he wrote, 'Tis better to have lured and lost than never to have lured at all.'"

So the pings continued merrily until, following a particularly frustrating day five summers ago, we tolled the camp bell and met in an emergency session and vowed to try to solve some of the problems that afflicted us. One of the more obvious, of course, was the constant physical difficulty of fishing the place. So we had another round of drinks and talked away and finally passed the hat and, presto, in a matter of weeks had installed twin rough-plank boardwalks running practically the pond's length on both sides. We also built a narrow footbridge to get across on without having to boat or walk 'way down around the dam. Finally we fashioned and set out a series of wooden casting docks, Lloyd surrendering his precious collection of old wooden beer crates for us to squat on during the frequent ritual of tying on still more tippets.

All this measurably improved both our balance and tempers as it also increased our pings, alas. But our growing frustration kept pace, for in making our improvements we'd also managed to lose our pet alibi for so regularly falling on our fannies — the now largely vanished difficulty of fishing the place. Some elusive thing was still lacking; we knew not what. Things came to a head just four seasons ago last July, on a memorable Saturday. To save time and rhetoric, I'll swipe most of the account from my old fishing notes:

———————————🦋———————————

Today we turned Frenchman's into a genuine gambling casino lacking only dice girls and slot machines. Here's how it happened.

When we reached camp around noon the pond had gone crazy. Trout were rising and rolling everywhere: big, little, medium. Hal said it looked like a hail of golf balls with a few bricks thrown in. We quickly rigged up and raced for the boardwalks and our favorite casting stations — mine being at a tangled jumble of ancient submerged logs which, in an inspired burst of creativity, we had labeled the Log Jam, located in the narrows just above our new footbridge. Naturally the Log Jam was a great hideout for big trout since they, like their human pals, generally grab up the best spots. Naturally the Log Jam was also one of the main pinging centers on the pond.

All of us fished like mad all afternoon until around five when someone mercifully tolled the camp bell. After the first round of drinks we took a creel census, followed by a stunned silence, for nobody but nobody had caught a decent trout. All of us had had plenty of action, though, either being cleaned out at least once on the strike or busted or pulled off during the day.

"Fine bleeping state of affairs," Hal finally said. "Guess we gotta mend our ways."

"How?" somebody asked.

"Like maybe talkin' things over to see what in hell we can do about it," Hal said. "But first another round."

So we had another round and talked things over and were well into the second fifth when we arrived at an intriguing plan. Beginning the very next day and from then on we agreed to place a standing bet on each fishing trip, every time out. The rules were simple as falling off a trampoline: The guy with the biggest trout ten inches or over would win a buck each from all the others. That was it. All had to be taken on flies, of course, and the fly produced.

During our huddle we kept reassuring ourselves that we weren't even faintly commercializing our favorite sport. Perish the thought. Merely trying to chase away boredom and stimulate zeal in what we all agreed was one of the toughest spots we'd ever fished. Then we had another round and huddled some more and, to add spice to the roll of the dice, further agreed that the losers would pay two bucks a head when the winning trout reached twelve inches or better, three bucks at thirteen and so on into the higher realms of fantasy. We'd simply gamble our way into a state of mingled bliss and more fish.

There were a few miscellaneous odds and ends: A guy could keep his qualifying trout in a live trap, if he liked, and return it after the showdown. Or sooner if meanwhile a pal happened to catch a still larger trout.

"But suppose I catch a twelve-incher and Hal noses me out with a thirteen?" I inquired. Don't I deserve a two-dollar credit for coming so close or must I also pay Hal three bucks along with the poor guys who caught a chill?"

"Close don't count, lads," Hal argued in rebuttal. "Main reason I gave up dancing."

So my suggestion was voted down with only my lone dissent. Next we agreed a guy couldn't hog a spot all day but was limited to a half-hour at a stretch if another guy showed up and wanted to give it a try. Finally we agreed that each day's betting would end with the ringing of the camp bell, summoning all parched fishermen to the first round of drinks, generally around five.

"To Frenchman's!" Hal toasted at the end of our historic huddle.

"Transformed from a pastoral boardwalk to roaring gambling hell all in one afternoon," someone said.

———————————— ✿ ————————————

'Twas the last day of fishing and all up and down the pond my pals and I scurried against the deadline at five. Four summers had fled since we'd started gambling at Frenchman's, and as I took my stand at the Log Jam and sat tying up a new tippet my thoughts wandered over the intervening years.

Our fishing had picked up remarkably from the very first day, whether from avarice or added concentration I cannot quite say. One thing was plain: All of us fished longer and harder with far more intensity. That very first Sunday I'd started at the same spot, hadn't I? Ah, yes, it was all coming back. We'd begun fishing around noon and on just about my first cast at the Log Jam I'd hooked and landed a plump twelve-incher — my first decent trout in weeks — and had admired and calibrated him and reverently placed him in my brand new live trap.

I recalled how, in my excitement, I'd spent most of the rest of that first afternoon boardwalking up and down the pond proudly telling my pals about my prize — and also making sure that none had excelled me. Then, only minutes before five, Hal had come ambling along and paused to admire my fish.

"Any more luck?" Hal inquired.

"Couple small passes," I lied softly, as I'd actually just busted off an even bigger trout.

"Mind if I give it a try?"

"My pleasure," I further lied, resignedly reeling in and moving away. "Don't catch 'em all."

Before I'd retreated ten paces along the boardwalk Hal had made a few false casts and popped out a little dry over my hot spot and — presto — hooked and splashily fought and landed what turned out to be the day's winning thirteen-incher. Meanwhile, I, always slow at math, stood there stupidly figuring out that instead of just winning ten bucks (five guys at two bucks a head) I'd just lost three, all in one lousy cast, a total net loss — let's see — of thirteen whole bucks, almost the price of two bottles of your favorite hypothermia therapy.

During these years I'd occasionally won a few bets, of course, for it's hard for anyone to lose all the time at anything, even when the cards seem to be stacked against you. And after all, wasn't it just as egotistical to believe in consistent bad luck as in good, both carrying their self-absorbed assumption that someone out there gives a damn? Yes, but wasn't it only last summer that I'd caught that dreamy plus-fourteen-incher when *none* of my pals had shown up?

I finished tying on my new tippet, then a small dry, at the same time ruefully wondering whether that distant first day of betting hadn't set the tone and pace of my piscatorial gambling career. True, our fishing had sharply improved, mine included, but why in hell did I so rarely win a bet and so often merely come close? Was it some sort of punishment for ever daring to suggest allowing that betting credit? Had my fate as our gang's favorite pigeon frozen me into a permanent role as runner-up?

Ker-plonk, I suddenly heard, scrambling up so rapidly I kicked over one of Lloyd's beer crates, stripping and whipping out line, finally lofting out the little dry, which sang past my ear, poised for a fleeting moment, and then settled like a wisp of thistle in the middle of the lovely ebbing circle left by the rising trout.

The trout instantly rose and took the fly, I struck — lo, there was no ping — and I all but skidded it out of the danger zone — the narrow Log Jam where all of us so regularly lost so many fish and flies — and in moments had landed it and stood hefting it in my hand — a nice drippy twelve-incher. I glanced at my live trap, and then almost furtively up and down the pond — no pals in sight — and suddenly knelt and slid it back into the water, where it lay working its gills for a moment and then, presto, was gone.

"Maybe that will break the spell," I murmured out loud, feeling for a moment like one of those legendary millionaires lighting up a cigar with a ten-dollar bill.

In the next hour at the same spot I took and returned two more trout about the same size, one possibly larger. Then I sauntered back to camp and sipped a slow can of beer, listened to a couple of innings of baseball, then sauntered down below the bridge to check on my pals. Also to see what in hell was keeping them glued below. Also to show them I hadn't used up my current half-hour at my favorite spot.

Fishing had been good below, too, I discovered, Lloyd having just been cleaned out at the Big Spring and Lou a little earlier at his favorite Weed Patch. Ted and Gigs were still out of sight, probably in the deeper water down at the dam, a sporty big-fish spot the two often shared, while, as usual, good old Hal stood teetering and casting away on a rickety wooden platform on stilts that we called the Diving Board, so I moved down his way.

"Any luck, pard?" I inquired. Hal grunted and gestured at his nearby live trap. "May I sneak a look?" I said, and Hal nodded and I sneaked a look. "Hmm," I said, for my hunch had been right: There lay a gorgeous trout, at least a fourteen-incher.

"Want to give my spot a whirl?" Hal said as I turned to leave.

"No thanks, pal, just came down slumming to see what I had to beat."

"Better get going," Hal said, glancing at his watch. "And don't catch them all."

"Have a nice day," I said, as I got going, "as total strangers keep chanting at checkout counters as they heist our dough."

Once back at my Log Jam I saw it was already past midafternoon and that time indeed grew short. Play it cool, I told myself. So I sat on my beer crate and went through some of the more chaotic of my fly boxes. Then I heard a good trout rise and glanced upstream and saw it spreading over the Top Log area.

Remembering our half-hour rule, I glanced at my watch and headed for the Top Log, pausing a good cast length below the sunken log, which today I could plainly make out running straight out and downward from the brushy shore where, in distant days when it was still a tree, it had once proudly stood.

First glancing back to make sure my favorite spot wasn't being invaded, I worked out line, false-casting, and finally sailed out a sizable dry just beyond the deeper end of the sunken log over one on the bigger springs. I glanced around to check on my pals and inadvertently twitched the fly and heard a watery explosion and then a sharp *ping* — and ruefully saw I had not only lost my fly buy nearly half of my lovely tapered leader.

Again I glanced at my watch — my, how the time flew — and stood there debating whether I still had time to tie on a brand-new leader or at least a couple lengths of new tippet. Better get back there first, I told myself, and then we'll see.

Back at the Log Jam I'd barely sat down on my beer crate when I almost fell over backwards as a simply whopping trout rose, sending out wavelets in all directions. Once again I glanced at my watch and emitted a whistle — make that a low whistle — and mentally shrugged and found and managed to tie onto the remaining half of my shortened hawser leader a duplicate of the big feather-duster fly I'd just lost.

"Only minutes more," I kept whispering as I whipped the fly back and forth, back and forth, my fly darting like a humming-bird, all but closing my eyes as I finally released both fly and whirling hawser in the general direction of the Log Jam, where it landed at the far end with a watery plop.

Nothing happened and then I remembered the magic twitch, so I gave my fly a little twitch and a trout rose. I struck, and to my dismay saw I was on to a plucky junior-leaguer that seemed scarcely larger than my fly. Again a glance at the watch — only two minutes more — someone campbound waved at me from the footbridge — so I reeled in furiously, hoping to get in at least one more cast before the final bell.

I'd skidded the small trout almost to shore when I saw and heard a sudden *ker-plonk,* and I reared back and struck more out of shock than anything, and found myself latched to an epic rod-bender that thrashed and churned like a retrieving spaniel.

The camp bell was still ringing as I finally towed him in close and batted him ashore with my net, for no way would he fit, falling on him and wrestling him just as he disgorged the smaller trout with my fly still in its jaw. Still wrestling, I managed to unhook my fly and slip the still-wriggling junior back into the pond.

"Looks like a dandy," Hal hollered across from the camp door-way, shading his eyes.

"Not bad," I modestly hollered back. "May need a licensed surveyor to measure 'im."

I left my big trout crammed and sulking in the trap, eyeing me balefully, and headed back to camp, now wrestling not with any trout but a flood of vexing questions. Had I really caught this monster on a fly? I asked myself. Or merely on a midget trout I'd already taken on a fly? But we had no rule against trolling or baiting our fly, had we, and wasn't this really akin to maybe adding a lone kernel of corn or a wee salmon egg to one's adroitly maneuvered fly? Or wasn't all *that* a lot of bull and shouldn't I confess and leave the verdict up to my pals?

"Looks like it's between us," Hal said after we and the other boys had downed our first round. "How big is your baby?"

"Don't know yet, Hal," I answered honestly enough, "but I'd guess at least somewhere between eighteen and twenty inches, maybe more."

"Wow! Whadya catch 'im on, man?"

I glanced down at the pond for a spell and turned and answered Hal.

What do *you* think I said?

KENNETH PETERSON

World class fly tier, champion duck caller, conservationist, renowned outdoor writer. Kenneth (Ken) Peterson was all that and more. As one peer put it, Peterson's death in May 1997 "left a hole in conservation journalism." Peterson started his writing career in 1951 with the Port Huron Times *after serving three years in World War II in Africa and Italy. He joined the* Flint Journal *in 1954, became outdoor writer in 1963, and held that position until he retired in 1985. Along the way, he served eleven years as a national director of Trout Unlimited, an organization he helped form. He was a founding editor of* Trout *magazine and president of the Michigan Outdoor Writers Association (MOWA). In 1977, he won the first Ben East Award for excellence in conservation journalism from the Michigan United Conservations Clubs. In 1992, MOWA presented him with the Gene Little "Papa Bear" award for lifetime achievement in outdoor journalism. Peterson was known for spending his days afield, building firsthand knowledge of the outdoors. As Dave Richey of the* Detroit News *wrote, "Ken Peterson was a man that any sportsman would love to share a boat seat with or to spend a week with in deer camp. And among sportsmen, there is no higher praise."*

STILL OF THE NIGHT

KENNETH PETERSON

"*A tranquility comes over one who waits quietly to put his fly rod into action at the right time. Sometimes it is a long wait, long enough to seemingly absorb the very night itself. The night begins to lie like a cloak draped about one's shoulders, wrapping around as if to take one to its bosom.*"

It was night on the river, and it was quiet. The last sounds of humans had disappeared, leaving no sounds foreign to the riverside. It was a quiet full of sounds, full of the sounds of nature going about her business.

The sound of the river dominated everything as I sat on the banks, wader boots awash in the slow edge current. To my right, upstream, was a backwater, a quiet shallows over deep muck, protected from the current. It was the home of the burrowing mayfly, incubator of the big bugs I was expecting to hatch and awaken the brown marauder who lived under the opposite bank.

The current spoke softly, as it must if I were to hear the sounds of the hatch and the feeding fish. For here, in the black silence, my ears took over for my eyes. I had located the seductive gurgle of the water as it was parted by a log just downstream. The log created a little run along the bank and a hiding place for big fish awaiting mayflies. Across the river, where the stream swept along a tag-alder-lined bank, a bowing alder fought reclamation by the stream. It bobbed constantly as the water washed sometimes over it and sometimes under.

Yes, and an occasional frog on my side of the stream jumped in with a croak and a splash and swam to a half-submerged log in the shallows. But I had that sound pegged, just as I had cataloged the noise of a common sucker rising to feed on the surface.

The sounds jumped out in the windless night and I duly recorded all of them.

A tranquility comes over one who waits quietly to put his fly rod into action at the right time. Sometimes it is a long wait, long enough to seemingly absorb the very night itself. The night begins to lie like a cloak draped about one's shoulders, wrapping around as if to take one to its bosom.

Just as one begins to be lulled by the peaceful surroundings, it comes: whip-poor-will! The shrill whistle splits the night sounds, knifing through my quiet nook and echoing through the hardwoods up the steep riverbank. Aha! Old friend! I warm to the sound, the signal to be alert for the rustle of whispering wings plying the river highway.

Whip-poor-will! Yes, it is time to perk up, to listen even more closely for the sound of those lumbering bodies heading upstream, those B-17s of the trout insect world.

But there is time to have fun, too, with the harbinger of the hatch. I purse my lips and imitate my unseen insect-seeking friend. Pretty good, I think, as my whistle echoes along the river. Pretty good, I guess! Suddenly, there is a flurry of wings right in my face. A hovering whip-poor-will — I could only hear it — was only a foot or two from me, so close I could feel its wingbeats. It studied me for only moments, but is seemed as though it spent a minute trying to figure out the source of that mimicking sound. It did not come again, but I had had my chuckle.

I do these things. It is part of absorbing and being absorbed by the wild. Earlier, I had a try at being a frog. That was not so good. But before dark I became a chickadee in my hidden spot, and one of those friendly little birds searched the bushes about me so long that I began to feel sorry for it and quit talking to it.

But now, the night was advanced. Now I had better pay closer attention to the night sounds. Then, I heard the fish splash across the river. It was out in the current where the bugs would quickly wash by. Another splash. The smaller browns were starting to feed. So, apparently the flight was upstream from me, for I did not hear those wings, either high or low, rustle by me in the dark. But it was enough to know that the flight was on and that mayflies were mating upstream, completing their life cycle and floating lifeless, or nearly so, into the jaws of waiting trout.

The long wait was over. Time to get up, get the kinks out and wade out to where I could cast into the quiet water, where I knew big browns sooner or later would come, either seeking hatching bugs or those that had floated from upstream. Again, my ears would tell me, sorting out the slurp of a feeding trout from the other water noises I had been marking all evening. Time to shake out of my reverie and join the predators of the night.

The next significant sound coming out of the still of the night would be that of a large, struggling trout on the end of my fly line. Then all would be still again — as still as it gets on a warm June night in trout country.

BOB LINSENMAN

Bob Linsenman lost his heart to fly fishing at age seven and to the Au Sable River at ten. He oper-ates a guiding business, literary agency and free-lance writing practice from his Rose City home. He hunts pheasant, grouse, woodcock and ducks about fifty days a year and will usually "sit in a tree with a bow another ten days or so." He has been involved in book and computer software publishing since 1965. He has co-authored two books, Michigan Trout Streams: A Fly Angler's Guide, *and* Great Lakes Steelhead: A Guided Tour for Fly Anglers. *He is the sole author of* The Au Sable River — River Journal. *His articles have appeared in* American Angler, Fly Fisherman, Wild Steelhead & Salmon *and other magazines. He also edits* The Riverwatch, *the publication of the Anglers of the Au Sable. Bob's son Marc lives in Chicago and daughter Ciree in Minneapolis. "My hideout is in Oscoda County about ten minutes from the Au Sable in Michigan's beautiful Northern Highlands," he says. "I have an old rusty Suburban, an old gray Labrador (Cobaka) and no money. I am the luck-iest man on Earth."*

HEXARITAVILLE

BOB LINSENMAN

"*They came from downstream in undulating waves numbering in the tens of thousands. They were forty to fifty feet above the water, and their wingbeats produced a distinctive, humming vibration. They came through pale shards of moonlight filtered by rolling clouds.*"

The geography of Michigan is easily understood if not widely appreciated. In the north the state is largely comprised of a few dry ridges surrounded by swamps, ponds and lakes and threaded, weblike, by rivers. South of "the line," which runs roughly from Bay City on the east coast to Muskegon on the west, there is a gentle roll of rich agricultural land that continues across the short borders with Ohio and Indiana. Elsewhere, the state's limits are defined by the vast sweetwater pools known as the Great Lakes. The lakes pump moisture into the atmosphere, feeding snow and rain into the system. This is damp country, but easy enough to understand.

The hard part in achieving appreciation of Michigan's total equation comes with a full comprehension of a deviant, social strata variable. To avoid embarrassment, the touring angler needs a working knowledge of the societal hierarchy, complex though it may be.

A few years ago, my sisters cornered me during halftime of the annual football riot between Notre Dame and Big Blue. The Wolverines were down by three points, due largely to the efforts of an officiating crew who had been (we speculated) flown to South Bend directly from the Vatican. The mood was tense. Only brother-in-law Don whooped heartily for the Fighting Irish, but he had previously bunked on a nuclear submarine for extended periods and we suspected some sort of cranial meltdown as the cause of his demented loyalty seep.

"I'm tired of telling your life story by way of explanation," sister Carol said. "You've been back home long enough to get it right." She pointed to an empty chair and continued as I sat. "People wonder why you get everything mixed up, and I tell them you moved away for a long time. They ask me why, and I tell them you were sick. 'Well he moved back, didn't he?' they say. 'Well then, he must be better.'"

"It's not really that hard, Bob," said sister Carlene. "Gerry and I have written it out for you." She nodded to Geraldine, who produced a yellow legal pad from thin air.

"Just read this and try to remember," said Gerry. "Maybe you could carry it with you for reference in case you forget," she added, patting me on the head and turning to the roar from the television as a Michigan tuba man took a roundhouse swing at a Notre Dame drummer. I would not take the time to present this overview of that crib sheet if it were not vital to your understanding of the human broth that comes to such a frenzied boil during the emergence of the giant Michigan mayfly, the *Hexagenia limbata*.

At the peak of prestige (and geography) sit the Yoopers. These are hardy souls who defy the elements and harsh terrain of the Upper Peninsula and who mostly cheer for the Packers and Brewers. Society's bottom rung is held by the Flatlanders, who live south of "the line," who root for the Lions and Tigers and who have jobs. In between you will find a mixture of Trolls (to a Yooper, anyone who lives below the Mackinac Bridge is a Troll), whose subspecies include Cedar Savages, Bush Weasels, Swamp Angels and Fudgies.

Cedar Savages live north of "the line," but south of the bridge. They could also be Jack Pine Savages if they live on one of the few arid ridges or near the sand barrens. The Bush Weasel's range extends from "the line" across the bridge into the U.P. Bush Weasels often appear suddenly at roadsides near the edge of a forest or swamp. They are identified by their nervous posture and furtive glances back and forth before they scurry across the trail, or back into the woods. A Swamp Angel cuts trees in the U.P. and works long hours. Swamp Angels are tough and can be sudden in their decision making. Fudgies are Michigan Yuppies, almost always Flatlanders and always from "down below," a generalized direction and place, referring to anywhere south of where you happen to be at the moment. The Fudgie drives a foreign car, says "Michiganian" instead of "Michigander" and comes north only to visit the shops in Petoskey or on Mackinac Island. Fudgies rarely fish and do not hunt, but they drop some serious coin on the locals and are therefore tolerated between Memorial Day and Labor Day.

So there you have it, without the complications of work-related moves (rare), or intermarriage (less rare). To sum it up, it is safe to say that a Yooper Swamp Angel enjoys much more status than a Flatlander Fudgie, who is roughly equal to an Alien from Ohio or Florida or New York. If the two extremes held the same job, the Yooper would say he was a Swamp Angel, perhaps a logger. The Fudgie would say he was an "independent forester."

But, the Aliens and all the Michiganders drop their pretense and caricatured posturing once a year, when they pack their fly rods and duffels and head to the languid, sweet-stream flow of the beautiful Au Sable River for the Bug Dance, the emergence of the *Hexagenia limbata.*

Benny (Bad Scene Benny) Coyne and I sat at the bar of the Northwoods Tavern just north of Mio. It was June 18 at 12:45 a.m. and the saloon was busy with anglers (Flatlanders, Yoopers, Aliens, Fudgies) just off the river, many of them showing early symptoms of "the stare." This is simply an insensate condition caused by trying for too long to force visual form to sounds and shapes that have been deliquesced into the gloom of foggy twilight. Marie, the bartender at the Northwoods, calls it the Hex Vex.

"The river rats got it bad tonight, eh?" she said. "That faraway look reminds me of the reaction I got from the IRS guy down below when he saw my bag of handwritten receipts. Benny, you got it, too." She moved to pour Bad Scene another tequila and I turned to my friend. His eyes were an unblinking, unseeing signal that the cerebellum was otherwise engaged.

We were waiting for other members of the fly angling underworld to join us. Our loosely bound fishing group, the Blazing

Waders, hosts an annual meeting we call the Burrowing Muck Dwellers Conclave during "the hatch," and Benny and I expected the momentary registration of our colleagues. Dan Donarski was on his way down from Sault Ste. Marie. Steve Nevala would drive up from Kalamazoo. Jerry Pytlik, the bamboo wizard from Bay City, would join us, as would my nephew, Rob Powell.

We would keep company with the hordes of other bewitched anglers, Buckeyes, Texans, Hoosiers, Swamp Angels and Fudgies, all bundled into an area roughly circumscribed by the villages of Grayling, Lovells, Roscommon and Mio. For eleven months of the year these burgs are independent and proudly competitive, but from early June through the Fourth of July, they bond and become Hexaritaville, USA.

So here we sat in a saloon at the eastern edge of Hexaritaville, waiting. Benny, the only trout guide I know with an unlisted telephone number, had earlier caught and released a twenty-two-inch male on an experimental spinner pattern. He was feeling powerful and expansive, and decided to request a double order of garlic bread sticks by making questionable hand gestures to the kitchen staff. Just then, the front door flew open and Dan muscled through the neoprene-clad zombies to our place at the bar.

"Hex smeared the windshield at the M-72 bridge on the South Branch," he said. "I had to stop and clean it by hand. I was there, so I fished instead of coming straight in. Caught a sixteen and a nineteen, and lost a big one above Dog Town. Hi."

"Hi," we both answered, and Benny asked, "When did you take up falconry?" In response to Dan's quizzical, distant expression, Benny pointed to Donarski's shoulder, upon which perched a large, live Hex dun, probably a size four.

"God, they're really out tonight!" Dan noted. Then solemnly, hat held over his heart, he plucked the big mayfly from his shoulder, tossed it into Benny's glass of chilled tequila and drank it down. "To the Burrowing Muck Dwellers," he toasted.

Marie observed dryly, "Well, Dan is here. So now we have Dan Donarski and the Burrowing Muck Dwellers right here in my bar. Sounds like a Yooper polka band."

By noon the next day our team was assembled. Jerry had roared up the driveway at 2:15 a.m. and parked his thirty-six-foot motorhome exactly an inch and a half from my brother-in-law Bill's tarp-covered custom Corvette. "I thought it was a woodpile," he said. Bill used to earn his pay doing mean things to people late at night in faraway dark jungles, and his son Robert had fainted at the sight of the lumbering RV skidding to a stop so close to his father's toy.

"I think he scraped it. You'll get blamed for this Robby," I had told him. He was still in a nervous, twitching sleep.

Steve Nevala was the last to arrive. As Michigan's official Curmudgeon Laureate, he had been required to issue several blanket disapprovals and sign a negative opinion statement before leaving Kalamazoo. He laid his gear on the porch and swaggered into the cabin, shaking hands, petting dogs and gesturing toward the table where fly-tying paraphernalia and coffee cups surrounded a sickly plant.

"Perfect pathos," he said.

"It's pronounced pothos," I answered.

"I wasn't referring to the plant."

We tied flies, both duns and spinners, but mostly the large hen-winged, cream-colored spinners with extended bodies. And we laid plans. We considered splitting into two groups with one party of three spread along the smooth, silt-banked flats near Parmalee Bridge, while the others concentrated on the big slot near the sand bank below Whirlpool access. We weighed the merits of floating the long stretch from McMasters to Parmalee against the walk-in approach, and finally decided on the latter. We would all stick roughly together along the three-hundred-yard glide below the sandhill slot.

Steve summed it up with, "I have an obsessive need to sit very still on the mud bank of that little island. I want to stare into the gloom and think Nobel-Peace-Prize-type thoughts until the fish start feeding."

By six that evening, Benny and Dan had tied enough flies to supply everyone in Oscoda and Crawford counties, Jerry had given Rob a casting lesson (and sold him a new Powell rod), and Steve and I had listened to the Tigers deliver a thumping to the Yankees while preparing dinner and some river snacks for later consumption.

Dinner was finished, dishes were washed and two well-worn Suburbans were fully loaded by seven o'clock. We needed two large trucks because, as the years had passed, each of our private checklists for the bare necessities had grown. My list required two fly rods — a nine-foot 5-weight and a nine-foot 7-weight — a waterproof camera, two flashlights, two pair of waders, an extra jacket, an extra pair of reading glasses, two extra reels, two cans of mosquito spray, two cans of diet soda, one Thermos bottle, two sandwiches, and so on.

I also like to take two dogs. With apologies to John Gierach, I must say that mine are a joy to fish with when I am alone. The Cookie Monster (a mutt) and Cobaka (a Lab) usually loll around on the bank and rarely criticize my casting. But, they would stay behind on this night. Cobaka worries if "her party" of anglers gets too spread out and will sometimes try to herd them back together. The Cookie Monster likes beer, Steve's brand of beer, and has been known to nudge him a little forcibly if her thirst needs quenching. A cold, wet nose pressed suddenly to the back of one's neck on a foggy, moonless night can be exciting, and a push from behind against a knee braced in the current is, at best, problematic.

Rob and Jerry piled in with Benny, Steve and Dan joined me in my truck, and we headed out to the Whirlpool on the Au Sable's mainstream between Mio and Grayling.

"I need to stop at the store and pick up some garbage bags," Benny called out his window. We would need at least one bag to carry out our own cans, paper and plastic, and possibly another for any refuse we might find along the river. Nearly all of the guides, and a high percentage of the anglers in my home area, now carry bags for trash removal as a matter of policy. It is painful to admit that this is necessary, but it is also heartening to note a positive effect, and that is a noticeable decrease in stream-side litter.

We were on the bank of the small island at eight o'clock. Thousands of dead Hex spinners, remnants of the previous night's orgy, were gathered into drifting masses in the slack water behind logs and in tiny coves on the shore's edge. A high overcast and a slight, shifting fog at eye level fostered hopes for early nightfall and the beginning of the evening's festivities. The previous day had been clear and hot, and the bugs had not appeared until shortly after full darkness at 10:50 p.m. We were anxious.

A few small trout started rising just upstream from our observation point and Jerry examined a tiny olive spinner drifting past his feet. It looked like a size 18 or 20, and he guessed it was a

Baetis vagans. Steve pointed to some larger, dark mayflies pulsing into a mating swarm roughly fifteen feet above the water and guessed (hoped) they might be the last of the brown drakes. They seemed a little small for *Ephemera simulans,* and as they dropped we discovered they were mahogany drakes, the *Isonychia sadleri,* that will occasionally tease an eager fish to the feeding point before the nightly Hex banquet.

Two larger fish slurped near the bank to our right. There, the confluence of two smallish side currents formed a vee and scoured a pocket of some depth next to an old, twisted stump. Rob tried to effect a demeanor of nonchalance and patience, but soon cracked. "Would it be all right to try those two? Would it disturb the bigger fish if I hooked one?"

"No, it shouldn't bother anything," I answered, and handed Rob a size 12 spinner with a slender, dark mahogany body, smoky wings and long, graceful tails. "Try this," I offered. "Sneak up the bank and stay low." Rob added a stretch of 4X tippet, tied on his fly and crept up the bank. Benny grabbed a handful of yesterday's Hex and tossed them into the main flow. "Chumming," he said. Dan rustled around the island like a bear in heat, finding odd bits of litter, stuffing junk into the trash bag and working himself into a frenzied snit. "I hate waiting," he muttered.

Steve stood, then froze and pointed behind us. Donarski's ramble had come too close to a hiding fawn. Her nerves had popped, and she stood trembling halfway between Dan, now motionless, and our cluster of philosophers. Dan took two slow steps back. The fawn broke fast to the edge of the island, splashed along the small, graveled channel, then scrambled up the bank into the undergrowth. The usually irreverent Pytlik doffed his goofy fishing hat, gazed upward and said, "Thank you God!"

I turned to check on Rob's progress. He was intent on his task and had not seen the fawn. His casts were low and accurate, but he had not yet matched his delivery to the feeding rhythms of the fish. He had the right fly. It would only be a matter of time before he hooked up.

Six, or seven, or eight wild turkeys thundered into a leaning white pine on the far bank. They fluttered and hopped and chortled and pecked their way to suitable roosting perches and settled in just as Rob hollered. We all turned in time to see a nice rainbow, maybe fourteen inches, somersault back into the water and run straight toward his waders. The line went slack and the fish was gone, but my nephew grinned widely as he sloshed back to us.

"Nice job," I said. He sat, still smiling, cut his leader back to 1X, and tied on a Hex spinner. It was getting noticeably darker by the minute, and the talk seemed directed more to the river, the fish, the sky, than to any one of us.

Steve's voice (dryly): "This is the time and the place for heavy thinking. Knee-deep in muck, mosquitoes, werewolves, loud-mouthed turkeys — what stimulation!"

Pytlik's voice (plaintively): "Maybe I'm a hopeless romantic, but I'd like to bring a lady friend down here. You know, on a date."

Benny's voice (knowingly): "I tried that once. It didn't work. She said the mosquitos were terrible, and she was afraid of the dark. But the Hex really made her crazy. They came in swarms and got down her neck. I asked her to try it again this year, but she said, 'No, let's have dinner instead.' She's a big-city girl, a Flatlander."

Dan's voice (as in thankful prayer to the heavens): "Yes, but she had the guts to try it."

Rob's voice (with serious, wild passion): "Jeez! Look at them!" They came from downstream in undulating waves numbering in the tens of thousands. They were forty to fifty feet above the water, and their wingbeats produced a distinctive, humming vibration. They came on, abreast, then passing, through pale shards of moonlight filtered by rolling clouds. The mix of visual images included a sky scene from a Dracula movie, the living, pulsing, lusting swarm of insects, the dancing fog and the quiet, inky flow of a large, ominous river. There was a long moment of awe-inspired silence, then a voice in the dark.

"Wow! This is why we're here. This is downtown Hexarita-ville!"

Steve, Dan, and Bad Scene moved slowly, quietly downstream and dispersed to fish the curling sweep of deep water next to the eroding sandhill on the far bank. Jerry, Rob and I stayed put to fish the more complex currents and troublesome wading of the heavy run at the head of the island. Three fish began to feed near the opposite shore below the dark current curling from beneath a dying cedar. Two more fish, seemingly quite large, slurped greedily just upstream and about fifteen feet out from Rob.

"Get 'em, Robby," I directed, but he was already stalking them, shaking line out through his rod, staring hard into the gloom.

Without discussing it, Jerry and I had somehow agreed that he would try the fish farthest upstream and I would work the riser that now fed consistently about fifty feet lower in the run. There was no talking now, only the soft swish of fly lines, the hum and flap of insects in the air, the soft, fluid gabble of the river, and the feeding sounds of very heavy trout.

I turned toward a heavy midstream rise, quickly followed by a gasping expletive.

Jerry waded unsteadily back to shore, turned on his flashlight, and muttered, "Missed him. Fly sinking. Bad Jerry." No commentary was expected, and I looked over in Rob's direction. He continued the short cast, short drift technique and seemed to be timing the feeding patterns of the two fish in front of him.

From downstream a voice exclaimed, "Got him!"

A few seconds later, "Steve's got one, too! A double! Both nice fish."

I turned back to my fish. It was still greedily sucking down protein every twenty or so seconds, and I resumed casting. Jerry waded back into position and hooked up on his third or fourth delivery. It was a female brown of about twenty inches, and she tore up the patch before Jerry released her in the calm water off the island. My fish seemed to have moved a few feet closer, but held its steady feeding pattern. I kept casting and made several false sets when he/she slurped a natural close to where I thought my fly should be.

The trout continued to torture me as another signal of success wafted upstream from our friends at the sandhill. I changed patterns, being careful not to allow the flashlight's tiny beam to fall on the water, and applied floatant. I checked the short leader for kinks and tangles. I took a deep breath and cast again. There would not be much time left. The spinner fall was over. The bugs still in the current were carried to us from somewhere upstream.

Out in the dark beyond my sight, the fish fed again and I lifted the rod. "We have ignition, Hexaritaville. We have liftoff." The trout was heavy and powerful, wild and wonderful. Rob and

Jerry joined me with camera and net for the last moments. The fish, another brown, surged and rolled and bored deep one last time before Jerry had it in the mesh. We quickly taped him at twenty-three inches and made a happy release as Rob snapped pictures that exploded the night with flashes of brilliant light. A small series of time slices, one-thousandth of a second each, were forever captured.

We slogged back to the island to join Steve, Dan and Benny, who had quit for the night and were sitting on the bank enjoying the show. Happy chatter abruptly ceased when one of the fish Rob had been working fed heavily, then again, and again. My nephew looked at me wildly, handed me the camera, and waded back to his original position. We followed, all of us. Rob had a coaching staff that, in numbers, would rival some small college football teams.

Rob quickly hooked and landed a fifteen-inch female, and we readied to leave when a tremendous, plungerlike sound erupted from a widening, frothy hole in the water not fifteen feet in front of us.

"Good God! Did a plane fly over and drop a bowling ball?" someone asked. "That was a very big trout eating a decent sized trout," said Benny, and added, "However big it was, it was big enough to stalk and eat a fish that was gorging on Hex. It's over for tonight. Let's quit. It's one-thirty."

We waded upstream to the path, then made the short hike to the parking area in silence.

"What now? Can we come back here, I mean right here, tomorrow night?" asked Rob.

"Can we go to the Yooper Square Dance in Grayling?" begged Dan.

"I want a hot bowl of chili and a cold beer," said Steve.

We drove back to the little cabin on the hill, hugged the dogs and tied some flies.

ANN R. MILLER

Ann Miller, "mother of three girls, wife of one man," lives in southwestern Michigan along Lake Michigan. She earned degrees from both the University of Michigan and Bowling Green State University in biology, specializing in "slime-cology," or the study of algae. While she still uses her microscope to look at swamp water with her kids, she is drawn more to macrofauna now, particularly fish. An avid reader, Ann became interested in writing after volunteering to become the editor of The Leader, *a 16-page fly-fishing tabloid representing the Great Lakes and Great River Councils of the Federation of Fly Fishers. When she isn't fly fishing or on active family duty, Ann plays competitive team tennis, designs and makes quilts, and enjoys nature walks, Jack Daniels, occasional cigars, and email. Her long-time fantasy is to meet author Jim Harrison on stream anywhere in Northern Michigan and trade flies for recipes.*

UNDER THE WEATHER

ANN R. MILLER

"I realize I am living my recurrent night-mare where I fall in and eventually get tangled in an underwater logjam. I am going to drown. This has always been my worst fear, and now I am living it."

The wipers swish in soft rhythm as my van turns from north to east, clearing the first light drops of mist from my windshield. It has been nearly four years since I have been up north, but countless previous trips with my husband remind me that this last leg of the trip will take another hour. We had spent innumerable hours exploring Michigan above her knuckles, an imaginary line on the mitten that happened to correspond with the birch line, close to the 45th parallel. We had camped, hiked, hunted mushrooms, bird-watched, photographed wildflowers, cross-country skied and fly-fished in much of northern Michigan, and now its moldy and pine-scented aromas tickle my nose through the cracked window, triggering recollections of previous getaways.

Pleasant memories are jolted momentarily as I pass a couple with a baby strapped in a car seat. I briefly dwell on the horrors of that night in the labor room and try to push the thought away. I look for a new selection from the cassette collection strewn on the floor between the front seats. *The Cars, Best of …* nothing morose about them. I crank the volume and am temporarily protected from ghosts of the past. I think of my two beautiful, healthy babies that I kissed goodbye hours earlier — really the first goodbye they have known since their births, seventeen months apart. In my eagerness to protect, perhaps I have smothered. Certainly I have suffered as much separation anxiety, and probably more, on this first trip without them.

I reach the outskirts of Grayling and watch for my turn north to Gates Au Sable Lodge. Grayling is a bizarre town, a mix of tourists and National Guardsmen from around the country who come every summer to practice bombing the daylights out of the local flora and fauna. Recently, the Guard missed a target and a piece of shrapnel punched a sizable hole in the roof of a home. Fortunately, the family was out and about and no one was hurt. I never understood the extensive bombing and war exercises, since the Guard's main job seems to be protecting towns that have been flooded or tornadoed or beset by other such catastrophes.

I find my turn and head north, hopeful now that the rain has ceased but still watchful of the early summer skies, which remain low and gray. Within minutes I am at the lodge, and I stretch my muscles after the long drive. Inside the fly shop, I am greeted by the proprietor's shy grin.

"You must be Ann."

Seems odd that he would know, but when I glance around for other female faces, I find none. It is an odd thing to be born with desires that some societies dictate as gender specific; I wonder if men in needlework shops squirm and make excuses. Feelings of anticipation erupt as I glance at the bins of colorful flies. I dwell on the moment, knowing that with my lack of skill this could be the best part of the trip. As I marvel at the creations in the dry-fly compartments, I ask the owner about water conditions and hatches.

"It's been cold," he says. "Everything is late, especially the brown drakes. Fishing is real slow."

Phhht. My balloon deflates a bit. I remember this from fishing B.C. (before children) — conditions are always better the day after you leave or were great until just yesterday. Before I die I will be there on the day that the fishing is just perfect.

After selecting flies (passing on the brown drakes), I decide to invest in a decent raincoat. I had forgotten how much it rains in this section of the state, and I make a mental note to bring a raincoat next time, regardless if it's seventy and sunny at home. I check into my room and am delighted. It is spacious and clean with a picture-window view of the famous Au Sable River. Instantly I am homesick and wonder again what possessed me to come up here alone. Thoughts of sneaking out and driving home begin to creep over me. The rain begins again and I calculate my arrival time if I were to leave now.

No, I can do this. I have to do this. Four years ago I could barely go shopping, go to work, leave the house. I need to prove to myself that I can do this on my own, to restore the confidence I once took for granted.

A shot of Irish whiskey coaxes one foot out the motel door. My gear is still inside the van, but I dash back to my room for my new raincoat and flies. I am off! To the river I charge. My heart races as my van accelerates out of the parking lot. A light rain dampens my spirits momentarily, but with each passing mile, my emotions vacillate between excitement and terror as I consider fishing alone for the first time.

I arrive at the river, leaping out to assess my domain. The rain has stopped and I have the entire place to myself. An old bridge extends across this section of the Au Sable, marking the upper boundary of the "flies only" water. I pull on my waders and boots and lug my heavy vest over outstretched arms. My vest is like my purse — both can always hold more even though I never take anything out. A final layer of raincoat and hat finishes my ensemble before I start to rig up my rod. The sound of tires on gravel makes me turn. *Damn.* The magic of the evening is spoiled — I am not alone after all. A man and two kids bounce out of the sedan and the man immediately comes over to speak.

"Don Stacey, Saginaw, Michigan." Nice to meet you and other pleasantries. He actually apologizes for interrupting my paradise. A nice enough man, especially if he is taking his son and daughter fishing. They plan to stick close to the bridge so that the kids don't have to do much wading. They invite me to join them, but I decline, heading in an opposite direction in my quest for solitude.

There is no path heading upstream, so I decide to cross the river and look for a trail on the other side. The current is steady here, especially in the middle, where I must hold up the bottom of my vest to stay dry. I cross uneventfully and easily spot the trail as I emerge from the river. I try to make note of the landmarks along the way as I tromp along and caution myself not to stay out too late. I cross a creek with an old fish weir and stop to examine both. The creek seems very small, and I wonder what the weir is supposed to block. The trail becomes more and more diffuse, and I consider stopping and fishing back to the bridge. It will be a long walk back in the dark. But I can still hear voices from the parking lot and I am urged onward as the trail angles into the woods.

I meander for some time through a plantation of white pine, probably planted in their nice, neat rows by the U.S. Forest Service fifty-some years ago. The trail winds out of the woods, paralleling the river; I pick a ninety-degree offshoot that eventually directs me to the water. Watching the surface for activity, I unzip my rainjacket, releasing the heat built up from the hike in. I start fumbling through my vest for fly boxes while I cool off. An occasional plunk increases my blood pressure and I hurry to unsnap the pouch with the dry flies. After the third try, I find what I am looking for, but as soon as I step into the river it starts to rain. Not lightly this time, but a real pail dunking. I laugh out loud at the weather and at myself.

Have I proven anything yet? Am I happy? Can I go home now? I pull on my hood and zip up, pondering these questions while searching for the perfect fly. A distant flash in the sky causes me to lose my concentration. Was that lightning or Camp Grayling?

Just then the rain lets up and a few fish start to feed. *Ooh.* I quickly scan the stream in search of flying insects, but see none. More fish are feeding now, perhaps seven or eight. My hands quiver as I select a small Adams and tie it onto my tippet. I roll cast my offering to a fish feeding regularly in the same spot, but it drifts by untouched. I try it again and again. Nothing. Fish are beginning to feed in a frenzy now, and I snip off my rejected fly and try something else. I cannot see to tie on my fly, and I search through my vest for a flashlight. Directing the light over the water surface, I find no sign of winged activity.

I try one more fly, this time a tiny caddis. Only caddis could escape unnoticed so quickly. Darkness is rapidly settling in and a light fog over the river makes it difficult to see my fly as I cast it out. Another roll cast to my friend, and this time a quick strike. And a miss by me. *Damn.* I cast again in the direction of another fish and notice that the feeding frenzy is gradually tapering off. Nothing. One more cast. One more cast.

A flash of light and subsequent boom cause me to look up in bewilderment at an approaching storm. *Where did that come from so quickly?* At the same time, my friendly fish takes the fly, hooking itself momentarily. I strip in several feet of slack line that I had let go when interrupted by the flash and boom. Too late, the fish is free. Felt like a nice one, too.

At least I got the fly right, I muse. I cast three more times in the direction of past splashes and come up empty each time. The fish have shut off now, and I suddenly realize that I cannot see across the stream. Yes, it is dark, but now the light fog has suddenly become as dense as smoke from burning leaves. Another flash of lightning; I start counting seconds to the boom, getting only to one-thousand two. This is not good, I think, reeling in my line. Why didn't I leave earlier? I should have left at that first flash of light. Deep down I knew it was lightning and not Camp Grayling exercises. *Idiot! Should have stayed at the bridge. Should have stayed at home.* Self-flagellation at a time like this is not useful, but I have to lash out at someone. As my mother used to say, "I yell because I care."

I finish cursing myself as I wade toward the shore, slipping on the muddy bank. The storm is building and the thunder and lightning seem practically on top of me. I grab an alder branch and pull myself out. I unhook my flashlight from my retractor and its light starts to falter. *Dammit!* I smack it and it seems to take notice. *Should have checked the batteries.* Should have, should have. That has been my life. Should have used another doctor. Should have insisted on keeping the monitors on...

I can't handle this abuse now. The storm is like a great beast beyond the river bend. It hasn't seen me yet; if I hurry I can escape it. *Lookit, God. I know I'm behind in prayers, but please keep me safe.*

I hurry now through the alders. *Where is the path?* It should be here. I stop as I am jerked from behind, my tangled line snatched by the brush. Shaking hands fumble with the snare, and finally I cut the leader. I take the rod down and stow the reel in a vest pocket. *Stupid.* Did I really think I might fish on my way out? Flash! Boom! Lightning and thunder are nearly synchronized now; I turn to go, scraping my cheek on an errant branch. *Ouch.* A tickle on my cheek suggests blood, and I wipe the annoyance against a wet shoulder.

I make better time now that my rod is down. *I can get out of here. Stay calm.* The flashlight falters again; the rain is coming now in buckets. The trail is difficult to see; it is somewhere in this mess of alders and grass. I shake the flashlight. Curse again. I have reached an impasse and realize that I am not on a trail at all. My mouth is completely dry, my heart is racing. I cannot think, I try not to cry.

Go back to the river. How brilliant! The river will get me back to the parking lot eventually. Can I be electrocuted if lightning hits the water? Probably. But it should hit the trees before it hits the water. *You will be safer in the water.* My mind is at least functioning, and I follow its directions, retracing my steps back to the river.

My first step into the river lands in a deep and mucky spot, but I don't have the luxury of looking for a better entry. I carefully place each step forward, gagging on the stench that is emitted each time I retrieve my foot from the decay. *Go slow, don't fall here.* The muck is knee deep, but getting looser, and I finally feel the relative stability of the river's shifting sands. The water prods me forward and I try to stay in the slower current. My feet maneuver around small stones and a few logs. Another thunderbolt. Has the beast spotted me?

The river gets deeper, about thigh high, the current a little stronger. I am wading faster, but still able to feel the bottom with each step. It is mostly sandy here with just an occasional downed tree and few rocks. As I approach a bend in the river, the water reaches above my waist and I calculate which bank I can make it to first. If I head for the outside of the curve it will be farther, but the current will be less strong. The inside bank is much closer, but it could be deeper and there might not be a trail there, anyway.

Which way? The water is above my belly button, and I switch from shuffling to tiptoeing. As I scoop up the bottom of my vest, a fly box pops out and is carried downstream. Dropping the left side, I reach out to grab the box, which, while still floating, is just out of reach. I start to bounce a little quicker on my toes — six, seven, eight giant steps. One more step, I grab the box and then abruptly pitch forward as I trip on a submerged stump.

The water is cold and I feel it as a dam bursting, flooding first my head and arms, then trickling down my back and into each leg. I'm flailing and sputtering wildly as my feet search for safety. I try to swim, but thrash helplessly with a fly box in one hand, a rod in the other. I think of my babies, growing up with just a dad, someday learning that their mother drowned while on a selfish fishing jaunt. Everyone will be sorry, but secretly pissed off at me, knowing that if I had just stayed at home this would never have happened.

I realize I am living my recurrent nightmare where I fall in and eventually get tangled in an underwater logjam. *I am going to drown.* This has always been my worst fear, and now I am living it. *Will my son be grown up in heaven?* A sudden memory of a Dave Whitlock video flashes in my head: There was Dave, floating down the river, calmly narrating what to do if you fell.

"Lean back and allow the current to float you to shallower waters. Don't try to fight the current ... "

I stretch my arms out while twisting around backward, allowing my head to bob to the surface. A deep breath restores my lungs. I try to keep arching my back. Within moments my feet are dragging in gravel and I swivel around and right myself. I make my way to the bank, half standing and half crawling, unable to walk upright with my extra ten pounds of water. I collapse on the bank, quickly losing an easy five. *Thank you, Dave.*

Still clutched in my right hand is the rod, the fly box in the left. These cursed weapons that I have paid hundreds for and protected so, all to pursue a fish that I will subsequently release, have nearly cost me my life. I should pitch the flies into the river, break the rod over my knee, bury it all in an unmarked grave. But practicality beats out capriciousness, and instead I consider the consequences of staying in this spot all night. Lying flat, I would not be struck by lightning, the rain would keep the mosquitoes away, I would not drown. I mull it over for a few minutes, but soon start shivering, reminded that hypothermia is no picnic, either.

The storm is so peculiar. While it seems that my escapade has lasted hours, the beast is still just around the river bend. Like a giant hunting dog, the storm wants to first flush me from the river, then finish me with a shot of lightning. Sighing, I pull myself together and up. I decide to walk for four minutes and if I can't find the trail, I will spend the rest of the night in the woods.

Such a simple proposal, but within moments the head demons are silenced. My heart has slowed, my saliva returns. After two minutes and some odd seconds, I find a trail and follow it downstream. The rain has turned to a gentle mist, and I wonder how long it has been this way. The flashlight's weak beam does not cut the fog, but it allows me at least to see my boots and a couple of steps in front of them. Within five minutes my feet stop at the little creek with the fish weir. *Thank you, God, and all you saints and angels.*

I look at my watch again. I know that I crossed the river and encountered the weir just afterwards. Was afterwards two minutes? Four minutes? *How long?* Crossing in the wrong spot could mean another dunking, and while I am already wet, I don't relish the idea of another near drowning. I will go for one minute plus, not as far as two. I can hear the river but can see no more than ten feet of it. I have to step in again, go across. The current will push me and I will have to be careful not to fall. Sixty seconds. I look into the fog. *Do I cross here?*

Suddenly I hear a car door slam. Voices. Oh, sweet Jesus. It is Don Stacey and family, my blessed intruders of the night. A faint glow across the water — car lights. *Thank you, thank you.* I step into the river, carefully angling my way across and slightly downstream. I call out to them and Don yells back.

"We were starting to worry."

Me too, I whisper, and aloud a little chortle. "Oh, there was a hatch and I couldn't tear myself away." Something all fly fishers can understand.

Out of the water we talk about the fishing. No luck at the bridge but the kids had fun with their casting. He is interested in my little hatch story, but I mention nothing about being lost, nearly drowning, the beast. I notice that they are packed up and realize that they have been waiting for me.

"Thank you for waiting for me. And for leaving your car lights on. You really are a lifesaver."

"Oh, we just got out. We didn't really wait long. Just a few minutes."

"If you hadn't been here, I wouldn't have known where to cross the river."

I think about telling him more, but the rain starts up again and we all hastily say goodbye and jump into our cars.

Both vehicles wheel out of the parking lot. Don turns left, I go right. I wish for my Irish whiskey. I wish for little arms to hug me, little voices to tell me they love me. *See, there are happy endings.* The rain is pelting down with a fury and I pull over to the shoulder to wait it out. Rain turns to marble-sized hail. The beast is loose.

JIM ENGER

Jim Enger has written for his supper since 1969, mostly in advertising agency creative departments, where he has worked on everything from beer to boats. He is an award-winning creative director. Along the way, he has been published in numerous magazines, particularly Fly Fisherman *and* Fly Rod & Reel, *where he has been a steady contributor since the founding of each publication. He is also the author of* The Incompleat Angler *(Countrysport Press), featuring tales of trout and salmon from the Arctic Circle to the rivers of Michigan to the rainforest streams of Central America. Jim is a founding member of the No B.S. School of Fly Fishing, "which has no meetings, no by-laws and no newsletter," and is a proud member of the Tennessee Squires. He is also a former member of the now-defunct Detroit Press Club, "gone to the dogs because they were still selling drinks for something like seventy-five cents into the early 90s." Jim grew up fishing and hunting in northern Ohio and moved to Michigan in 1966. There he discovered trout streams and advertising, "and any possibilities of a steadfast life went right to hell."*

*

GETTING OUT OF DODGE

JIM ENGER

"*Reality now? It's driving to work (a fly shop where I will meet a client) and seeing fourteen turkeys, seven deer, one porcupine, one coyote, a sharp-shinned hawk and not one car in the course of twenty minutes.*"

There I was, sitting on a hummock at dusk a few hundred yards into a northern Michigan marsh next to a sweet little creek. The creek came out of a distant cedar swamp. For as far as I could see there was nothing but waist-high grass, an occasional swale of what we call tag alders and a lone spot of high land sporting a few red pines.

We go from season to season, river to river, hatch to hatch, searching for that perfect pool, and I was beginning to think I had found mine. Behind me the sun was sliding beyond the tops of the cedars, turning a line of mare's tails an outrageous pink. I turned often to see it and I knew that others were watching, too; fortunately, not where I was. All over the north, on clear lakes and rivers, from cottage porches, from atop the dunes along Lake Michigan and in the lakeside villages, from bluffs above the old Indian town of Cross Village, the pace slows as people stop to watch the dramatically colored tendrils sweep high into the sky. The tourists enjoying dinner on the world's largest veranda at the Grand Hotel on Mackinac Island were getting their money's worth this evening.

Back in my bog the yodel dogs started to sing. There seemed to be two families of coyotes that lived and hunted in the swamp, and when one group started to sing, the other agreed that it was a fine evening for some music. There were puppies in both groups, and the combination of serious, adult wailing and the comical breaking voices of the pups created a festive atmosphere, just the right prelude to what I hoped would happen shortly in the air over the stream. Motivated perhaps by the Michigan Tourist Council sunset, the two families set up a racket. One pack seemed to be moving up the creek toward me, and I longed for a glimpse of the gang, especially the pups.

I did not see them, of course. Coyotes are extremely wary, and I was smoking a cigar (an extremely good imported number I had saved for a moment like this one), sending AWACS-like signals to Wile E. and his merry band.

In Michigan, you mostly see them from the car as they dart across the road. They are not nearly as numerous as in the western states and do no harm. But for years they were responsible for all sorts of witless antics on both floors of the state legislature in Lansing.

The Michigan legislature comprises politicians from one of the largest cities in the country, and politicians who represent areas so remote and wild that a very high percentage of their constituents practically live off the land. That the state is divided in half by water adds another dimension. The legislators from the top half, as well as many of the folks they represent, not so secretly believe that the Upper Peninsula is its own state every way but legally.

For years there has been a bounty on coyotes in Michigan. And each year, mostly in the U.P., several dozen are killed, their ears turned in, and the small bounty paid as prescribed by law. (Pointy-eared dogs in certain parts of the U.P. have learned to look over their shoulders.)

For reasons not entirely clear, the politicians from downstate would annually mount a big effort to get the coyote bounty repealed when the legislature reconvened and new bills were introduced. It wasn't long before Lansing-watchers began to look forward to the yearly battle between the slickers from the big city and the representatives from across the Straits of Mackinac.

The downstate politicians were never successful, despite all sorts of chicanery in the smoke-filled back rooms of Lansing. The politicos of the U.P. are elected term after term, have seniority and chair important committees. Thus, the distinguished representative from distant Dollar Bay might suggest to the distinguished representative from Detroit that if the good citizens of the Motor City really wanted those nifty road improvements, the good citizens of Dollar Bay ought to be allowed to collect the bounty on a few ky-oat-eez.

The year the big-city mob came closest, one U.P. legislator left his hospital bed to reach the floor in time to vote, while another stood in chambers embracing a stuffed baby deer. The gentleman with the taxidermy said that every spring there were plenty of these (he holds stuffed fawn aloft) in his district, but if the bounty were repealed his folks would be ass-deep in coyotes. As everyone knew, he said, they bred indiscriminately. Once again, the downstaters retreated with their tails between their legs, so to speak.

The sky deepened and now the fireflies were out and about. Ten yards in front of me the creek curved sharply, and within the curve there was a deep hole. What I was waiting for while sitting on the hummock, watching sunsets and fireflies and listening to yodel dogs, was the appearance of Mr. and Mrs. *Hexagenia limbata*. This little creek gets a tremendous hatch of the giant mayfly.

This is an intoxicating piece of water, and over the summer I had become addicted to it. It can be fished up or down, it is wide open yet remote, and it holds browns and brookies. A friend had been nice enough to show it to me and we often fished it together, sharing a rod.

It was almost dark, and still the big mayflies didn't come. This isn't at all unusual for the Hex, but they had come just at dusk two evenings in a row, and I am not much of a night fisherman anymore. Over the years I have come to fish for reasons that often have little to do with catching a lot of trout or timing probable hatches to the second. The reasons have more to do with going when I'm genuinely in the mood and when I'm likely to see things. I have come to use the sport as an instrument to bring me a variety of pleasures, and a trout taking a fly is just one of them, no more or no less important than any of the others.

This has not always been the case. For a while, but not for long, the sheer number of hours spent in the river meant everything, and the only object was to catch a lot of trout. A group of us ran together and we fished very hard. When we weren't fishing we raised hell. Everything was done to excess and we were very good at it — all of it. There was nothing contemplative about those days.

I had no desire to hang around until midnight, which diehard Hex fishermen routinely do, waiting for the hatch or spinner fall. I decided to give the bugs an honest hour. I was armed with beer and smokes, and the mosquitoes weren't bad.

It was then that the enormity of what I had done struck me. Here it was, the end of June, and I had not worked a single day since February. I had about sixty dollars to my name and the immediate prospects for any more dough were slim.

In February I had spent a weekend with a friend at her cabin on a river in northern Michigan. It turned out to be a watershed weekend for both of us. She decided that her marriage was worth saving and I decided that it was time to call in the dogs and piss on the fire. Twenty-two years in the advertising trenches were enough.

I called my secretary that Sunday, dictated my letter of resignation, and thus removed myself from the world of commerce. I had done this before, but always on a temporary basis. And directly or indirectly, trout and trout country were almost always responsible, much to the consternation of a variety of bosses, no less so to wives and girlfriends. But advertising types are supposed to be a touch distracted. And when the chips were really down, a decent portfolio always landed another writing job.

I had written about cars, bread, car wax, plastic shipping pallets, conveyors, fishing tackle, public transportation, lubricants, marinas, beer, storage racks, robots, pest control, a restaurant, rocket engines, spark plugs, light bulbs and quickie tuneup centers. When I made the phone call in February I had worked at the same job for nearly four years. My friends thought I had either gone straight or crazy, but they all agreed it was a miracle.

Still no sex-driven Hexes, and my head was full of the past.

They want a new approach to their TV stuff, the boss is saying. I am gazing out the window. It is a Thursday evening and I can see it coming. I was scheduled to be off the next day. It was May and there was a sparkling little meadow stretch of the Boardman I wanted to fish. I wanted three uninterrupted days in the sunshine 250 miles north to fish Pale Morning Duns and #16 Adamses to the gorgeous little browns and brookies that lay in ambush there. I wanted to sit in the greening meadow and drink brandy from my flask and write letters to the woman I loved. I had a momentary vision, imagining her next to me in the meadow, her raven hair flashing in the sunlight. But the boss is saying that he has made arrangements for me to ride with a bread-truck driver. From my eleventh-floor window I can see a hawk circling a suburban neighborhood. The boss is saying that if I ride one of the bread trucks maybe I'll get some new angle we can use for TV spots. Be at the bakery at 2:30 in the morning.

I spend half the night riding a bread truck. Not only don't I get inspired, but I get hot and sweaty because I end up helping the driver, who is overjoyed at having company. I see the inside of more grocery stores in eight hours than I expected to see in a lifetime. We get back to the bakery and I am tired and angry. I notice two women in the mailroom putting loaves of bread into special cardboard boxes. Oh, that, says my driver. When people move away from Detroit, a lot of them still want our bread, so we mail it to them. I can't believe it. I rush back to my office and rough out two thirty-second spots, which I leave on our art director's board.

* * *

The sky over the cedars had turned to deep purple and the first Hex of the evening makes its appearance, not in the sky overhead but on the surface of the creek. It rides the current silently and alone, the huge wings prostrate in the surface film, its body twitching, struggling as do all living things in the fight against the inevitable. It floats into the deep corner of the bend and hangs for a moment on the cedar post that had been driven into the creek by the German seaman who had jumped ship on the East Coast around the turn of the century. The German found his way to the deep pine woods of Michigan and lived his life on the edge of this swamp. There are signs of his handiwork along the creek — the pilings for what must have been a footbridge, the remnant of a small diversion dam that would have kept the water there from freezing in the winter. He knew his wood: All the pilings are cedar and will still be there at the turn of the next century.

The current sucked the big fly away from the piling and it began to float over the deepest part of the pool and I knew that eyes other than mine were watching it. But the appearance of just one fly wasn't quite enough to trigger an attack, and the spent Hex floated out of sight down the chute below the bend. I changed from a dun to a spinner, a pattern with double badger wings that on the water wiggle better than a hooker's ass. Even in the gloom I had no trouble making the change, thanks to 0X and a #2 hook. Another fly came down, and then another. Around the bend upstream I heard a splash. There were spinners falling up there, but I wasn't about to move. I had business with a resident of this pool. We had sparred the evening before and I suspected that if enough of these pork chops floated by his doorstep there was a good chance for a rematch. In the darkness I had not seen the trout, but if it was a brown it was a good one. If it was a brook trout, it was the grandpappy of all brook trout. I had heard stories, on the sly of course, about brook trout that had come out of this creek. One of the village elders, who grew up near the creek and knew the old German sailor, once confided that he had speared brook trout in the creek that were over twenty inches. Speared them, for God's sake.

So I waited. Spinners began to float by in greater numbers and the kids began to slurp. I thought about my friends in the city and my children and how much I missed them all. I wanted my son to see this creek and what happens here when the Hex comes off. I recalled with pleasure the not-too-distant time I was able to put him and his two sisters — the freckled princesses — in a TV spot, the fun they had "acting" and goofing around on location. They were three of fifty extras but thought they were the stars, and that's all that counted. I also recalled a certain dog, key to a certain scene, that decided to take care of business not just during one take, but during a succession of takes. Then a car alarm went off somewhere close and the dog said *adios*. The thirty-second epic-in-the-making came to a halt while trainer, cast and crew sprinted down a Detroit alley after a hundred-pound white wolfhound that appeared to have the speed of an F-15. Then the cops started badgering me about how they couldn't keep the street blocked off any longer. Then the head of the merchants association began to scream about all the business they were losing and loudly mentioned the word "litigation." Not for the first time did I begin to have thoughts of trout streams on a permanent basis.

The big guy fed and I swear the hair stood up on the back of my head. Imagine standing next to a small creek in a swamp on a dark, quiet night. Imagine that someone you don't see throws a brick in the water near the opposite bank. Imagine the sound that brick would make, on this quiet, dark night, when it hits the water. Imagine that, and you have the sound of an outsized brown trout (God, maybe a brookie!) taking a Hex. Except for one thing: You can't duplicate the *savagery* of the sound. When a big trout takes a Hex the sound has overtones of barbarism that make you think about great white sharks or man-eating tigers.

A coyote ripped a good wail close by and I thought I was coming straight out of my waders. But I was standing and stripping line, the big pattern whizzing by my ear as I lengthened line and dropped the fly near the opposite bank. The attack was almost instantaneous and I reefed back to bury the hook. There was a tremendous gusher of water as the trout slued around to get under the bank. Just as fast it turned again and bolted upstream in six inches of water, leaving a wake that reached both banks. The reel howled, and behind me in the bushes I heard noises moving away. The trout was around the bend above and I was in the creek, running after it. At the bend the trout was still on, but I spooked it up to the next bend. This time I stood my ground and, remembering the heavy tippet, leaned on the fish. It slowed but I couldn't turn it. This bend was almost a double-back and the fly line was across the grass as the trout again tore upstream. I came around the bend and discovered the big slob heading right for the pilings of the old diversion dam, and then it was in there and that was all she wrote.

I think a fisherman is entitled to all sorts of childish behavior when he loses a large fish. Personally, I don't give a rat's ass about streamside decorum as long as I'm not bothering anyone. I think if you want to yell and swear and kick things and chuck your fly rod up the bank (or into the river), that's your business. I think those posturing bullshit artists who stand around in fly shops and say things like, "I raised my rod in salute to the big fellow and knew I'd never forget him" have either caught more big trout than all of us put together or haven't caught any.

I went down and popped a beer and when the toes on my right foot quit hurting I went looking for my fly rod. I found it in a small stand of sumac and reeled the line in and put the light on the tippet. It was frayed about six inches from where the fly would have been. OX. I drove the truck to Jack's place where the lovely Kim got me straightened away with a beer and a double shot of bourbon. I consoled myself by reminding myself that I could go back every night all summer and try again for that trout.

As it turned out I went back plenty of times, but never hooked it again or even saw the fish feed. I have visions of a thirty-inch brown trout (sometimes it's a twenty-five-inch brookie) dying of old age, turning belly up in that little creek out in that swamp, washing downstream with the current, lodging in some logjam or settling into the silt, the big spots fading forever. All I wanted was to see it.

Dodge City. That's how advertising people in Detroit sometimes refer to their turf, where mega-million-dollar car accounts dominate, competition is fierce and the stakes are high. I never worked directly on a car account, but I've gotten out of Dodge.

I grew up in what was then a relatively small town in northern Ohio. There were woods and fields across the road, farms five minutes to the south, and Lake Erie five minutes to the north. Growing up, I hunted and fished as much as I wanted to. I am sometimes overwhelmed that I can do it again, if only in the evening. In the summer I hang out in fly shops and hustle guiding jobs. In the winter I chase words. There is still the business of keeping something in the larder and storing enough acorns to get through the winter, which in northern Michigan is long and cold.

During moments of reflection, I realize that I always knew it would come to this. You have an intuitive sense of priorities or you deliberately set them. Some people get hooked on money and power; I got hooked on woods and lakes and trout streams. And words. So, no midlife crisis here, sorry to report, or any quarrel with the ad biz. I had some great times and worked with some gifted people, many of whom became good friends. But woods and water and trout kept getting in the way and increasingly I yearned for a simpler way of life. There were times on Sunday evenings or early Monday mornings as I drove south on the interstate back to the city that my depression was as big and gloomy as an empty boxcar. And I didn't need a shrink to tell me why. So here I am, but not without some pain and sacrifice, and I do not stand alone in that regard.

Reality now? Well, since you asked...

It's driving to work (a fly shop where I will meet a client) and seeing fourteen turkeys, seven deer, one porcupine, one coyote, a sharp-shinned hawk and not one car in the course of twenty minutes, the record so far.

It's going to the bank where the two tellers know me and not having to produce twenty-eight pieces of identification to accomplish a simple transaction.

It's having your life depend to a large extent on the whims of mayflies, caddis flies and stone flies. I explain to a friend that I can't come downstate to her birthday party because the brown drakes are about to come off, and I'm booked. A city girl, she is incredulous. "Bugs! Bugs! You mean your income depends on little bugs that live in the water!"

It's Huey, my mailman, routinely delivering letters so vaguely addressed that they might read, Jim Enger, Somewhere in Northern Michigan. Then we talk for ten minutes about my new bird-dog puppy and his new black Lab.

It's the luxury of having time to explore some wild places and finding four remote beaver ponds, three of which have brookies.

Even phone calls tend to be of a different nature. Eddie Golnick calls from his trailer on the banks of the South Branch. Eddie once knew every beaver pond in three counties but doesn't get around so well anymore.

"Not floating today?" he asks.

"Not today, Ed."

"It's probably just as well. The river may be too low."

"Why do you say that?"

"Well, two trout just knocked on the door and asked for a glass of water."

STEVE NEVALA

Steve Nevala is retired after twenty-six years of teaching high school English in the Kalamazoo area, where he still lives. His wife Judy and daughter Terese teach school; his older son Matt is a sportswriter; his younger son Curt a college junior. Steve was born and raised in the rural area of Waterford, Michigan. "My brother and I virtually lived our youth outdoors with slingshots, tree forts, stick bows, snares, rafts, fishing poles and the like," he says. Cub and Boy Scouting ring pleasantly in his memory, and a gift of one of the first Fred Bear recurves fostered a lifetime passion for the serenity of bowhunting. Steve has co-authored two books, Michigan Trout Streams: A Fly-Angler's Guide, *and* Great Lakes Steelhead: A Guided Tour for Fly Anglers. *He has also written various whimsical pieces based largely on recollections from more than forty years afield. He ties flies, cooks wild game, builds arrows and fly rods, and "chases steelhead, whitetails, golf balls and young grandsons."*

❧

ARE YOU THE GUYS
WHO TAKE OUT CANOES?

STEVE NEVALA

"*The good Lord, to hear it told by my tutors, had a cruel sense of humor. He provided beautiful spots for His children to recreate, but couldn't resist adding tempering elements. To the trout anglers, he gave rising trout in sparkling, pristine rivers, then infested those waters with canoers.*"

I realized at an early age that while bluegills, sunfish and rock bass were fun to catch, they rarely appeared ablaze in color on the covers of outdoor magazines. They lacked glamour. Even I could catch them. In my sports-cluttered young mind, they were the 1950s Cleveland Indians of the piscatorial league.

But trout — hook-jawed browns, vibrant rainbows, boldly speckled brookies — these more often appeared as cover girls, invariably pictured leaping or slashing at a fly or baitfish as colorful and streamlined as themselves. They were the pinstriped Yankees, classy, cool and aloof.

I grew up in southeastern Michigan, a region that has about as many trout streams as Ted Nugent has Christmas cards from Cleveland Amory; therefore it only made sense that I should want to fish for trout above all else. The classic lure of the unattainable had me. I read every related article I could find and pumped information from more fortunate friends who claimed to have actually caught a trout. Then I discovered that a couple of my dad's friends had even fly-fished. I still recall the enthrallment of listening to one of these demigods talk of taking trout on dry flies during the "big caddis hatch" on the Au Sable.

And I garnered several useful bits of lore through this early, vicarious approach. I learned that to catch larger trout, it was smart to fish at night; I learned that one should walk softly along streams so as not to send alarming vibrations; and I learned that I should treat any canoers who might blunder by as the misbegotten sons of Belial they really were.

The good Lord, to hear it told by my tutors, had a cruel sense of humor. He provided beautiful spots for His children to recreate, but couldn't resist adding tempering elements. To the golfers He gave lush fairways and verdant greens, but threw in yips, shanks and pull hooks. To the hunters He gave the unparalleled glories of autumn foliage, but added wood ticks and Lyme disease. To the trout anglers (on the surface his chosen people) He gave rising trout in sparkling, pristine rivers, then infested those waters with canoers. This plague, of course, outdid anything, including the minor inconveniences inflicted upon Job or the dampened contemporaries of Noah.

It was quite some time before I encountered any of the Canoemen of the Apocalypse. But I accepted as Gospel that they must indeed be a nefarious sort put on earth expressly to foil the noble pursuits of the pure-hearted troutist.

"Yeah, it was going to be perfect," some pipe-smoking veteran fly angler would say in a profound and long-suffering tone. "The hatch was nicely under way, old Mossyback was already into his feeding rhythm, and I was just easing into casting range. Then here they come. Must've been fifty of 'em. They came sideways and ass-backwards and every which way. Had the whole river, but where did they pass? You got it. Right over my fish, the whole paddle-clankin' armada. And that was it. The fish quit feeding, the bugs stopped hatching, the river turned mud-brown and night fell two hours early. I packed up and went home."

And so for a time, apt pupil that I was, I carried the banner. The surly words I muttered at paddling "intruders" now make me cringe. To the innocent "Catch anything?" I would likely reply, "I was before you came by," or simply snarl, "Nope," and look put upon. I left prime stretches of river only because a couple of canoes had eased by.

It wasn't until I did some fishing with Jim Scott of Whitehall, Michigan, that I began to realize much of what is given as Gospel should be suspect. Jim liked to fish the Pine River in Lake County, so I'd go along in spite of that stream's reputation as a canoer favorite. What the heck, I would think. I might see somebody tip over and flounder around and teach me new words. I knew I wouldn't catch any fish.

But Jim caught fish, and soon I found I could, too. "Trout get used to the traffic," Jim said. "I've hooked browns when the wake of a canoe was still sloshing. And if you fish your chosen river stretches with a little forethought, you can be there well before or after the majority of canoers."

So began my mellowing. It was nurtured by a combination of circumstances, not the least of which was the realization that canoers often provided unsolicited and inexpensive entertainment.

One late June evening I was nestled in some thick, streamside bushes on the Boardman River, hoping to hit the spinner fall of the big Hex hatch. This sultry weather should turn them on, I thought as I leaned back against the tag alder saplings with only my feet in the water. I was vaguely contemplating the countless hours of my life thus spent waiting on bugs that, often as not, never showed. At least I was in a pretty spot, screened from the world by an encircling bower of shrubbery and trees, watching the sunset.

I was a bit puzzled at being brought out of my reverie by the metallic *tunk* of a canoe paddle against an aluminum hull. Canoers were usually well off the rivers by this time. As the single craft came even with my hidden person, paddles dug in and it grounded against the meadowy little point of land not forty feet away and directly across from me.

Wonderful, I thought. They're going to set up for the night right where I want to fish. Why me, God?

But unless starting the evening fire by friction really works, camping wasn't what these two had in mind. The close embrace they immediately fell into was discussed in no chapter of *Selective Trout*. Now, here was a dilemma. I would eventually have to step out into the stream to cast. Such a sudden, unannounced appearance could be unsettling, yet if I revealed my presence now and the bugs never showed and the fish didn't feed, then I would have interrupted them for no good reason. I may be several things, but a spoilsport is not one of them.

Also, one must be circumspect about speaking abruptly from the gloom, I quietly mused. I did not want to be responsible for two cases of cardiac arrest. So, too, choice of words needed careful weighing. If I sounded disapproving in the least, they might well take me for some sort of irascible snoot-tilter and think ill of trout fishermen in general. This I could not have on my conscience. What a quandary! As I wrestled manfully with possible courses of action (what to do, what to do) I leaned forward — only to better see if that was a leaf or a Hex spinner floating by — and the girl saw me. Her eyes immediately took on that classic deer-in-the-headlights look.

"Hi. Any big mayflies upstream, did you notice?" I asked conversationally as I stepped into the flow and began stripping line. "Should be a perfect night for them."

"We didn't know you were there," she squealed as they scrambled about. They departed hastily in a state of huffy discombobulation, unaware of the mental struggle I had just been through on their behalf. "Ingrates," I muttered.

Late afternoon and evening interactions between canoers and anglers are not uncommon, but the aluminum hatch is primarily a daylight occurrence. The true dark of night on Michigan rivers belongs to the wheeling bats, swooping owls, cruising trout and a few skulking fly fishermen. Occasionally this eerie soup is spiced with the emergence of a nocturnal canoer, an invariably interesting phenomenon.

One July I reached "my spot" on the Big Sable River shortly after dark and stood streamside for several minutes at the top edge of a six-foot bank. I was listening intently for a decent feeder when a noncommittal voice from the darkness asked, "How ya doin'?"

An unexpected voice in the dark usually makes me start, and this one came from directly beneath my feet. The owner of the voice had his feet in the water and had been reclining against the bank, his camo hat just inches from my muddy wader toes. I caught my breath, we exchanged the usual pleasantries, and I asked if he'd mind if I moved above him about fifty yards. "No problem," he assured me.

This short remove provided a ringside seat for the next event. It began with strange muffled voices, clankings, swishing of brush and the like, and culminated in the launching of a canoe directly over my newfound, reclusive friend's hat. When the exclamations and low mumblings and apologies died down, I could hear the now-stealthy paddler and his woman companion heading upstream against the gentle current toward my hold in the murky shadows.

"How ya doin'?" I asked as they glided five feet in front of me in the gloom.

"Aacck!" the woman replied, executing a respectable sitting high jump.

"Jeez!" the guy exhaled as he semi-deftly shifted and back-paddled to avoid capsizing. Then, apologetically, "We'll get well above you."

"No problem."

As I got my night senses going again, I thought idly (but seriously) of what an exciting, memorable experience any novitiate to this sport could have on such a night, and hoped they'd hit some active fish so she would see what drives an angler during the Hex season. A scant fifteen minutes later came the sound of that dipping paddle.

"Sorry again," the guy said.

"I just got too scared." This the young lady declared unabashedly, in the firm and forthright manner of one who had made the only practical decision; no alternatives were even to be considered.

"That happens," I offered lamely. And they left, as did the much-beleaguered hat-man below, leaving me to fish in peace (to no rises) and once again ponder the vicissitudes and vagaries of romance during the major hatches.

Another valuable step in my adaptation to canoers came when I realized it just plain makes one feel good to be helpful. Faithful fishing companion Bob Linsenman and I were sprucing up our camp after a pretty much fishless and chilly day on the Little Manistee River when we heard voices. As they and attendant canoe-bonking sounds came closer, we could separate them into distressed feminine tones and lower, grumbling, more masculine voices.

When these intrepid souls came into view, it was evident their day's adventures had provided unforeseen pinnacles of pleasure — assuming that being soaking wet, cold and thoroughly honked off at one another are measures on the pleasure scale. (I suspect they are among casual canoers as so many of them travel in this fashion.) The fine art of capsizing had reached a point where the guys were no longer even trying to stay in the canoes and paddle; they were walking them down. Their girlfriends remained aboard, soaked and shivering, eloquently commenting on mankind and life in general.

"How long before dark?" one of them yelled up at us when we waved a tentative greeting from our high bank overlook.

"Oh, about an hour and a half. Where are you getting out?" "Six Mile Bridge. How far is that?" This question in the most plaintive, hopeful voice imaginable.

"Oh, about three hours."

There ensued below us a conversation that ran the gamut of decibel levels, much of it in Technicolor. Bob and I, happy to have been helpful in fomenting inspirational dialog, gazed warmly down on the riparian rhapsody.

"And by the by," Bob called as they slogged and babbled their way around the bend below our camp. "Since it'll be getting dusky soon, watch carefully for the sign that marks the portage trail around Dead Man's Falls." He assumed they had heard this hoary bit of river levity before, but thought a token attempt at humor might lighten their spirits.

It was well-received.

"Falls? Dead what? What did you say?"

The noise from the river current and gusting breezes obscured most of what was said as they slowly moved on, but some moments later the wind shifted. Faintly but clearly we could make out some of the words of a canoer plainly near tether's end:

"Kidding? I don't think so! ...heard...say falls! Oh...perfect. If...think...ever again...!"

"Man. Helping them was nearly as much fun as that tuber last year," Bob observed.

Tubers are a peculiar race who drape themselves across various-sized inner tubes and float down rivers at the whim of the currents. They are a kind of bargain-basement, less-skilled relative of canoers. Lacking paddles, they need not know the intricacies of the J-stroke or synchronized switch. However, they are arguably superior in one respect: They take the worry out of when they are going to get wet by doing so immediately, and they stay wet the whole day. Inside and out, often as not.

The reference to last year's tuber involved one of a group who had careened by us down this same river on a hot August afternoon. They were all dressed as pirates. Sporting head scarves and painted-on scars, they yo-ho-ho'ed by in convivial disarray. The main freebooter flotilla was a good five minutes by when a lone eye-patched straggler rounded the bend above me, all spread out across his tube, blissfully puffing on a slender cigar.

"Your friends are going to be long gone before you hook up with them at the takeout spot," I ventured.

"Nah. They'll wait for me. I got the beer — what's left of it." He was towing a second tube, in the center of which was lashed a large cooler. "And hey, if that's your buddy upstream back there, tell him thanks again for the smokes."

When I fished up to Bob later, I mentioned the encounter. It seems the guy had seen Bob lighting one of the cheap, wine-smoked cheroots he occasionally used to keep the gnats away. "He churned his way over here like a side-wheeler steamboat and offered me five dollars for a puff," said Bob. "He'd left his cigarettes at the place they put in and hadn't had one all day. Five dollars." Bob shook his head.

"You didn't," I said.

"Of course not," he replied indignantly. "You know I wouldn't take advantage of anyone like that. Fact is, I gave him two whole, unbent cigars, and I only had two left."

"Gave? You?"

"Yeah. Well, as much as did." He sloshed over to the bank and lifted a 12-pack out of the shade of some ferns. "We engineered a mutually beneficial trade."

"Eminently fair from where I stand," I said in admiration. "You are generous to a fault. It should also make for an entertaining session around their campfire tonight when your buccaneer buddy explains this deal to his hot, thirsty crew."

Now, there have been some hitches in the mellowing process. The term "sorely tested" is too strong, but there have been some little jolts that required forbearance. I hit one of these fluvian speed bumps one evening at the Whirlpool Hole up on the main branch of the Au Sable. A middle-aged lady who had clearly had her fill of a day on the river sat in the bow of an approaching canoe, talking a mile a minute, while her teenaged son, a pasty-looking, overweight sort, occupied the stern. They came into the pool and rested, letting the circling current move them as it would. Their concern was the whereabouts of the pickup spot.

As they circled and jabbered in the revolving current, Bob clumped over from our vehicle where he had been stringing his fly rod and stood on the tree-shrouded bank beside me. The anxious woman spotted us and shrilled in a voice that would have set Ethel Merman's teeth on edge, "You must be the men who take out canoes."

We looked behind us, assuming some stealthy livery personnel had crept up.

"You two in the tight rubber pants," she shrilled again. "Is this Louie's Landing? Do you take out canoes?"

"Bob," I asked, *sotto voce,* "is your 20-gauge still in the truck? Let me take out just one canoe." He looked at me, but didn't answer. Instead he pleasantly explained to her that, no, we were not the men she sought, and no, this wasn't Louie's Landing, but if they paddled on downstream they would reach it in about forty-five minutes.

They left and we sat and watched the water for emergers. "Bob," I remarked after a few minutes, "Isn't Louie's Landing just a couple hundred yards upstream? Couldn't they have gone up the off-current side and been there in five minutes?"

"I suppose," he answered. "But when they're not at Louie's, the livery guys will check the other landings. They'll find them, eventually."

Any lack of magnanimity in the misplaced landing incident is partially excusable in that we were not long recovered from a more severe test of our equanimity. The two young Sierra Club types who launched near us as we were steelhead fishing that early April day should perhaps have guessed we were sincerely ignorant that this section was closed to fishing (we honestly, ignorantly were). They did not have to answer in the affirmative an hour later when a couple of conservation officers standing on Three Mile Bridge asked if they had passed any fishermen. But they blew the whistle long and loud, and we were shortly absorbed in a serious confab with the local wardens.

The officers were very nice and allowed as to how we did appear to be honestly misinformed, which did explain our malfeasance, but (and they were right), this did not excuse it. Shortly thereafter we drove back to our cabin much lighter of wallet and considerably heavier of heart. It was a while before either of us would even nod politely to a canoer.

In the couple of years since "the big bust on the Little M," our aluminum encounters have been few and unremarkable, except for one. It was so brief, almost ephemeral, that I sometimes ask myself if it really happened. Bob, my brother Dennis and I were way up near the headwaters of the Big Manistee checking out fishable water. After a hot, grueling hike, I hit the stream in a remote, beautiful area. Rings on the water showed fish were feeding on a fairly regular basis.

Aha! Grasshoppers! I could see them skittering around meadowy clearings at the water's edge, clinging to weed stems like large, twitchy heads of wheat. And I had the definitive imitation in my fly box. I fairly chortled as I knotted one of the little beauties on a 6X tippet. Then, from upstream, came the rasping clash on canoe paddles on metal gunwales.

"Doggone it," I muttered to the heavens. "I can't believe anyone would put in this far up." Wading to the near bank, up to my scuppers in this, the deep side of the slight bend, I awaited the onslaught. This didn't seem right. I had worked too hard to get here to have to wait for the fish to reactivate after these interlopers disturbed their rhythm. I wanted to fish now, I wouldn't be able to, and I felt more cranky and petulant by the moment. My responses to the inevitable passing remarks rang terse and insincere.

"How's the fishing?"

(Okay.)

"Beautiful day, hey?"

(Yep.)

God help me, was I regressing to the intolerance of my callow youth?

Then the last canoer saw my bank-hugging form and altered course so he would pass a scant foot or two from me. Good grief. The others had at least tried to favor the far side. As he closed, I rehearsed scalding remarks, debating whether to shrivel him with sarcasm, leaving him to limp away and suffer, or to bombastically blow him from the water, finishing him on the spot. My rancor and spite grew as he drew ever nearer.

"You look like you could use a cold beer," said the paddle-wielding saint, handing me a sixteen-ouncer as he slid quickly past. "I trout fish, too," he called back over his shoulder at the stammering doofus left in his wake.

Brother Den came wading down some time later and found me perched on a streamside pine stump. "Not fishing? What deep mystery of life are you brooding over that has your fly in the keeper ring and you out in the hot sun?"

"No mystery, Den. Maybe ... maybe an epiphany." I pulled the tab on the can and held it out, chalicelike. "Here's to canoers. May they live and prosper. And if you ever hear Bob say another disparaging word about that noble breed, take umbrage. Have you noticed how he's been a bit cross-grained and curmudgeonly over the years?"

NORRIS McDOWELL

Norris McDowell now lives in Florida but spent most of his life in Michigan. As a journalism student at Michigan State University, he wrote for the Lansing State Journal *and the* Clinton County News; *after graduation he edited the* Grand Ledge Independent. *He joined the Michigan Department of Natural Resources in 1973, where he wrote news releases, position papers and speeches, and helped develop Michigan's Report All Poaching (RAP) program. He was the DNR's environmental information officer for several years, and saw plenty of action in the late '70s during Michigan's infamous PBB contamination turmoil — considered one of the nation's most troubling agricultural disasters. He spent the remainder of his career as editor of the award-winning* Michigan Natural Resources Magazine *and feels privileged to have edited the works of many fine writers, including his friend, the late John Voelker. Norris returns to Michigan each summer to pursue his dream of catching a 12-inch bluegill ("which will be mine one day") and each fall to tramp aspen slashings and cedared hills in search of grouse and woodcock.*

IF TROUT COULD TALK

NORRIS MCDOWELL

"*Back on the road, he drove at a possum's pace, straddling the white line on the right side of hard-surface byways, which he avoided whenever possible. He said he would drive for miles out of the way on a two-track road to avoid stoplights.*"

Renowned author, respected jurist, champion of his beloved Upper Peninsula, master of the roll cast and king of the cribbage board, Michigan's John Voelker left his inimitable mark in many ways and on many people. But perhaps the most remarkable thing about this rare man is that through it all — from one accomplishment to another and even in the winter of his years — John remained at heart a little boy who liked to go outside and play.

There's a narrow, winding road near a place in the woods that was dear to John and his playmates, a place known by his readers as Frenchman's Pond. The old road runs doggedly through rock-strewn gullies, up and around conifered crests and under towering hardwoods. John knew these rocks and trees well, often slowing his old Jeep wagon "fish car" to admire them and share witticisms and wonder about them with his traveling companions. If they could talk, those rocks and trees, what stories they could tell about John, who spoke so often of them as he prowled the backwoods.

And what of the feisty chipmunks at Frenchman's Pond, whose underfoot scurries were predictably entertaining on warm days? What would they say of this man whose wry "fifty-cent epigrams" and laughter so often rang from the cabin, to the boulders, then across the shimmering waters? If trout could talk, the brooks at Frenchman's could spin the best yarns of all about John, who wooed them patiently, wrote of them passionately and spoke to them pleadingly. Yes, he talked to trout, this Voelker. And when they shunned him he would marvel at their intelligence and call them graduates of the Harvard Business School. When he did catch a trout, he was apt to apologize to the fish for the inconvenience, then release it "with only its feelings hurt."

When fishing was slow it became cribbage time, and countless games were played in John's tiny cabin by the pond. The contests were spirited in more ways than one, thanks to the maestro's patented old-fashioneds — the fabled bourbon from a tin cup that "always tastes better out there."

Losing a cribbage game to John cost his opponent a quarter, upon receipt of which the former Supreme Court justice would cackle appreciatively. Then came his famous down-the-nose, blue-eyed leer and the question: "Care to try another, lad? I do believe it's your deal."

Regrettably, I knew John neither long nor well, although I feel blessed to have known him at all. Our friendship grew from a note he sent me early in 1986, while I was editing *Michigan Natural Resources* magazine. He asked why we were offering his book, *Trout Madness,* for sale, but not his more recent *Trout Magic.* John's note, in green felt-tip pen on yellow legal paper, was the first of many he sent me over the following five years. I was surprised and delighted to hear from him, having heard that after *Anatomy of a Murder* made him famous, he became reclusive or, as he put it, "fled the baying hounds of success."

We began listing *Trout Magic,* and a few months later, on October 28, John wrote to say thanks. He enclosed the latest issue of *Rod & Reel* magazine, which contained both an article about him and an announcement that he had been named Angler of the Year. The article mentioned John's love of cribbage, my favorite card game.

Call it fate, coincidence or whatever, but just two hours after receiving that copy of *Rod & Reel* from John, I saw the first perfect cribbage hand of my life. At lunch that day, I dealt it to my friend Larry Folks, with whom I had played the game for fifteen years. The chance of holding a perfect hand is so slim that a player who does get one often frames that lucky jack and four fives.

Euphoric that afternoon, I wrote to tell John of my good fortune. A few weeks later I received the following response, which Larry framed along with his perfect hand, and which has hung in his den since.

"Dear Larry Folks and Norris McDowell," John began. "I've been playing cribbage since the early 1920s and consider two-handed cribbage the most fascinating card game dreamed up by man, mostly a game of luck, alas; but, in a close game, often decided by skill, a game not only of position but essentially one of *relative* position, something even a lot of old timers never quite learn.

"Some old timers never held a 29 (perfect) hand; I've held three, the last one out at fishing camp ten years ago. Even holding the chance for it is quite a feat. I dealt the last 'biggie' and held three fives and the jack of hearts; Hank sighed and cut and, presto, I turned over the five of hearts. The hand is now immortalized and framed under glass and hanging in camp, and do come up sometime and behold it and then take on the sly U.P. cribbage champ — sometimes spelled 'chump.' Regards, John Voelker (Robert Traver)."

And so it was that I accepted John's invitation and drove the following spring from Lansing, where I lived, to his hometown of Ishpeming. He suggested that I meet him at the Rainbow Bar, where he liked to start the day with a few games of cribbage. It seemed strange to walk into a bar at 9 a.m., but I did and, sure enough, there he was, playing cards with pal Ted Bogdan. The only other person there was Pollie the bartender, absently polishing glasses as he watched John and Ted peg their way around the cribbage board.

Soon it was my turn to face the maestro, who quickly trounced me twice and took my pair of quarters. "'Tis mostly a game of luck, lad," he said graciously, perhaps trying to make me feel better about losing, perhaps setting me up for further drubbing later.

Then he rose and announced that he was going to the post office to get his mail, then "out to the camp." Would I like to ride along?

"I'd love to, Judge Voelker," I said. He nodded, turned for the door, then spun around to face me.

"Do call me John," he said softly. "It's been a long time since my days in the black nightshirt. Then he smiled and placed a hand on my shoulder. "I was paroled," he explained.

Any self-respecting crow could make it from Ishpeming to Frenchman's Pond in forty-five minutes. Our trip that morning took John and me about three hours. As promised, he stopped at the post office ("I still get a royalty check from *Anatomy* now and then. When you write your bestseller, lad, make sure to nail down a good deal on the movie and TV rights.")

Next, he stopped for gasoline. Then he pulled into the parking lot at a new supermarket and asked me to go in with him. Inside the store, John led me to a long produce counter brimming with leafy rows of cabbage, lettuce, celery and other vegetables. He paused and surveyed the bounty. "The Russians would love to have something like this," he exclaimed.

Following him from aisle to aisle, I began wondering what, if anything, he was after. Finally, he stopped at the meat counter and carefully selected a package of side pork. When we returned to the Jeep, John wordlessly stowed the pork in a Tupperware bowl behind the driver's seat. It took him a few minutes to find the bowl, which he finally spotted, then dug from a mound of assorted cardboard boxes, fishing gear, clothing, glass bottles filled with dried pussy willow along with other flora, and other treasures.

John offered no explanation for his side pork purchase, and I was not about to seek one. Later I theorized that is was contraband, destined for consumption at Frenchman's Pond or on some other remote trout stream where John's blood pressure and cholesterol levels were of little concern, at least to him.

Back on the road, he drove at a possum's pace, straddling the white line on the right side of hard-surface byways, which he avoided whenever possible. He said he would drive for miles out of the way on a two-track road to avoid stoplights. I thought he was kidding. But after an hour or so of bouncing along rutted logging roads and across rickety bridges, it became clear that he was serious about pursuing the least-traveled passages. More than once on our way to camp we were stymied by tree trunks that had fallen across the road. I jumped out of the Jeep and dragged them aside while John sat patiently behind the wheel.

He talked throughout the journey, sometimes to me and sometimes to himself, as if there were a third passenger. "Why did you take the right fork back there, John?" he asked. "Well, we've turned there before and never been lost in here," John replied.

As we bounced along, he pointed out unusual rock formations and ancient white pines reaching for the clouds. Stopping beneath one, he led me to its massive trunk and declared, "This one was here before Washington, Jefferson, the Revolutionary War … "

Pushing on toward the pond, John continued his gentle, rambling commentary about the wonders of nature, all the while scanning the wooded roadsides. At one point, he reined in the Jeep, handed me a bucket and sent me toward a clump of ripe blueberries. "Looks like we beat the bears to those," he laughed. "Go get 'em, lad."

Finally, after unlocking a thick steel cable that hung across the road, we chugged around a bend and down a steep hill, and there, glistening in the late-morning sun, was Frenchman's Pond. While I explored, John got out his fly rod and fished silently from shore, clearly at home in this "solitude without loneliness."

We lunched on pasties I had bought that morning in Negaunee, then played several games of cribbage, all at my expense. John sat facing a window to the pond, watching for rising trout. As we played, my mind kept returning to the words of something he once wrote: "I fish because…I suspect that men are going along this way for the last time and I for one don't want to waste the trip." It struck me that of all the things this man had done in his life, wasting the trip was not among them.

Frenchman's Pond was never the camp's real name. John guarded that like a forty-niner his pouch of gold dust. Only when he came to know and trust someone would John divulge the actual name, locations or other details about his fabled hideaway in Michigan's Northwoods. One afternoon he surprised me by inscribing the pond's real name in my copy of *Trout Madness*, his first book of fishing yarns. Since he'd had other chances but never before offered to share the name with me, I was quite pleased. Every now and then, I flip open that book to cherish a memory from August 4, 1988, when an old fisherman (as John often called himself) winked and shared one of his treasures.

Considering John Voelker himself a treasure worth sharing, I often took Michigan writer friends to meet him on what had become semiannual jaunts to Frenchman's Pond. Artist Paul Grant told me how he and John had bounced along countless twisting backroads in pursuit of trout, mushrooms, blueberries and other things wild and elusive. I imagined these two adventurers topping an October hill, golden aspen leaves dancing in the wake of John's faithful blue Jeep, just in time to glimpse the rippling flag of a startled buck or the thunderous farewell of a ruffed grouse veering into the pines. Paul seemed to read my thoughts with his artist's eyes.

"People ask me, 'Why do you spend so much time riding around in the woods with that old man?'" Grant said. "I don't even try to answer."

Why indeed. Perhaps for the same reason a longtime Voelker friend named Charles Kuralt has referred to John as "the greatest man I've ever known." What was it about him that inspired such admiration?

Jerry Dennis wrote: "He had presence and charisma, the kind that fills a room." Eric Sharpe: "Forty years from now, when I'm nearing his age, I'll be able to say, 'I knew John Voelker.' And that alone will cause knowledgeable people to look at me with at least a fraction of the awe with which we looked at him."

Tom Carney: "I wonder how many more of us he fooled, like brook trout rising to an artificial fly, this extraordinary man, into thinking he was common."

I went up to see John each spring and fall through 1990. We corresponded regularly during that period, and I will always treasure his letters. Here are excerpts from a few of them:

"Wishing you all the joys of Christmas and the chance to get back up here for a low-tuition graduate course in cribbage."

"Storm's over, sun's out, John's rarin' to prowl through a newly plowed tunnel of white. Snow in a city is an affliction; up here, poor city lad, it's a glittering trip through fairyland."

"I once knew places where dozens and scores of wild orchids once grew but the loggers — softer tissue for milady — have chased most of them and most of the mushrooms far, far away."

"Opening day was typical ... cold, damp, boozy and virtually fishless. Picture seventeen adults loaded with fortunes in gear and fly patterns but not catching even one adult keepable trout! I love it. P.S. I won a little at cribbage after thawing out."

"The Utica lads have come and gone and we had a ball and I showed them some of our trees. Tomorrow five fishermen arrive from sylvan Chicago."

"Yesterday Paul Grant and I went moreling near a secret spot where we often fish, and fortune smiled, and we emerged parched from the search with visions of six-packs dancing in our heads and damn near half a bushel of prime morels in our baskets, the biggest and most exciting find we've had in years."

And, finally: "The more I prowl the woods the more I realize how little we people really know about the planet we vainly think was made for us to tinker with and plunder."

In fairness to John, it should be noted that he usually beat me at cribbage. He was the best player I've ever encountered. But on the other hand, it should also be noted that when I did beat him, I did so soundly. He hated to lose, perhaps even more than he loved to win. After one of the few games I won, he said, "It's tomorrow you're heading home, right?" I nodded. "I suppose you plan to go out tonight and spread humility all over the peninsula," he said, trying in vain to hold back a smile.

John invited photographer David Kenyon and me to his home one day to photograph him for an article written by our Marquette friend Dixie Franklin, which was later published in *Michigan Natural Resources* magazine. The day before, I had come out ahead of John at cribbage, and I knew he was still smarting from it as Dave asked him to sit at his big oak desk and pretend to write something, in green felt-tip on yellow legal pad, of course.

"But what shall I write?" John asked.

Ah, it was the perfect opening, and I pounced. "How about an affidavit?"

John looked puzzled, but only for a second. Then he smiled and mumbled that he had not written "one of these things since my days in the black nightshirt."

And, as Dave snapped away with his Nikon, John wrote, "John D. Voelker, being first duly sworn on oath, deposes and says that prior to yesterday he reigned as the undisputed cribbage champ of the U.P., that during yesterday those downstate eliters sent a crafty man called Norris McDowell up here to beat me; and beat me the man did, winning games and quarters and even skunking the deposed champ, who, with lumpy throat, now signeth off; further deponent sayeth not, dammit.

"Signed this 20th day of August, A.D. 1987, John Voelker, former chump."

Whenever I read those words it is my throat which grows lumpy, and it is my heart which fills with hope that sometime, somewhere we will play again. And it is my soul that longs to hear those words, "I do believe it's your deal, lad."

Autumn

*"As the harvest moon
sheds extra light on
farmers a month earlier,
the hunter's moon provides
hunters some extra
illumination as they
traverse the fields near
day's end — a sort of
blessing from the gods
of the hunt."*

TOM CARNEY
From "Woodcock Wanderers"

TOM CARNEY

Tom Carney has lived his entire life in southeast-ern Michigan. Therefore, he must take road trips to gather story material. His GMC Suburban reg-istered 100,000 miles in less than four and a half years, "not bad for a part-time writer." Tom teaches high school English and journalism; his wife Maureen is a community college Instructor of English. Whenever possible, they and their English setters, Maggie and Lucy, head to their cabin in northern Michigan. Both of Tom's books, Sun-Drenched Days, Two-Blanket Nights *(1994) and* Natural Wonders of Michigan: A Guide to Parks, Preserves, and Wild Places *(1996) won the Michigan Outdoor Writers Association's Harold "Opie" Titus Award for Best Book. He is at work on a third book,* Bird Dogs and Betty Cakes. *Tom, a resident of Utica, has contributed to national and regional outdoor magazines since 1980. His weekly column appears in the* Oakland Press, *a suburban Detroit daily. He is also a contributing editor to* Michigan Hunting & Fishing *magazine, and his column, "Compass Points," appears on the back page.*

WOODCOCK WANDERERS

TOM CARNEY

"*Conversation lasts well beyond total darkness. Why not? After all, the woodcock, a gentleman's bird, encourages hunters to sleep in, unlike the white-tailed deer, which insists that daylight find hunters in the swamp.*"

"If the bird is a nomad, then we shall be nomads, too."

So goes Chapter I, Verse 1 in our revised bible of woodcock hunting. There is a simple premise at work here, one that stems from a three-pronged logic: The realization that woodcock are migratory, the situation of a lengthy Michigan along the migration route, and an indignation that spawns the thought, "Why should deer hunters have all the fun?"

Spliced within is the decision to enhance our woodcock chasing by traipsing after the bird throughout the state and setting up mini-hunting camps several weekends each fall. The camps have come simple: a two-man-and-a-dog mountain tent pitched on the state land where we parked for the evening hunt in Michigan's Thumb, water from canteens, bread and lunch meat from the last party store before we left the paved roads, cribbage games by campfire light.

Some camps are more elaborate: a travel trailer set up as a base along a stream in northern lower Michigan, bottled water transported from a supermarket, meat-and-potato meals prepared over the old stove fueled by the twenty-pound propane tank, the art of cribbage explored within the shelter of that weary pre-Air Stream metal trailer which, for all its unsightliness and cramped quarters, still keeps us dry and warm.

The granddaddy of the camps is the most elaborate because of the number of men involved, the distance traveled to get there, and the quality of the cuisine. For four days each autumn, about ten of us meet in a rustic campground in Michigan's Upper Peninsula and strain together as we erect the Army surplus tent that serves as our dining room/social hall. The water, we pump into five- and ten-gallon jugs. The gourmet meals — make no mistake, they are gourmet in quality and presentation — are prepared over a couple of Durango grills with secondary dishes warmed on Coleman two-burners.

Starting from scratch after a full day's hunting, the camp cook gives new meaning to the term performance artist as, by lantern light, he creates meals with entrees like southern hickory smoked ribs and Creole fried oysters with horseradish cream sauce. For the rest of us, dish-washing detail usually lasts about an hour. Cribbage games sputter only when the lanterns do. Conversation lasts well beyond total darkness. Why not? After all, the woodcock, a gentleman's bird, encourages hunters to sleep in, unlike the white-tailed deer, which insists that daylight find hunters in the swamp.

In many other ways, though, our camps resemble the traditional deer camps that will soon quietly and instantly sprout in the woods like morels in spring. The camaraderie, the good humor, the thrill of the hunt, the love of the game animal: these qualities are the same. The chief difference, aside from the variation in firearms and hunting apparel, the one that sets our camps aglow, is that we have dogs.

Purely and simply, dogs are the reason most of us hunt. They spark the passion that directs us into the woods. If a triple logic spurs us on our woodcock wanderings, then a three-tiered appeal draws us to the bird in the first place. The woodcock challenges us poor shooters and brings wonderful flavor to the table. It is also a wonderfully patient and helpful teacher's assistant when young dogs are around. When its space is invaded, a woodcock will usually hold tighter than a ruffed grouse will. Also, woodcock do not suffer the population cycles that grouse do. Consequently, many fine grouse dogs first honed their pointing skills on woodcock.

Observe Lucy, my English setter puppy, in the northern Lower Peninsula a week before her four-month birthday. Not much would be expected from the little orange-and-white butterball that first year, only that she lighten my spirit and take my mind off my old setter, Paddy, whom we had lost to cancer the previous Christmas. Imagine our thrill when she pinned a patient woodcock for two of us. We were so grateful to the bird that we dutifully missed all four shots we tossed its way when it finally flushed.

See Lucy on the last day of the big camp in 1993, giving three of us another treat, pointing fifteen of the nineteen woodcock we flushed in an hour and a half. See Lucy cementing the bond with me in 1994. I, poor of shooting skills you must realize, enjoyed one of those fabled hunts: a half hour, seven birds pointed, a five-bird limit taken. Lucy would trot into the scene, then patiently wait as I floundered through the thick spruces where they mixed with aspen. Things went so well this day that I even dropped one bird with one shot while crouching beneath the spruce boughs, and not until after the bird fell did the top of a small aspen tree tumble to the ground. I christened this covert Promised Land, for the birds erupted into the heavens like loaves of manna headed the wrong way.

Thank Lucy for the patience she showed in 1995, when I went zero for ten shots during one stretch of our hunt in Promised Land. The day would produce thirty-nine flushes, at least nine of which came from what would have been opportunities at triples had I carried something capable of holding more than two shells, and had I not missed the first bird of each group with both shots. A couple of chances at doubles met the same fate. So, counting the birds I did not shoot at, I was sitting on a zero for nineteen score, and Lucy just kept covering the ground and pointing out more birds.

Thank God for Lucy, not once but twice in 1996, when she pointed grouse that just sat there on stumps or logs. Certainly, though we migrate in an effort to cross blades with timberdoodles, nothing in our code forbids our taking grouse when we can.

If the truth be known, the big camp started out being called Grouse Camp. And if the truth be more completely revealed, of these two grouse Lucy stalked to attention, one adroitly placed a tree between itself and the barrel of my friend's shotgun at the moment he pulled the trigger.

These are just my most recent images of dog work in camps. Another member of the big camp, Jim Ekdahl, has other visions. His upland hunting memories were originally consecrated by a performance turned in by Paddy, costarring a woodcock.

If rotten luck had greeted us in the guise of a locked gate on the road to a traditional hot spot, then blind, mystic luck guided us to a covert we now call The Place Between Two Rivers. A few minutes into a hunt that would grant us twenty-one woodcock flushes in forty-five minutes, Paddy held point on what remains my only double on the birds. But that was only prelude; the crescendo was yet to come. A lyrical snow began falling, like at the end of the movie, "McCabe and Mrs. Miller." Among the aspens, Jim walked up to find Paddy, riveted to the spot, nose to beak with a woodcock. Jim watched and savored for a long minute until the bird flinched.

Actually, Paddy's work was nudged from the position of Jim's top memory by his own dog Kelly five years later. Child of an unplanned pregnancy, Kelly is half English setter, half Brittany spaniel, but she looks completely English. While I was discovering the Promised Land, Jim took Norris McDowell and Jerry Dennis on a journey that led them to the covert now called Triple Limit.

Of the sixty birds they put up that afternoon, Kelly pointed or otherwise rousted about twenty. She was, indeed, a full-blooded bird dog, but Honest Jim (he is a conservation officer, you see) kept calling her "half English/half Brittany."

"Why don't you just tell people she's a Hastings setter," I asked.

"What do you mean?"

"Well, William the Conqueror invaded England at Hastings. He was from Normandy. That's close enough to Brittany for you to name this breed after the spot where the English and French first mixed it up."

"I'll give it a thought," Jim said, though the effort to promote the concept remains mine alone.

A year later, Kelly and Lucy led us through both Promised Land and Triple Limit, stitching their way through the woodcock-infested coverts like monomaniacal cobblers.

My favorite story about someone else's dog takes place on a cold, sleety, rainy, freezing, "You've got to be nuts to go out in this" kind of day in the big camp. Tom Huggler had loaned Holly, his ten-year-old arthritic yellow Lab, to Jerry and Randy Carrels. By late afternoon, everyone else had returned to camp and was dry and warm. Darkness sidled up, and with it, concern for Holly.

Not to worry, though, for a few minutes later, the three barreled into camp. Two of them just gushed over how Holly had hunted like a schoolgirl again. For them, camp had climaxed in fine style with Holly's finding, flushing and retrieving more birds than they had seen all week. While they lavished praise and hugs, Holly just grunted and stood at the door to Tom's tent until he unzipped it so she could curl up in his sleeping bag.

An equally important aspect of such woodcock pilgrimages, these attempts to intercept the bird along its migration routes, is that they offer insights not always available to hunters who simply return to the same spots in their states each weekend, hoping to ambush some flight birds. One year during the big camp, I shot a banded woodcock. It was my first, and also the first for anyone in the group. We crunched some numbers and estimated that hunters have a two-tenths of one percent chance of harvesting a banded woodcock. Subsequent details from the U.S. Fish and Wildlife Service indicate I had found the bird in the general vicinity where it had been banded a year earlier, thus supporting the theory that woodcock return to the same territories each year.

Another time, we arrived just in time to set up a pup-tent camp at a turn-out near a river. We sat cross-legged on the ground cloth eating our sandwiches as dusk faded almost entirely into the shadows. A pair of woodcock flitted by, following the dirt road that was growing lighter as the surroundings grew darker. That observation supported the theory that full-moon nights encourage woodcock to move, ostensibly because the north/south roads and river bottoms of their migration routes show up better in the moonlight. Maybe that is why Van Morrison's "Moondance" has become my theme song for late in October. He sings:

> *"Well, it's a marvelous night for a moondance*
> *With the stars up above in your eyes*
> *A fantabulous night to make romance*
> *'Neath the cover of October skies."*

He can only be speaking of the hunter's moon. As the harvest moon sheds extra light on farmers a month earlier, the hunter's moon provides hunters some extra illumination as they traverse the fields near day's end — a sort of blessing from the gods of the hunt.

Of course, our camps deliver more than just good dog work and the chance to learn more about woodcock or to speculate on theories. Something special — call it a privilege perhaps — anoints the camper at this time of year with the unction of autumn: brilliant days drenched in warmth and clarity of thought, nights that urge you deeper into your sleeping bag where clear and brilliant dreams await.

Yet there is more. In the big camp, the year before we softened up and opted for a dining tent, we were hovering around the overflowing picnic table eating the third or fourth course of one of those gourmet meals. Beyond the ten-foot diameter of the gas lantern's reach loomed utter darkness. Now and then, those of us not wearing hoods would get a leprechaun's handful of sleet down our necks. Then came the call, the guttural, primeval "Kar-r-r-o-o-ok" described by Aldo Leopold as "the trumpet in the orchestra of evolution": sandhill cranes migrating in their pin-wheel formation. The sky was so dark we could see no silhou-ettes; however, by following the calls, we would glimpse stars momentarily eclipsed by moving figures.

Another time, if we had not been in camp, and if Paddy had not been dog-tired, and if I had not run back to get a camera while Jerry and Randy made one last sweep through the woods before dinner, we would not have obtained photographic evi-dence that a chipmunk will eat a smaller mammal. And if we had not been in camp, I would not have earned my stripes as a bird dog on that same sashay.

"Jerry, head down into those alders," I called, just up the slope from him.

"Why?" he asked.

"There's going to be a bird in there."

"What are you talking about?"

"Just go down there and you'll put up a bird."

As he sized me up and considered my command, the alders flut-tered to the lilt of a woodcock making his escape. The next time I made a similar prediction, both hunters trusted me and one of them dropped a bird.

Often, the blessing springs from the pleasant juncture of time and place: Michigan Thumb towns like Cass City, Almont and Vassar seem particularly suited to harvest time. The wind picks up on Main Street and curbside leaves skip through town like so many trick-or-treaters making their annual rounds. Afield lies the chance for a grand slam: woodcock, ruffed grouse, ring-necked pheasant, and in favorable years, bobwhite quail.

If the day approaches perfection and the wind is right, the scent of apple will drift onto the tent fly, a hunter's moon will delay darkness, and "Moondance" will haunt from a radio free of static.

JERRY WARRINGTON

Jerry Warrington is a full-time free-lance writer who calls northern Michigan home. The fourth generation in a long line of storytellers, he differs from his predecessors only in that he spends more time crafting the written word than the spoken. In keeping with past generations, he's been known to spend an inordinate amount of time doing "field research" on a favorite hole on a trout stream or waiting for the evening flights in a duck marsh, often to the chagrin of his editors. The father of two daughters (who appear in the accompanying story) and a fancier of Labrador retrievers, he thinks he's convinced his significantly better half that one can never have too many dogs, guns, fly rods, decoys, et al, and that hunting ducks and geese or fishing a new trout stream are merely part of his job. "Don't bet the farm on it," he says. At any rate, Jerry is often found on the pages of Outdoor Life, The Retriever Journal, Ducks Unlimited, American Hunter, Chevy Outdoors *and other publications.*

🖋

SAME TIME NEXT YEAR

JERRY WARRINGTON

"*They once were 'Daddy's little girls,' anxious to do anything if it meant spending
time with their father. Every trek afield, every
streamside or woodland trip, was an adventure.
Things changed, however, when the latest hairstyles and how best to wear a bit of makeup
took on a new importance in their eyes. In the
blink of an eye, the two had become 'Mom's
young women.'*"

The phone slipped easily from his grasp, his mind sorting
through the possibilities as he considered the direction of his most
recent conversation. Good old Arnie, true to his word, was letting
him know that the geese were in full molt; Arnie expected him
and his two daughters to help, as he had promised, at the Fish
Point Refuge's annual banding outing, come Saturday morning.

Arnie's kindly reminder merely rekindled the memory of his
commitment when cornered at a local conservation banquet
some seven months back. In the wake of the months passing so
quickly, he'd totally forgotten to check it out with the powers that
be: the Speaker of the House, and the teenage twosome who so
gently reminded him of her.

He hadn't meant to be so verbal at the dinner. The words just
seemed to find their way into his mouth when chided about the
fact that he had no sons to inherit the marsh; no one to whom he
could teach the art of duck calling or how best to set a spread of
decoys when the birds were winging it south. Pushed about his
lack of male heirs, he'd risen to the occasion and flatly stated his
daughters could cut it with the best of them, male or female. His

pride had gotten the best of him, and now he was faced with the prospect of not being able to uphold his end of the bargain.

It wasn't that he feared broaching the subject with his teenagers. Far from it. The girls had always enjoyed the after-hours stories of the day afield and the conversation of his like-minded friends. Still in all, he wondered how they'd feel about being active participants as opposed to casual bystanders in an endeavor somewhat far removed from the normal Saturday activities of most kids their age. Banding Canada geese was an arduous and sometimes messy job, and hip boots and marsh wading were a long way from fashionable jeans and spending the afternoon haunting the shops at the local mall.

At one point in his life, there would have been little question in his mind that their collective response would have been in the affirmative. As the saying goes, they once were "Daddy's little girls," anxious to do anything if it meant spending time with their father. Every trek afield, every streamside or woodland trip, was an adventure. He had reveled in his role as teacher and counselor, and the outings had given him a feeling that his observations and his ethics had made a difference in their young lives. Things changed, however, when the latest hairstyles and how best to wear a bit of makeup took on a new importance in their eyes, and boys began to hold more attraction than an afternoon spent tying flies or repainting decoys. In the blink of an eye, the two had become "Mom's young women."

For a while, it had bothered him some, the thought of dog training and shotshell reloading being displaced by hours of motherly advice about makeup and long phone conversations with girlfriends. The realization that they were growing up and their priorities had changed had been a hard pill to swallow, even in light of his acknowledgment that they were indeed becoming more mature. They'd been youngsters for far too short a time, and in a way, he had longed to reverse the process and return to the way things had been early on.

Now he faced the possibility of putting them in a rather awkward position. He knew from experience that they normally reserved their weekends for household chores and spending time being typical teenagers, and he wondered if he shouldn't just swallow his pride and take his lumps at the banding seminar. After all, maybe the girls no longer had any interest in the outdoors and all it encompassed. Bird banding had been his volunteered pastime in recent years, and seldom had they expressed any desire to go along. Then again, nothing ventured, nothing gained. With that, he made up his mind.

Their reaction to his announcement about the banding seminar was far different from what he expected. As he mentioned the early hour involved and the commitment of at least four or five hours on the upcoming Saturday, the younger of the two made a dive for her closet, coming out with an old Ducks Unlimited hat he'd won at a banquet years before and subsequently had given to her. Perhaps shamed by her sister's immediate response, the elder pondered for a moment before deciding to go as well. For a mere shadow of a moment, things again felt like old times.

Saturday morning found him up earlier than usual, working on a batch of sourdough pancakes, a favorite with his daughters whenever they'd gone afield before. As he tested the griddle's readiness, his mind worked over the possibilities signaled by their willingness to join him at so early an hour. Had he misread their expanding horizons, interpreting them as replacements for the values and appreciations he'd sought to instill in them rather that what they truly were — mere additions to their everyday interests? He wondered, almost aloud, if he had denied himself the pleasure of their company because of what some would call a "failure to communicate." It was a consideration that disconcerted him a little.

As agreed, both daughters reported for duty at the appointed hour of 6 a.m. They finished breakfast in record time, and the truck swayed in an easy side-to-side motion as they made their way along the two-track leading back into an area of the refuge not normally accessible. And, with every flock of waterfowl sighted by the twosome came questions. What would the day's events bring? How did they capture the birds? Did they bite? When was lunch? The inquiries came in a flood that washed over him in a satisfying way.

The inquisitive attitudes continued as they stepped from the truck and got their first look at the holding pens. As the biologists conducted a brief seminar on capturing techniques and explained how the bands would help them gather information on migratory patterns, harvest data and the like, the daughters continued to cross-examine at will, firing an almost endless barrage of questions that proved just how much of their early teachings they'd retained over the years. It was obvious that their interest was genuine.

The group broke up in anticipation of the arrival of the first birds. It was then he took his first good look at the day's participants. A few of the faces were familiar, men he'd seen throughout the previous seasons while gunning the bay, including Bud, an elderly gentleman who'd been a fixture around the area for years and a welcome addition at any duck camp. Greetings exchanged, he turned to find his daughters already assigned to their tasks. One would record band numbers and vital statistics while the other would help transport birds from the pens to the banding area, and then release them back into the water.

At first, everyone got involved in the process. Birds came faster than the biologists could comfortably handle them and a waiting line developed. He soon found himself doing more watching than working, awed by what was transpiring before his eyes. The girls were handling each and every situation like seasoned veterans rather than first-timers, and they seemed to be truly enjoying the work. They were doing him proud, and he couldn't help but allow himself a knowing smile.

As the day wore on, his daughters lost little, if any, of their enthusiasm, and he found his respect for the kind of ladies they'd become growing with each passing minute. While a few of the early arrivals headed home a couple of hours into the day, the bulk of the crew stayed on and continued to assist in the banding, the older men driven by their desire to give a little something back to a resource that had given them so much, and the youngsters taken with the process as a whole.

As the sun fell toward the western horizon, the last of the goslings were released to rejoin the family group, bringing the grand total to eighty-five birds banded. Watching as his daughters then took on the task of helping to collapse the holding pens, he hardly noticed as Bud made his way through the crowd to his side. The old man's words were complimentary without sounding the least bit patronizing. He spoke of the pride a father could take in such a fine pair of kids; of how pleasant it was, in this day and age of youngsters who cared little for the outdoors, that he could point to his daughters as having made a positive difference.

That said, he turned to leave, then hesitated. Reaching deep into his jacket pocket, he pulled forth two aged bands, silvered by years of being worn around his neck on a lanyard that held his duck calls. Turning back, Bud held them for a moment before turning them over, softly stating something about the girls having a "keepsake" by which to remember the day. The sentiment acknowledged and understood, he watched as the old gentleman eased his way back toward the remaining members of the banding party.

The long ride home was a direct contrast to the morning trip. Where the truck had been filled with nonstop chattering and anticipation early on, the silence now was overwhelming. Worn out by the day's events, both girls had succumbed to fatigue, leaving him alone with his thoughts and the sound of their gentle breathing. More than he had in quite a while, he felt hopeful that he'd made a difference and touched their outdoor souls in a most positive way.

It wasn't until later that fall that he understood how much their day together had meant to his daughters. Just as the after-dinner conversation was winding down, his ears detected the shrill cry of a small flock of Canada geese making their way down the lake. Quickly excusing himself from the table, he stood on the back deck and watched as the group flew over the house, their wings beating in near-perfect unison as the flock's leader defined their flight path. Despite his years, he never failed to find a childlike awe in the sights and sounds of migration.

As he stood listening to the last of their cries, he realized he hadn't been alone. Just to his side stood his daughters, their eyes straining for one last glimpse of the now-distant flock. The younger of the two reached into her shirt pocket and pulled forth a necklace, a thin band of gold boasting one polished and aged goose band. Rolling the band between her fingers as if giving careful consideration, she asked, "Can we do it again next summer, dad?"

Same time next year, kiddo. Same time next year.

BEN EAST

Ben East, regarded by many as the dean of American outdoor writers, was best known for his true accounts of outdoor adventures. He began his career as outdoor editor of the Grand Rapids Press, *moving on after twenty years to* Outdoor Life, *where he spent the next thirty-seven years. In his sixty-year career, East wrote more than a thousand magazine articles, along with several books, including* Survival: Twenty-three True Sportsman's Adventures, *from which the accompanying story was taken. He also produced a number of highly regarded outdoor films. East covered many major Michigan conservation stories and was an advocate for outdoor causes. He was a driving force behind creation of Tahquamenon Falls State Park, Porcupine Mountains State Park and Isle Royale National Park. The Michigan United Conservation Clubs named its coveted outdoor journalism award after him. East was 92 when he died on August 1, 1990.*

✦

Reprinted by permission of the family of Ben East.

DEATH WALKED
THE DUCK MARSH

BEN EAST

" *H* is legs and body were stuck in the md
as fast as if encased in plaster. There
was no way he could raise himself an inch to
escape the rising water if it came. A foot or two
of it over the mud would be plenty to drown
him like a muskrat in a trap, and he knew it. "

When the Michigan duck season opened in October of 1965
there was a fairly good flight of blacks, mallards and blue-winged
teal in the Pointe Mouille marsh at the west end of Lake Erie, and
hunters had good shooting at the start. But it tapered off toward
the end of the month, and when Edward La Fountain and his two
cousins, Dave and Tom Venier, headed out into the marsh before
daylight on the morning of the thirty-first they didn't expect to
kill many ducks. It was a Sunday morning, however, with no
school and no work to think about, and that was reason enough
to go hunting, whether there was a feather in the sky or not.

The Pointe Mouille marsh is a big, state-owned public shooting ground, laced with creeks and cuts and channels, on the Lake
Erie shore a few miles south of the mouth of the Detroit River.
Before Michigan acquired it in the early 1940s, it was a private
marsh, belonging to the Pointe Mouille Hunting Club. It's one of
the top waterfowl areas between Detroit and Toledo.

The La Fountain family lived on the western edge of it, a dozen
miles north of Monroe, in a neighborhood that local people call
Bucktown, because of the deer that were killed there long ago.
The La Fountains had been hunters from way back. One of
Edward's grandfathers hunted and trapped the marsh all his life,

and the other was a watchman at the club for years and knew every foot of the place as well as he knew his own dooryard. Edward's dad, Albert La Fountain, was a punter for the club before he married, and he had plenty of chance to hunt there. But he was forty-three in 1965, working for the Monroe County Road Commission, and not finding much time for hunting.

Eddie and his brother Jim grew up on the marsh and started hunting ducks as soon as they were big enough to handle a shotgun. Jim was nineteen that fall and went into the Air Force right after hunting season. Edward was sixteen, a sophomore at the Airport Community High School at Carleton, and had hunted since he was twelve. He started with a Stevens single-barrel .410, but by then he had made enough money driving a tractor on his uncle's farm and skinning muskrats for a local fur buyer to get himself a 20-gauge Model 870 Remington pumpgun.

His two cousins and he had their duck boats at their grandfather's boat livery on Mouille Creek, a couple of miles from the La Fountain home. They loaded their decoys and other gear into the boats and were on the way down the creek at 5:30 that morning, Dave and Tom in one boat, Eddie in another. Dave was 19 and working in a factory at Romulus. His brother Tom was 14, a freshman in high school. They lived at Rockwood.

In the hurry to get an early start that morning Edward didn't take time to eat breakfast, and when they left the boat landing he forgot the hot dogs that his mother had fixed for his lunch. He'd have plenty of reason to be sorry about that before the day was over.

The morning broke clear and sunny, but at sunrise a high wind came up out of the northwest and within an hour it was blowing thirty to forty miles an hour, with very strong gusts. The boys knew that that wind, blowing offshore, would mean low water and poor shooting as the day went along. A strong wind from the west blows the water out of that end of Lake Erie and drains the Mouille marsh down as much as two or three feet, exposing mud flats and leaving many of the cuts and channels almost dry. It's hard to find a place where ducks will decoy on such a day.

The shooting was no better than they expected. They got their decoys out and sat hour after hour, watching the water drop lower and lower. There were almost no ducks flying and those few didn't come their way. About an hour after noon Dave and

Tom came to Eddie's blind and said they were going in. They had one bufflehead between them. Eddie had not shot a duck.

He hated to go home skunked and he liked to hunt alone. He figured that if the wind died in the late afternoon and the water started to rise, there'd be an evening flight and maybe he could knock down a couple of blacks before quitting time, so he stayed on.

But about 2:30 he decided he had had enough. He had missed both breakfast and lunch and was getting hungry, he hadn't fired a shot, and there were no ducks moving anywhere within sight. So he picked up his decoys and headed for the mouth of Mouille Creek.

He had only about five hundred feet to go and made it without any difficulty. But once in the creek, he ran into trouble. The wind had uncovered much of the channel, and he was still a mile and a half from the boat landing when he came to a place where he had to row through black, sticky mud instead of water. Then, up ahead, he saw Dave's and Tom's boat, resting on the mud fifty or seventy-five yards from shore, and when he got close enough he could see their tracks where they had abandoned it and wallowed to the marshy bank. Edward decided he'd have to do the same thing. The idea of getting into trouble didn't enter his head. If they had made it there was no reason to think he couldn't.

He tugged the oars and the boat slid ahead a few inches at a time, but the water was even lower now than when his cousins had come in, and when he got about twenty feet from their boat he couldn't go any farther. He left his decoys and gun, took the two oars to help him in the mud, and stepped out.

He sank knee-deep in thick, slimy muck, about the consistency of chocolate pudding, but he was wearing hip boots and that didn't bother him. He floundered ahead a few steps and when he was about halfway between the two boats, no more than three or four steps from either of them, with no warning at all, he suddenly went down to his belt. And when he tried to pull his legs free he couldn't.

That scared him. He had never bogged down in mud before and didn't like the way it felt. He laid the oars on the muck in front of him and tried to pry himself free, but only succeeded in pushing them down the length of his arms. He never knew what finally became of them, but in his struggles he sank them so deep that they were not found.

His uncle, Sam La Fountain, told him afterward that many times he had shoved a twelve-foot punt pole down its entire length in places in the mud of Mouille Creek, and Eddie must have hit one of those places.

He peeled off his hunting coat and laid it on the mud in the hope that it would hold up enough of his weight to let him pull his legs out. But the coat went down just as the oars had, until only a small corner of it remained in sight. He knew then that he wasn't going to get out by himself.

About the same time the thought hit him that if the wind died in late afternoon, as it usually did, the water would come creeping back across the mud flats and up the channel of the creek, and cover him. When they had rowed out that morning there had been at least a foot or two of water where he was stuck. He had sunk deeper and deeper as he struggled. He weighed 155, and his weight had pushed him down, but to him it felt as if the muck were actually sucking him under. He was buried to his armpits now, his outstretched arms resting on the wet mud, and they and his head were the only parts of him that he could move. His legs and body were stuck as fast as if encased in plaster. There was no way he could raise himself an inch to escape the rising water if it came. A foot or two of it over the mud would be plenty to drown him like a muskrat in a trap, and he knew it.

He quit struggling, because it wasn't doing any good and every move he tried to make seemed to sink him a little deeper. After a while he looked up the creek, and in a big pool of open water about a half-mile away he could see a hunter moving around in a duck boat. He knew the man wouldn't come down the channel where he was, because of the mud, and he yelled at the top of his voice. But the wind was against him and the fact that only about a foot of him was sticking out didn't help matters any. The stranger paid no attention, and finally he rowed out of sight around a bend. For a little while Edward thought maybe he had been heard after all, and the other hunter was going for help. But when nothing happened in the next half-hour he knew that wasn't the case. He felt worse than ever then.

He didn't yell anymore, for there was nobody in sight and there was too much wind for him to be heard. So far as he knew there were no other hunters out in the marsh who would be coming his way, either. All he could do was wait for some of his family to come and find him, if the water would give them time.

He wasn't cold. The muck, pressing his boots in around his legs skintight, even felt warm. He was tired from trying to get out and he got drowsy a couple of times, but was afraid to go to sleep, so he fought that off.

The afternoon dragged along, and he thought about his mom and dad and the rest of his family. He remembered things he had forgotten, things that happened when he was a little kid seven or eight years old. And he said every prayer he had ever learned. One thing bothered him greatly. He belonged to St. Charles Catholic Church at Newport, and he had skipped Mass to go duck hunting that morning. If he got out of the mud alive he wouldn't do that again, he promised himself.

He prayed mostly that somebody would get worried and come looking for him before it was too late. He had always urged his mother not to worry when he was out hunting. Now he hoped with all his heart that she would.

He had told his brother Jim that morning, kidding, that if the water was low and the shooting poor, maybe he'd stay out in the marsh all night and be there at daybreak. What if the family took him at his word and didn't search for him until morning? Long before morning the water would be over his head.

Toward sundown the wind started to die away, just as he had feared. He watched the channel and after a while he saw what he was dreading: an inch or so of water creeping very slowly in over the mud. That was about an hour before dark, and the 16-year-old boy gave up all hope then. He knew he was going to drown.

The water came in more slowly than he thought it would, however. He never took his eyes off it as long as he could see, and at dark it had covered only a little of the channel and was still nowhere near him. But the wind had died completely now and that meant it would soon be coming faster, like a tide.

Eddie was getting cold, too. Waiting for the water now that he could no longer see it, and wondering how fast it was creeping toward him, was the worst part of all, and he prayed harder than ever.

His family didn't worry about him until it started to get dark. His mother drove down to his grandfather's boat livery toward sundown, intending to wait and take him home. When he didn't come in at the usual time she thought maybe he was lost. That has happened to more than one duck hunter in the cuts and creeks of the Mouille marsh. But his cousin Dave, who was still at the grandfather's wasn't concerned on that score. He thought instead that Edward was staying out late because of the low water, waiting for it to come back into the channel so he could row in.

It was full dark at 6:30, and Mrs. La Fountain really got scared then. Dave went out in the marsh a short distance and yelled and when he got no answer she phoned her husband, back at their house, and asked him to come and start a search. He was as alarmed as she was. He hurried to the boat landing in his pickup, and at seven o'clock he and Dave started into the marsh on foot, the only thing they could do because of the low water, to look for Eddie. They were wearing hip boots and carrying a flashlight, but the flashlight was dim and they could see only a few feet ahead with it. They came to two muddy cuts and had all they could do to flounder across. The found an old length of weathered plank in the marsh and Dave had the presence of mind to pick it up and take it along. Every little while they stopped and yelled as loud as they could.

Their voices carried, now that there was no wind. It was about an hour after dark when Edward heard Dave calling his name. Dave and the father were still a quarter-mile away, and it was a pretty faint hail, but never in his life had Eddie been so glad to hear anything. He yelled back and after a minute or two they heard him. He was calling, "Hurry up, hurry up!" and they both took off through the marsh at a dead run.

Dave got to the edge of the cattails on the creek bank first. When Albert La Fountain reached him he had his boots off and was piling them on his coat, watch and billfold on the bank, and was shouting to encourage Edward.

They were on the wrong side of the creek. At that point it's about a hundred yards across, where it widens to open into the lake. To get to the trapped boy they'd have to cross it, through the mud, and then come out from shore on his side. The couldn't see him and he couldn't even see their flashlight, for his back was to them and he couldn't turn around. But his father kept calling, and Dave shoved the plank out on the mud for support and started to wade and crawl that hundred yards.

Nobody ever knew how he made it without getting bogged down, but he did. Once he reached Eddie's side of the creek he hurried to the spot where he and Tom had waded ashore early that afternoon, and then inched out to his cousin.

He reached Edward at about 7:45, almost exactly five hours after the boy had left his boat and gone down in the treacherous sucking mud, and he found Eddie exactly where he had taken his last step, upright as a post and just about as helpless, halfway between the two stranded duck boats. In all his struggles, Edward had not moved an inch back toward his own or ahead toward Dave's and Tom's. But the water had not yet reached him.

The first thing he said to Dave was, "Boy, am I glad to see you."

"And you better believe I meant it," he added afterward.

"Do you feel all right?" Dave asked, and when Edward said yes, Dave wanted to know what he could move.

"Just my arms," was the reply, and he flapped them up and down on the mud to demonstrate.

"I'll have you out of there in a jiffy," Dave promised.

"Where's the water?"

"I don't know, but it's not back in here yet."

Dave gave him the plank, to make sure he wouldn't sink any deeper, and then lay on his belly and literally swam along on top of the mud to the stern of Edward's boat. He got behind it, still stretched out flat, and kicked and pushed with his feet and shoved it ahead over the wet mud a little at a time, until Eddie could reach the front end. Then he climbed in, hooked his arms under his cousin's and heaved.

He might as well have tried to lift the bottom of Lake Erie. The sticky mud that had seemed to suck Edward down earlier held him now like a vise. Dave tried two or three times and Ed did what he could to help, but couldn't budge an inch.

After a minute the father yelled and asked whether Dave could get Eddie out. Dave shouted back that he couldn't, so Albert La Fountain peeled off his boots and started across the creek to help. But he had no plank and before he had reached the middle of the channel he realized that if he kept going there would be two to rescue, so he turned around and floundered back to shore. "I'll go for help," he shouted.

He didn't even wait to put his boot back on. He said afterward he had too much mud on his feet and legs. He took off for the boat livery barefoot, and once he got there he touched off an all-out rescue operation. He knew, as well as Dave and Edward did, that the incoming water would only allow so much time.

He phoned his brother Sam and Eddie's brother Jim, and urged them to come a-flying. Sam was twenty-six and both he and Jim knew the marsh well. Next Albert called the Monroe County Sheriff's office. Deputy Thomas Hoffman and a special deputy, Don Jennings, responded, and they also alerted the Newport Rescue Squad. Later the sheriff's office requested a helicopter from the Naval Air Station on Grosse Ile, fifteen miles away, but the boy was safely out of the mud before the copter got into the air. Nobody thought it could have pulled Edward out, anyway.

It was almost an hour after Albert left the two boys before anything happened. They heard Jim shout then. Dave admitted afterward that that was the longest hour he could remember.

"All I could think of was that water creeping back up the creek," he said. "I knew I couldn't get Ed out, and if it had come in fast I'd have had to get into the boat and watch him drown." That was a terrible thing to think about. He didn't mention it to his cousin at the time, but he didn't need to. They both knew what the score was.

Dave spent that whole lagging hour in the mud with Eddie, holding onto the boat so he himself wouldn't sink down, talking and joking to keep Ed awake and encourage him. Jim and the uncle, Sam, and a neighbor boy, James Hurd, were the first to get to the bank of the creek. Jim had been out on a date when his dad's phone call reached him, and didn't take time to go home and change his clothes for the rescue job.

He and Sam La Fountain started out to the boys, across the mud. Sam bogged down halfway, but he was carrying a rope. He threw it to Dave, Dave tied it to the boat, and Sam managed to pull himself out. He left his boots in the mud and they were never found.

He and Dave and Jim went to work to get Edward loose. The three of them couldn't pull him out, so they got in with him and dug the mud away with their hands. They worked as fast as they could, for the incoming water was only a few feet away now and rising faster. It took them half an hour to free one of Eddie's legs. The other one came out of the muck with a loud plop, and they boosted him into the boat. He still had his boots. Jim and Sam and Dave had done their best to pull his feet out of them but hadn't been able to. The mud and water had kept them pressed against his legs as if they had grown fast to him. He could stand up, but was too cold and numb to walk or move around.

When his three rescuers climbed into the boat with him there was enough water under it to float it, and there was enough to take them across the channel to the opposite side of the creek, too. When the whole thing was over, at midnight, Dave and Albert La Fountain went back to look for the boots and watch and billfold they had left in the marsh. The water had reached the bank then and was a foot or two deep out where Eddie had been stuck.

By the time the boy was freed his predicament had stirred up a lot of excitement, and some fifty spectators had driven out to the marsh in addition to the rescue people. There were cars stuck in fields all over the area.

Eddie stumbled when he tried to walk, and had to be helped to hard land, but didn't have to be carried. There was a levee running out into the marsh, and the sheriff's officers had a patrol car waiting there. They rushed him to the highway, where an ambulance was standing by to take him to Mercy Hospital in Monroe. It was close to ten o'clock when he got there. Somebody said afterward that all they could see that looked like a boy at that point was his eyes. The rest of him was encased solidly in mud and slime, from the soles of his boots to the top of his head.

They didn't even try to undress him at the hospital. They cut his clothes off and threw them away, and put him under a hot shower. Then the doctors checked to see whether he had suffered any damage from being buried almost seven hours in the mud. There was nothing wrong except that his legs were stiff and sore and he was awfully thirsty and hungry.

He was home by midnight, and before he went to bed he drank four bottles of pop and two glasses of milk, and ate two big bowls of hot soup. He'd had nothing to eat or drink since supper the night before, and nothing in his lifetime had ever tasted better.

He didn't sleep at all that night. Nobody at the La Fountain house did, for that matter. And Edward didn't go to school the next day. He was more shook up by that time than while he was stuck in the mud. But he was extremely thankful to be alive, and he knew how lucky he had been. If his dad and Dave hadn't found him when they did, nothing could have saved him from drowning. Another hour would have been too late.

He didn't give up duck hunting, but he resolved not to go out by himself any more, and to stay in his boat no matter what happened. "And I won't ever skip Mass again just to get an early start on Sunday morning," he told his family. "That's for sure."

TOM HUGGLER

Tom Huggler was born in Detroit, grew up in Flint and, at 52, has progressed as far west as Sunfield, Michigan, where he lives with his wife, Laura. Their home is "in the middle of twenty-seven acres in the middle of nowhere, sort of below a line from Lansing to Grand Rapids." Tom, a former president of the Outdoor Writers Association of America, has appeared on the masthead of Outdoor Life, Chevy Outdoors, North American Hunter *and* North American Fisherman. *He writes monthly columns for* Michigan Out-of-Doors *and* Woods-N-Water News *and contributes to several national magazines. He is also a videotape producer and the author of fifteen books. Tom spends time back in the woods in a writing shack he and Laura call* The Pout House. *When not working or traveling somewhere in the world to hunt gamebirds, Tom putters around his property, trying to make it wildlife friendly. He also aspires to "be a better cook, speak fluent French, grow magnificent roses, and play the piano."*

❧

Excerpted from *A Breed Apart*, copyright © 1993 by Countrysport Press.
Reprinted by permission of Countrysport Press.

SOMEWHERE ON POINT

TOM HUGGLER

"*You kill the bird, a young cock, for your dog on a crossing shot. Her perfect retrieve means she has forgiven you. The law allows two more birds; instead you unload your gun. You have learned that when the cup will hold no more, it is time to stop trying to fill it.*"

English setters gobble more ground in less time than any other breed of bird hunter. The brain, or maybe it is blood genetics, tells the dog to run hard and run long. Those that are mostly white float like elegant spirits over prairie grass and flash through aspen slashings. Their first points are pup clumsy, the legs misshapen, the body corkscrewed. You can mold such a young dog on point as though she is Play Doh in your hands.

"Cock that foreleg now. Keep the head up. Up, up. That's it, girl."

You will also not resist closing fingers around and stroking that magnificent tail. Like the feather plume on a musketeer's hat, it should be carried proudly high.

I played with setters long before I understood these things, certainly before I was old enough to hunt, with a gun at least, behind them. The first was Queenie, a big out-of-control runner that my father cursed loudly and often. Queenie was bold, stubborn, unmanageable in the way that only setters can be, but I suppose that was mostly my fault. On autumn afternoons when the elementary school bus deposited me in front of our rural home, I'd race to change clothes and unleash the excited dog. Then we'd head for the big fields beyond our lawn. We knew our roles well: Queenie's was to chase pheasants, mine was to chase Queenie.

I remember one time when she slammed, unexpectedly, into a pose as rigid as the lion statue on our front porch. She had been racing, pink tongue to the wheat stubble. Had she struck an invisible wall? Her body flag flew up and somehow she managed a pretzel bend to stare back over her shoulder at me, or so I thought until I approached close enough to see she was staring at a pile of old cornstalks. The pile suddenly ignited, and a big cockbird, all on fire, came roaring out. I think that was the day I fell in love with English setters.

Queenie's last big run occurred a couple of years later when a farmer shot her for trespassing. That is what our family was told, anyway, but could never prove.

When you are grown, you know it has to happen, but you wish it could be later and not sooner. Hunting dogs are born, they grow up and they die in the time it takes some people to get a college degree. That time is too short, or too long, depending on your point of view. For me, the eight years I owned a setter named Lady Macbeth were much too short.

Macbeth's death was unexpected and for no known reason that my veterinarian could determine. I found her dead in the kennel at feeding time one evening. There were no signs of suffering. I could not bury her on the farm where she was born because I had to leave for a long trip the next morning, and there was an autopsy to do. The autopsy proved nothing.

Those are the facts. They are easy to explain.

The evening before, we played on the back lawn and she pretended there were birds hiding under the roses, just blooming. Macbeth's tail chased her nose, wormlike, as though the hunting was for real. When I told her about our plans for the fall, she made that silly grin again. Our travels would take us to many places in search of native North American grouse. Some of these, such as blue grouse and ptarmigan, Macbeth had never seen. But I was confident that she could handle them, as she had learned to hunt Mearns quail and mountain quail and other gamebirds on a long trip that we had taken earlier. She was confident, too.

At first, I thought about canceling the grouse journey. What was the purpose, I asked myself, if I couldn't take along the partner who had shared so much with me in the past?

Some of those experiences have been coming back at strange times and in strange places, a not unusual occurrence when loss is both fresh and great. Scenes when Macbeth would retrieve birds that I couldn't get to — a pheasant that died in the middle of a duck pond, a grouse that fell into a shirt-shredding tangle. The day she learned to hunt brushy fencerows for bobwhites by vacuum cleaning them toward me. Her first taste of prairie grouse in Nebraska. How frustrated she grew with sprinting scaled quail in New Mexico.

And other things that were irritating or humorous but are part of any partnership, too. Her general bitchiness with other dogs and sometimes with children as she grew older. Her refusal to eat the supper I prepared in a hubcap, pried loose from my pickup, because I had forgotten her regular dish. That evening in the baggage terminal at Chicago's O'Hare Airport when she barked the instant she recognized me.

Macbeth was the progeny of a field trial mother and a gun dog father. Her permanence in my kennel was a fluke of sorts. By telephone, I had sold her as a pup to a friend from Kansas, after first choosing a male from the litter I was raising. I had her vet's certificate in hand and a reserved spot on an airplane leaving the next day. For want of a better name, I called her Ron's Star Point. That night the phone rang. It was Ron.

"I can't take the dog after all," he said. "My wife left me this morning and I don't know what I'm going to do. But it would be dumb for me to invest in a dog now."

So I kept her, changing her name when an editor and hunting companion sent a letter telling me of his own setter, Shakespeare. "You can't get any more English than that," he wrote. "Can you?"

The best dogs are those that form a special bond with their owners. I don't know how to explain that except to say that Macbeth and I had such a bond. There were times when I believe she could read my mind, and there is no doubt that I could read hers. She had ways of letting me know when she was happy or not. The most recent example occurred last fall when I came home from a sharptail hunting trip in North Dakota. I had not taken Macbeth because it was a short trip, and a sudden blast of frigid weather had me concerned about her safety in the cold belly of a DC-10.

I came home to Michigan on a Sunday afternoon in early November with just enough time for a woodcock hunt in some local coverts. After being able to see forty miles on the treeless Dakota plains, it seemed strange to be tramping through aspen bamboo where I could see only forty feet. Also strange was the behavior of my dog. She didn't want to hunt with me, striking out on her own a number of times without checking back. Punishing her did no good, and so we drove home in stony silence.

Later, I realized I was wearing the same hunting clothes I had worn in North Dakota. No doubt there were lingering odors from birds Macbeth had not stickpinned, the smells of other dogs that had competed for my affection. I washed the clothing before we hunted again.

Macbeth could be headstrong, sure, but only to the degree that you hope for in a bird dog. A dog that does not test the obedience limits once in a while is not worth putting your name on its collar. I shot my last grouse over my dog on December 31; my last preserve pheasant in early February. I was proud of her both times, and I think she approved of my shooting.

No matter how open or tight the cover, a pointing dog *has* to check in. Unless I had done something to annoy her, Macbeth always checked in. Except when she was on point.

Now, try to picture how it was for me that time in southwest Kansas. Imagine a thirty-knot wind trying to unbutton your hunting coat. The wires between hunters and quail dogs are certainly down this day. First Mike loses his golden retriever for a frantic twenty minutes. Then it is Macbeth's turn to disappear. You watch her chase the busted covey she had overrun from the upwind side. She is embarrassed, of course, and so she runs two errant birds downwind for a quarter-mile, finally vanishing as a white speck over a little rise in the cut field of grain. You wait three minutes. Four minutes. Five minutes. No Macbeth.

The tension mounts, along with your anger. "Excuse me," you tell your hunting partners. "I have a dog to punish."

But you should be the one spanked for not trusting your dog. There she is, another four hundred yards farther on. Locked up! The wind stirs her tail feathering, and it is your turn to feel foolish. You apologize as you creep into shooting position, but Macbeth admonishes you with those nervous setter eyes. They dart from you to the bird and you know what she is thinking.

"For Pete's sake, what took you so long? Here's the quail, right under this milo stalk."

You kill the bird, a young cock, for your dog on a crossing shot. Her perfect retrieve means she has forgiven you. The law allows two more birds; instead you unload your gun. You have learned that when the cup will hold no more, it is time to stop trying to fill it.

And so that is how you will come to accept the loss of this dog, your favorite hunting partner. You had her at her absolute best, and, in spite of your many screw-ups, you were also the instrument for some of her success. You know she wasn't great, at least not in the way the experts grade hunting dogs, but she was better than good and she made *your* bird dog hall of fame. What else matters?

This fall you will walk those mountain saddles and aspen whips and windswept plains after all. There will be other dogs and other hunters, but you will hunt alone. You will be looking for a white setter with black speckling to check back with you. She was right here, only a moment ago.

When she doesn't come back, you will realize that she is on point somewhere. You just haven't found her yet.

DR. JAMES W. HALL, III

James Whitney Hall III, M.D. (known to readers as Doc Hall), retired in 1993 "from thirty-one wonderful/stressful years of practicing internal medicine." He spends much of his time traveling, hunting and fishing, and writing about his experiences. He is the host of "Doc Hall's Journal" TV program shown in Oregon, and his book by the same name was published in 1995 by Wilderness Adventures Press. Jim began his outdoor career at his father's side, fishing, bird hunting, hiking and camping in Michigan and Canada. He studied for his medical career at Dartmouth College, Harvard Medical School and the University of Minnesota, and was an assistant professor of medicine at Stanford, before moving to Medford, Oregon, where he served patients until his retirement. Along the way, he expanded his interests to include advanced skiing, river running, dog training and fly tying. Jim, who now lives in Central Point, Oregon, has published scientific articles, stories about medical practice, and magazine pieces on the outdoors, and he wrote the foreword to The Corey Ford Sporting Treasury.

From *Doc Hall's Journal*, by James W. Hall, III.
Reprinted courtesy of Wilderness Adventures Press, P.O. Box 1410, Bozeman, MT 59771.

DUCKS: MY PREP SCHOOL

DR. JAMES W. HALL, III

"$\mathcal{I}$ was finally in the mysterious wilderness. Black ducks plunged miraculously from cold skies, twisting through tree trunks among clouds of blackbirds. All that I'd dreamed about, and wondrous. When and where would I be old enough to hunt them?"

I'm nine years old when it begins: my fascination with the wildness, freedom and wonder of waterfowl. I've wandered away from mom, dad and brother Tom at an outdoor concert on the Lake Michigan side of Michigan Avenue alongside downtown Chicago this evening to a little boat harbor at dusk.

Mom, bless her, took Tom and me to a lot of concerts in those days, mostly at the Symphony Hall for matinees in her efforts to mold us into little gentlemen with appreciation for classical music. But I recall now having learned the most from the other kids also stuffed into tight collars, neckties and scratchy jackets who sailed paper airplanes folded from the programs throughout the hall. Piano lessons were part of our indoctrination. Tom remembers best his stimulation thigh to thigh on the bench with various Miss So-andSo's, as do I, along with frozen fingers and blurred vision when called to the piano for recitals; however, some things did take root for me and remain — an ability to play by ear, as long as there are not too many sharps and flats, and the love of jazz.

But tonight in the dark, the music of Bach or one of those old guys is back sounding against the skyscraper lights reflecting on the inlet black waters, and here they come. Ducks. First whistling wings announcing their twisting, tumbling flight, looming bulky and graceful, skimming little patches to scatter the water-lights.

I'm enthralled by them, and that feeling has only gotten better ever since. I suppose now that my mind was prepared by a gaudy calendar rendering of a too-brilliant greenhead pinned to a wall of our small walk-up apartment, or by stroking feathers of a duck on our kitchen table — the odd one harvested by dad on his infrequent, brief escapes from the city — and his excited talk of each adventure. But here they were, alive, mystical, wondrous creatures from somewhere in the mysterious North, where Indians lurked in green-black forests and spooky lakes stretched to polar bears and ice.

I think today that my attachment to and fascination with wild animals, imagined somewhere out there beyond our apartments and the junk-strewn vacant-lot playgrounds, sustained me as a constant goal, through the confusion of multiple inner-city grade schools. There was a new school every year as we moved between Chicago and Detroit, necessitated by dad's fledgling medical career. Then he was suddenly in a khaki-brass, shining Army uniform when the radio boomed news of Pearl Harbor, and Franklin Delano Roosevelt's precise, cultivated tones called our country to arms. With each school there were new bullies to fight — I found them all — subjects either totally new to me, as were multiplication tables, or that repeated what I'd learned at the previous school. I think I was subjected to precisely the same short period of American history for seven years. Therefore, I'd sometimes be skipped ahead a grade, only to be suddenly dropped back one at the next institution.

The constant — the promise of country and wilderness — was sustained when Tom and I could stumble after dad toward a little pond or marsh near the cities, slowing him constantly as we gawked at a frog, turtle or garden snake. We'd arrive there, it seems every time, after carsickness in the back seat on our way through the black petroleum gloom of Gary, Indiana. We'd also follow him with our beautiful English setter, Jodi, in pursuit of brilliant pheasants in roadside farm ditches.

When I was ten years old, dad and his closest companion, Dr. Joe Sanderson, along with two other close friends, ventured into Lake St. Claire on a stormy late November day to hunt the ducks that funnel together in that great marsh from the Atlantic and Mississippi flyways. Dad returned very late, fiercely anxious and tearful: The boats had become separated, and the other two men were missing. Their bodies were found washed up on an island the next afternoon. It was my first experience with death close to us. Dad stopped hunting waterfowl that season, but did take me along seeking pheasants.

Another constant, it turned out, was Kathleen Sheldon, a little red-haired girl, like Charlie Brown's obsession in *Peanuts*, with whom I fell totally in love in kindergarten at Bradwell School. She had the audacity and unfaithfulness to accept a Valentine from Allan Pratt that holiday, so I naturally pounded his fat body and head on the playground asphalt and got my first school suspension. We returned to that school unexpectedly in 1945, while dad was serving in the Philippines. We were housed, mom and I, with her sister Marge and family (I slept in the laundry room and Tom with mom's mother). I was re-enrolled in Bradwell — seven years later. Rounding a hall corner in a crowd of strange students, I bumped into Kathleen. Instant recognition, blushing by us both — and we steady dated with the fervor of our twelve-year-old enthusiasm. I realize that I am digressing from ducks, but this is part of the story of my outdoor initiation.

Dad returned in his uniform at Christmas after the Japanese surrender, at discharge one of the youngest colonels in the Army, and, characteristically (Corey Ford would have loved it) re-honeymooned with mom by taking us all to a rustic lodge at Reelfoot Lake, Tennessee. Tom and I rode the narrow boat with dad and guide "Birdie" through tall drowned timber and dangling vines in swamp fog and skim ice of that giant backwater duck paradise of the Mississippi River. I was finally in the mysterious wilderness. Black ducks plunged miraculously from cold skies, twisting through tree trunks among clouds of blackbirds. All that I'd dreamed about, and wondrous. When and where would I be old enough to hunt them?

Dad agonized about where to begin medical practice. In Chicago, the only home that he and mom knew? Or in Cairo, Illinois, at a clinic (good quail hunting)? Or go north to Traverse City, Michigan, where he'd once fished, to start a solo practice? There, he would be the first specialist of internal medicine in a community of about 8,000 people at the foot of Grand Traverse Bay. We went north — I thank God. And I've been going north ever since, whenever I can.

Grand Traverse County was the far northwoods for us: crystal lakes and streams, actual hills that seemed like mountains, white pines and untracked snow so unlike the slush of city gutters, and just a two-lane highway stretching south to Detroit. Stores closed on the season openings of trout, birds and deer. My bike took me to grouse and woodcock coverts, to brown trout in the Boardman River, and, finally, to the edges of Lake Michigan where I could shoot ducks.

I wrote an outdoor column in our junior high school newspaper, *The Watchbird*, that was reprinted several times by the state conservation magazine, naming me "Michigan's youngest outdoor writer." I reached puberty and rode the train back to Chicago twice to see Kathleen. But she soon disappeared into the sunset riding behind a guy on a motorcycle. So, with all my city contacts severed, I was at home in the north.

Dad said then, I think with real wisdom, "It takes a man who's been raised in cities to most fully appreciate the outdoors. The farmer usually wants to go to town on Saturday night."

It's 4 a.m. this Saturday when dad bangs on our bedroom door. "Get up, boys." I'm bruised, stiff-jointed and groggy from our junior varsity football game against Ludington last night. I'd smashed against a huge farm boy defensive tackle for sixty minutes on frozen turf, then rode back, knees stiffening under my chin in the cramped school bus for two hours. Mom fetched me in the cold parking lot at 1 a.m.

Tom and I layer on woolen clothes, then plastic, holey waders beneath galoshes in the kitchen, and I stumble into the car with our 14-foot boat trailer behind and piled with decoys. We're driving through blowing snow to Bagg's Landing at Round Lake. We're stopped with the car lights shining a light-wall in the falling snow when a jackrabbit runs from the right and leaps high over this bogus barrier.

We're into the wave chop with ice spray in our faces out a half-mile, and with flashlights we locate our deep-water blind built on two floating telephone poles, framed above with 2x4s and chicken wire woven with cedar branches. The whole rig is anchored by a long chain to a cement-filled radiator thirty feet deep on the clay bottom.

We motor about upwind, waves slapping, to unwind and untangle and throw out fifty bluebill decoys and two Canada goose attractors. Back to the blind, we scramble onto the bouncing, slippery platform. I'm already very cold and my knees won't straighten reliably. I'm only artificially awake, but excited "as hell" (my first swearword) and warmed a bit by the thrill of the Stevens shotgun I hold tightly. Tommy's freezing, too, but he got some sleep and holds his BB gun at the ready.

The sky begins to lighten slightly, and the snow changes to intermittent squalls. A little blur of orange blush shows northeast over the Torch River outlet. Dark shapes flash at eye level, nearly brushing the blind. Thirty bluebills, sprung from the wavetops.

Dad: "Okay, Jimmy. Load your gun now. Watch your safety and your footing. Only shoot on your side. Remember to try to pick one duck and swing ahead through it, about fifteen to twenty feet in this wind. Deep-water ducks are hidden in the waves until they're right on us."

I've never yet hit a duck. Loading up and tense, I temporarily forget to shiver. It's lighter now. I can see a few duck string-specks weaving against the dawn toward the Skegemog marsh eastward.

Boom, boom. Blasts behind me, flinching me forward. I twist around to see dad grinning, jamming fresh shells into his double 12-gauge, and spy the white-bellied duck bobbing in our decoys and another splashing away with one wing. *Boom.* Dad quiets it.

"Good start," he shouts. They are beautiful: two plump greater scaup drakes with snowy bellies, blue-black backs and purple heads.

"Get ready again, boys. If you see any coming, yell '*Mark.*'" I'm staring about hard on my side. Suddenly two small ducks streak across downwind, bank sharply, knife back low to the decoys.

"*Mark — mark,* dad." I shoot twice, spraying water behind the leader. Dad pivots and misses them going away.

"Bufflehead, Jimmy. They're a beautiful duck, but very small and fast, a hard target to hit." I know he's only trying to cheer me up, but I like it anyway. Dad's so darned big, and he knows everything about the outdoors. His large nose is dripping steadily over his grin.

Then: "Dad, dad — hey, Mark!" yells Tommy. Twenty bluebills are blistering in, fanned out with wings cupped wide right over the decoys. Dad's gun booms twice. I shoot at the middle of the flock and, amazingly, nothing happens.

"I got two on my first shot, boys. Really lucky."

I keenly remember those first ducks on my first real hunt that morning, but the rest of the day's events blur together. The snow stopped; Round Lake turned from black to blue, torn by a stronger northwest wind. Scattered bunches of ducks swept into us pretty regularly. I didn't clearly hit anything, although dad credited me once when we shot simultaneously. Picking up, we were one shy of two limits, including one canvasback drake and a whistler with its majestic golden eye. The beautiful "can" especially intrigued me.

Round Lake (now called Skegemog Lake) was and is a prime stopping place for deep-water ducks migrating ahead of storms from Canada. With proper feed for them, it's wonderful hunting for the week or two of their visit before they head south. The ducks are mostly greater and lesser scaup, goldeneye, bufflehead, ruddy ducks, some canvasbacks and redheads. Good mallard numbers frequent the marsh. Dad killed a few Canada geese in his early years there with us; their numbers have increased much since then. Few swans would brighten the sky when I was in high school, but later they became very numerous.

I hunted there for five seasons. This included building several new deep-water blinds during the summers, because late-winter storms drifted off our structures, despite lots of experimenting with various anchor systems. The most arduous, wet, cold task was to pick up six-dozen decoys in the waves, untangling and rewinding each fifty-foot cord. We never found gloves that could keep our hands dry. Of course, there were days of slow shooting between flights when we'd take a merganser or two in frustration.

On the extreme eastern part of the lake is big Skegemog marsh: bogs, crisscrossed logs and dead, standing trees with alleged quicksand and huge Michigan rattlesnakes. It's a mysterious, scary place, made more frightening by the big muskies that spawn in the shallows. I was sure one of these fish could engulf my lower leg.

But mallards and teal took refuge there. When the diving duck migrations were scanty, we'd venture into it. I still keenly recall feeling the cold when once dad deposited me on a tree stump during a storm and motored off elsewhere for several hours. I flexed my legs up high (the muskies). In spite of mallards flying close regularly, my fingers were so numb that I couldn't get the safety off to shoot.

Dad's standard response to Tom's and my observations about feeling frozen was, "You just think you're cold." For years I trusted his absolute wisdom unreservedly — he was surely infallible — and undoubtedly passed on this controlling philosophy to my own four children much later. They seemed to reject this with much speedier insight.

Dave Wing and I skipped school today. Dave's my closest friend. His father was severely disabled in an automobile accident years ago and was often difficult to care for at home; therefore Dave, as the only child, was thrust into a "man of the house" role early on to help his mother. Dad kindly included him in our outdoor adventures.

Dave's a husky six-footer with crewcut blond hair and a very pale complexion that flushes brilliant crimson with any stress. Today we've broken away from school and hatched a scheme. Up long before dawn, I "borrow" the frail wood-canvas kayak that dad had lovingly handcrafted long ago in our Chicago garage. Fitted with a small sail, it had enabled him to briefly and hazardously escape from the city onto Lake Michigan.

We bound along a little two-track woods road to the edge of the Torch River, which links Round Lake to Torch Lake. Fierce snow squalls blot out the marsh and water intermittently — a dandy day for waterfowling — and Canada geese (then rare) honk all about. One flock beats low just over our heads as we're launching the kayak. Neither of us has ever been close to a honker, much less shot one of these seemingly untouchable creatures. Our teenage blood lust propels us to set out decoys among the sharp stump snags in the delicate and cramped kayak.

We're set up now. Immediately, two mallards form through the snow with cupped wings into the decoys. Dave and I fold the greenhead, probably both firing all our shells, and miss the hen. Shortly, a dozen more streak downwind low outside our stool. Four shots at the middle of the flock score nothing. God, we're excited by all the mallard chuckling and goose honking so close, but most of the birds are hidden by the driving snow. When we do see them, they're suddenly big, looming in front, and gone.

Lots more hurried and missed shots, but before too long we have three more mallards belly-up in the decoys.

Another blast of snow stings our faces when four huge geese-forms burst through right at us. We both shoot instantly. Two crash down with giant splashes. I scream, "Geez, Dave — they're swans." We're terrified, and feel instantly guilty. The swans are inert with enormous white wings spread.

Dave says, "We've got to get them out of here, fast!" We paddle out furiously as sunlight briefly floods the whole, awful scene. We rip a hole in the little kayak, and the shipped water rocks us sideways. The swans are terribly heavy to lift aboard. There's another tearing sound on my side and more water about my legs, and with the swans in our laps we wobble back now, taking on more icy water over the gunwales.

"Hurry, Dave. We've got to hide them somewhere, quick."

What do we do? There's an old outhouse near out parked car. We slip the swans inside, down the holes.

"Jim, let's get the hell out of here."

We retrieve decoys between dumps of water out of the listing kayak, shove the boat on top of the car, back around and head out. Suddenly ahead there's a red light blinking toward us through the windshield wipers. A dark green car blocks the road, and Mark Craw, the fearsome game warden, strides alongside. He's really tall — about ten feet — and smiling peculiarly.

"You boys doing any good?" Dave is sitting rigid as a totem pole, speechless, face bright red. I feign adolescent casualness.

"We've got some mallards, officer."

"I'd like to check 'em ... and see your licenses."

I unpack the four mallards. Dave can barely move to fumble out his wet wallet.

"Well, everything looks okay, fellows. You've got the stamps and all."

I've got to push Dave back into the car, sick-weak with relief. A siren shrieks behind. I slam on the brakes. Officer Craw leans in the window. "One other thing, fellows. What'd you do with those two swans?"

Craw later says a grouse hunter across the river on the hill saw us knock down the swans. "You know, these birds are pets around here," he said. "People feed them and have names for each one. It's a federal offense to kill one — $500 apiece." That's more than Dave and I earn each summer by hard, manual labor, and I've stolen dad's prized kayak, ruined it, and we've both skipped school. Our blackest day.

My memory of the events that followed is a despondent blur. We follow officer Craw to his office and sign confessions that seem like death warrants. I stumble home, show dad the remains of his kayak, and tell him all. Front page news in the *Record-Eagle* paper announces our crime: James Hall, son of Dr. James Whitney Hall, Jr ... $500 fines were imposed ... " etc. Thereafter follow some letters by local homeowners who've adopted the small swan flock. All this when dad is establishing his first medical practice and a well-deserved reputation as a fine sportsman and staunch conservationist.

Well, Dave and I suffered fully as we went with dad — hugely embarrassed — to court. The judge was most frightening to me, towering up over his bench (but I think he was, like Officer Craw, probably chuckling a bit inside). He rendered the $500 officially (for the press) but privately reduced Dave's portion to $50 (he was 16) and waived mine because I was underage at 15. He was probably aware of our already deep trauma.

Dave shortly thereafter had a poster printed that read, "Jim Hall, Swan Killer" and distributed it to our 200-person student body — most likely an important negative influence when I ran a close contest for class president later. I won anyway.

There is a wonderful inland marsh named Petebogo that stretches three hundred to four hundred acres north-south along Lake Michigan just forty minutes from our home. I've covered it for a year. Mallards infest it, but when I approach over the low sand dune on the inshore side, they always flush away, and the surrounding cattails are skimpy.

So, I hatched another clever scheme. I've come alone this early morning in full winter sunshine, a strong wind blowing. I drag and carry our canoe to the water — it weighs about two hundred pounds now due to fiberglass overlay of the canvas and multiple patches. Three good-sized bunches of mallards wing off. I hike back for chicken wire, stakes, a steel mallet, machete, gun decoys and so forth. I load up, now sweating a lot, pole and paddle the whole mess to the far end of the marsh, and build a major blind of cattails woven closely through the mesh. I set a dozen of grand-father's hand-carved wooden decoys out front, adjusting them three or four times. Most of them are lined along the reeds, plus a couple paced out a bit as attracters. Two hours' labor, but now it's great to settle in the bow, facing the stern, so well hidden that I can hardly see the far shore and just a glint of the big lake over the dune. Will it work? Will the mallards return?

An hour passes. Flies buzz about. Finally I see them again — about eighteen big ducks crossing from the lake into the marsh on my right. I catch the flash of bellies and underwings, then they near, and I can pick out bright-green heads. I tensely advance my shotgun ahead while staring fixed on them as they bore straight to the decoys. I mutter low feeding calls, and they're suddenly all right in front with the leaders skimming into the water. I snap up the gun, *and lift the whole blind skyward!* I've shoved the barrel end through the chicken wire.

Flaring wings, startled squawk-quacks, a pandemonium of ducks scattering while I'm jerking mightily on my impaled gun! It's suddenly over and I'm shaking. Those poor terrified mallards must have thought they were landing on an earthquake.

I did learn gradually, and did get some great duck shooting sometimes, mostly when dad was in charge. Grass Lake near Traverse City is a lovely, good-sized marsh that's hidden in a swamp forest and headwaters of the Betsie River. Standing, water-killed timber thickens the eastern shore. We got several fine opening-day shoots there on local mallards and teal. It was there I downed my first bull pintail (rare for this area) and stroked its beautiful plumage and dramatically long tail. This species became my favorite of all ducks ten years later when I hunted the great Pacific Flyway, and its nickname, "sprig," became the name of my second Labrador retriever.

Once we were set up in the canoe there in dense ground fog close to the trees with dad looking left, and a bird zipped across from my right. I snap shot it — a ruffed grouse. Later that same morning, fog thicker, two teal dive-bombed into the decoys. Dad shot, there was a yell from beyond, and two hunters appeared, swearing. Dad's shot had bounced off the bow man's glasses! I aggressively defended dad, while he attempted earnest apologies.

This is a dandy marsh to hunt, especially early in the season for local ducks; however, most of the mallards, and flight birds later, headed back into the flooded timber area that is unapproachable because of two hundred yards of bog with a thin mat of meshed weeds that won't admit a boat but will accept a wader leg, immediately, to the crotch.

I pondered this problem during the falls when I was in college at Hanover. Kay and I married at the beginning of my junior year at Harvard Medical School, and we, by some miracle, got a week free at Thanksgiving and drove the thousand miles to Traverse City. And I hatched another clever scheme.

Kay (on her first waterfowl hunt experience) and I pushed the canoe into Grass Lake on a cold, wind-driven, rainy morning, and paddled to the edge of the bog. But now I'm armed with my secret weapon — snowshoes. I wedge into the bog-mass as far as possible, struggle on the snowshoes over waders (it's tough to do), and step cautiously out — one foot, then both feet. The floating landscape is bouncing up and down, but holding me, swaying. Kay's quite worried, for some odd reason.

"This feels great, Kay! Hand me the gun ... you cover up with the poncho while I hunt." I'm taking a few shuffling steps: Heel lift, slide, lift again forward, and gaining maybe twenty feet. "So far, so gooooood!" Right snowshoe sinking — it suddenly breaks through, plunging my whole leg deep. I pitch face down, gun outstretched, left snowshoe wedged upright with the tip stuck. Loud, peculiar noises from Kay somewhere behind my mud-stuck eyes. I'm sinking deeper on my right side, the whole bog gyrating like a trampoline.

"Throw me a paddle — quick — and my knife!" She does. The bog holds miraculously for a bit, while I struggle to finally cut free the right snowshoe deep underneath. I slide, prone, to the canoe, stretch up to get in, and the left snowshoe plunges through. Holding the gunwales, I can finally cut it free and roll aboard. Score: Me, zero, ducks and swamp, two snowshoes.

Three years later, Kay and I and our four little children, Jimmy, twins Diane and Debbie, and infant Wendy, flew back to Traverse City for Christmas from northern California where I'd begun medical practice, and experienced a little bit of duck and goose hunting on that marvelous flyway. This afternoon, following gift giving, Dave Wing (now an engineer), Tom (training in urologic surgery) and I, with dad behind us, are crouched in a little shore-wood blind on the east shore of East Grand Traverse Bay, mostly just to get outside and digest our holiday turkey. It's sparkling sunshine with a spanking wind. A few ducks, mallards and divers, scoot out of range. Then, from the north, a brilliant white speck appears.

Dad: "Here comes a swan. They've multiplied enormously around here since you and Dave killed two of their ancestors." He's never forgotten any of that. The bird's getting closer, but a good fifty to sixty yards offshore. I see something special about it — the wing tips.

"Dad, I think that's a snow goose. I've shot a couple of them in the Sacramento Valley."

"No! It can't be. They don't migrate through Michigan. Don't — for God's sake — shoot!"

The white bird is now out front, beating hard upwind. I'm pretty sure now about black on the wing tips, and a shorter neck than a swan's. I rise forward, gun swinging up. Dad's trying to push my shoulders down. I shoot, and the bird collapses. All the others are yelling at me now, convinced I've repeated history and swan murder. We rush out in the boat and lift aboard the only snow goose dad has ever seen in twenty years of gunning northern Michigan. *Ha!*

STEVE SMITH

Steve Smith lives in the grouse and woodcock, duck and goose country of Michigan near Traverse City. Fittingly, those game species hold the key to his livelihood as an outdoor writer, magazine editor and book author. Steve is editor of The Retriever Journal *and managing editor of* The Pointing Dog Journal. *He is the former editor of* Gun Dog *and a columnist for* Shooting Sportsman, *a magazine he founded. Steve has written a dozen books on dogs, wingshooting and upland bird and waterfowl hunting. His titles include* Just Labs, Just Setters, Outdoor Yarns and Outright Lies, Reflections on Wingshooting, The Whispering Wings of Autumn, *and instructional books on hunting ducks, geese, pheasants and woodcock. He finds time each year to hunt in "half a dozen states and a foreign country or two."*

THE DOGS IN OUR LIVES

STEVE SMITH

"*Men trifle with their politics and they trifle with their careers, but they do not trifle with their sport.*"

Try this. Walk into a tavern and announce, in order:

1. "Anyone who voted for Bill Clinton is a jerk."

2. "Anyone who doesn't wear a tie to work is a loser."

3. "Anyone who spends time walking behind a bird dog is an imbecile."

See which one of those gets you punched in the mouth.

You see, when it comes to gun dogs, upland shooters and waterfowl hunters have never been wired up exactly like they should be — haven't been since *familiaris* stopped being *lupus* and moved into the family cave on this side of the fire, and probably onto what passed for the Neanderthal version of the good sofa.

I know one guy who has a female setter that breaks point, chases birds, eats the few my pal manages to scratch down and at nine years old hasn't quite got the housebreaking thing mastered. He dotes on her. The same guy is just finishing up a divorce to his third wife; this one couldn't get the toothpaste cap drill right. In any event, you get the picture.

So, it stands to reason that if you aren't used to hunting with dogs, you should realize there are several types. There are those that find and point game — pointing breeds. There are those that find and retrieve downed birds — retrieving breeds. There are those that find and flush birds for the gun — flushing breeds.

Now, on any given day, each of these lines can become blurred. Dogs that are supposed to point will flush, those that are supposed to retrieve can flush and (rarely) point, and all of them are supposed to retrieve after a fashion, even though only the retrieving breeds will do it with any degree of regularity.

The lines become further blurred by the retrievers and the pointers and the flushers being wrapped up into one package called the "versatile" dog of Continental extraction, which means the mutt will flush when he should point, point when he should be chasing, and eat downed birds like God's going to stop making them.

Then there's the type not often discussed: the Other Guy's Dog, a breed apart.

You see, there is something special about the Other Guy's Dog, and you have to realize that right off. And hunting with this beast is usually an exercise in self-restraint you could use to train for the Olympic Water-Torture Team. I mean, you can go to this man's house and he hands you his newborn son to fondle. You can turn up your lip, recoil and cringe, and mutter something like, "Get the little bugger away from me — he's all sticky," and the guy will shrug his shoulders and pass the kid off to his wife. But comment after a couple of drinks that the guy's two-thousand-pound shorthair is cutting the circulation off to your knees after sitting in your lap for the last four hours, and he shows you the door. And I mean right now.

I've got a pal who's got a mutt name of Sam — big English setter. Dog's a moron. Everybody knows it, including my pal, who got him as the result of a bet he lost or something. Or, maybe he's serving community service for kiting a check a few years back. That's the only explanation for the bond that exists between these two. The beast has two talents, the same two that are exhibited by English setters everywhere: eating and sleeping. Sam's world-class. Except, that's *all* he does.

Oh, my pal takes him hunting, all right. Sometimes when I scrape up the nerve or can't get out of it, I go with them. We hunt grouse and we hunt woodcock. Mostly we hunt for Sam, who gets out of the truck and just sort of leaves. About every twenty minutes, my pal starts shrieking at Sam, takes off through the cover like he was catapulted, and tackles Sam, who is heading for the epicenter of magnetic north. They wrestle in the leaves for a bit, and my pal wins because he's in better shape than Sam. Then, Sam hunts a while — maybe even points, although that's not guarantee he smelled anything or knows even a trifle more than we do about the whereabouts of any birds. Then, Sam splits again, and the scene is repeated.

But if you can stay with my pal when he goes after Sam, you'll get some shots, because the guy's the best flusher I ever hunted with. Hands down. Now, naturally, I don't criticize old Sam. He's doing the best he can with what he's got, poor soul. And besides being cruel to the dog, criticism would have a tendency to set my buddy's teeth on edge to the point that you watch the enamel splinter. You see, he doesn't trifle with his sport.

Spotting a felon among the changing cast of characters you'll hunt with in a year is easy, once you know what to look for in the Other Guy's Dog. First tip: the name. Now, folks who run a lot of dogs over the years have sort of run out of names, so they give them people names: Fred, Bill, Sally, Poindexter, you know. A dog handler at a Southern plantation with fifty dogs doesn't have time to sit around and think up cutesy names.

But, our hero is different. The cuter, the more autumn-is-the-smoky-colored-umber-smelling-earth-in-its-majesty sounding the name is, probably the worse the dog is. The inverse is usually true also: the simpler the name, the better the dog, because he's been named and trained by a guy who ran out of those sweet little names thirty dogs ago. There are exceptions (see Sam above) both ways, but it's a good staring rule of thumb.

For example, if your hunting pal introduces you to his new Lab Misty Morning (Missy for short), be ready for the canine equivalent of the Hillside Strangler. Good Labs are named Maggie and Tar and Jake. If the man's chiseled-headed setter looks like an Osthaus painting and has a name like October Delight, think about spending that particular Saturday at the Christian Science Reading Room.

There aren't many things I know too much about, but I learned a long time ago not to verbalize my true opinions of The Other Guy's Dog. You'll forgive me if I give you advice without informing you of the exact details that give me the right to give it. Trust me when I tell you it is hard-won knowledge I paid for in dashed friendships, bad hunting trips and the odd rearranged facial feature. Innocent little remarks on my part, I tell you, but the opposition does not trifle.

So, for your enlightenment, here is the advice: Develop an alternative vocabulary, commit it to memory, and use it when you discuss the Other Guy's Dog with him. Use these terms only when called upon. Volunteer nothing. To wit:

Good range. This means the dog can actually be seen on clear days if you're on a hill and he's passing over the next. Replaces previous usages like "coyote" and "smoker."

Thorough. This refers to the dog that thinks the birds are most likely found between your feet or eight yards behind you. Avoid here the use of the terms "bootlicker" and "gun-shy."

Intensity. Another term you can use to admire the Other Guy's Dog. This is best used after you've had a tug-of-war to get a bird away from him. Substitute for "hardmouth" and "jarhead."

Good conformation. Use this when the dog at least seems to vaguely resemble any one of the following: the sire, the dam, the breed, a dog. Avoid at all costs discussions of "papers" and the "Field Dog Stud Book."

Staunch. Admire the mutt's "staunchness" if you notice he has a tendency to doze off while on point.

Drive/fire. These can be used interchangeably in referring to a dog who can't stay on the ground when birds are in the air. To the Other Guy, "steady to wing and shot" might as well be "byziliop nugerlow epilimbot."

People-oriented. This means the dog will spend at least a portion of what he considers down time in the field trying to hump your leg. Admire his friendliness. Comment on how he's "bonded" with humans. Kick him when the Other Guy isn't looking.

But for all their faults, of course, what would we do without them? Who would share our duck-blind sandwiches? Who would care enough to take the time to ask how we feel each morning? Who else would put up with us the way we are? And as they age, and some of their fire cools and we catch on to their schemes, they become, as we all know, the best companions we can have.

Old dogs, especially old hunting dogs, are indeed a rare breed — rare as in remarkable, singular, irreplaceable and precious. There is something uniquely elegant about old dogs. They become, in their last years, so much more human than they ever seemed before.

The old gals become fastidious little clucking hens, set in their ways, sometimes a little crotchety, but mostly a little frightened, like a widow from the old neighborhood that is changing as she herself changes. Males, for their part, get to aching and paining, and sometimes they aren't in the most pleasant humor, but mostly they, too, mellow with time. There is an elegance in age that is a bittersweet potion made up of equal parts shrewdness, serenity and sweetness. They become so much more in tune with our moods, adjusting theirs to fit ours.

I have a good friend who has such a good friend, an aging wirehair. Time was, she was a crackerjack pheasant dog. She could go all day and ask for more, pinning running roosters and the odd covey of quail on the Iowa prairies. These days, her favorite outings are bass fishing with her somewhat aging partner. She really likes bass fishing, likes the boat rides, likes watching the line part the surface of the lake as the bass takes the plastic worm and runs. Mostly, she likes the carpeted deck of her friend's bass boat and the warm June sunshine.

My own setter, Jess, with miles beyond her dozen years, has taken lately to following the sun across the living room floor, and the back steps are sometimes a little steeper and icier than she'd like, an opinion she'll share with me through a sometimes bewildered look when the night winds spring up cold and melancholy. Old folks feel so alone at such times. As Guy de la Valdene said in his wonderful *Making Game*, "She once was strong; now she is very wise."

These old dogs, these old friends. There is a certain sadness, an emptiness that comes over us as we watch them dream by the hearth, doing the things again in their musings that they did once in their youth. The paws moving, the eyes flickering, the flews lifting in a barely audible little woof now and then. This is their world now, and it is not a cruel one. We can only hope for pleasant dreams and warm hearths when the last of our hunts, too, are but memories.

Now, I dislike sappy, saccharin dog stories as much as you do. You know, the kind where Old Rufus gives up the ghost after a life of faithfully finding birds for his master, pulling part-time duty as a guide dog for the blind and rescuing wagon trains lost in that big blizzard eighty miles out of Fort Laramie.

But the truth is, as Ben Ames Williams said in *Fraternity Village*, " ... dogs will die and men will weep for them so long as there are men and dogs."

Take Jess. A gentler soul, human, canine or otherwise, never lived. She's a great house pet, companion, world-class beggar at the table (total strangers being her favorite target), and more than a passably good bird dog. In her eleven seasons, she hunted in maybe thirty states and a half-dozen provinces, and slept more than one night under the stars with me in some Godforsaken woodcock camp tucked away very close to the edge of the world.

She's still with my wife and me, though, and she did a fine job of raising our daughter through med school and marriage and our two sons into college. She did it with a cool head, sagacious judgment, loving discipline when needed, and the firm belief that no bed is complete after there's a kid in it without a seventy-pound orange belt on one end of it to keep it from floating off during the night. When my daughter and her husband visit, Jess still hops on their bed, the better to keep the evil things of night away from the girl-now-a-woman she loves so well.

So, what follows isn't one of those this-is-how-Old-Jess-bought-it stories. This is about Jess's retirement party.

I had been off for a four-day pheasant shoot in Michigan's thumb, fine pheasant country, and I had intended to use Jess with her roommate, Maggie, my son's four-year-old Lab. But the CRP grass fields were thick and the weather rugged, so I left her back each day. Good thing, too, because Maggie could barely move after the hunt. It would have killed Jess. But she asked at the door each day to be taken along.

So, when I got back home to Traverse City, I knew I owed Jess a hunt. I also knew something she didn't — this was probably her last one. I knew a place where there were a few grouse, so after work I loaded her in the car and headed for one of the spots near home. I was using a little Parker 20 I just got, and I hadn't even fired it yet, so I sort of planned Jess's last hunt to be the Parker's first. Fitting, I felt, because most of the birds I had shot over her in her long career were woodcock and grouse, and I had shot them with my old 16-gauge Parker.

We moved no grouse the first half-hour, and the going was slow, her arthritic hips making her dawdle around deadfalls she once vaulted with aplomb or smashed straight through. As I watched and waited for her, I thought how I wished I could transplant that magnificent heart and mind and spirit of hers into a young body. Hell, I wished I could do the same thing for myself.

Making a swing toward the gravel road to hunt the other side back to the car, Jess came on point. She doesn't have the style she once had. It's more like, "If you want one, there's one right there." Though her nose is still what it always was, she's about deaf, so when I told her, "Steady," it was out of old habit.

I walked into a patch of bracken fern, and a hen woodcock rose through the bare aspen branches. The shot was easy and true, and Jess sort of speed-shuffled toward the downed bird. Now, I should explain here that Jess was gun-shy when she was young, a fault she cured herself of because she loved me and loved hunting more than she hated the sound of gunfire. But while we were working through the gun-shyness thing, we sort of skipped the retrieving thing. She never had any propensity toward being a natural retriever, so it would have been a force-breaking operation. After she came back for me over the gun-shyness, I didn't have the heart to force-train her to retrieve. So, over the years, we perfected this little ritual:

1. Jess points.
2. Smitty shoots.
3. If (big if) bird falls, Jess runs for the bird to grab it and munch on it.
4. Smitty sprints after the dog.
5. Dog, Smitty and bird arrive at the same place at the same time. Face mask and unnecessary roughness penalties follow.
6. Smitty stuffs what's left of the bird in his coat and the hunt continues.

For a few years, it was easier. My sons hunted with me and they were faster than I was, and got faster than Jess as all the players either grew into their prime or aged out of it. Hell, I even got faster than she was. Jess got very few munchies in before someone had the bird, a circumstance she found vexing.

But this time, I didn't race her. I let her amble over, find the bird in the dead and browning leaves, and flash-point it. I sat down, leaned against an aspen trunk, lit my pipe and watched as she slowly dropped to her belly, stretched her neck forward and gathered in the bird. She munched a few times, raising her head to look for me. I got up and walked over, and she feigned innocence, but her flews covered with feathers gave her away. I picked up the bird, pulled a few tailfeathers and put them in the empty 20-gauge shell, and we walked back to the car.

I poured Jess some water into the pushed-down crown of my old tweed hat — she especially likes water from my old tweed hat — and as she drank, I took the Parker apart and put the shell with the feathers from Jess's last bird in the case. I'll never open that case without remembering that shot, and someday, before too long, I'll look at that shell and use it to help me remember the dog that made that shot and so many others possible.

Anyway, I took the bird home with us, trimmed off the meat, fried it with a little bacon and some garlic (Jess likes a little garlic) and fed it to her in pieces off a fork. She asked why we didn't think of this custom eleven years ago.

So that was Jess's retirement party. She's been a companion and a friend and a drinking partner for so many years that when the season comes next fall, life will seem different. And not for the better. There will probably be a new pup, but there will never be another Jess. I just thought you'd like to know.

JERRY DENNIS

Jerry Dennis was born in 1954 and has spent most of his life in northern Michigan, where his grandparents farmed cherries and made maple syrup and his father realized a lifelong dream of owning a house on a lake. He started writing about the outdoors after he and his wife, Gail, took a year off from college to travel North America "in a camper van that kept breaking down near trout streams." Jerry became a full-time writer in 1986, and his work has appeared in The New York Times, Smithsonian, Gray's Sporting Journal, American Way, Audubon, Sports Afield *and others. His six books about nature and fishing have been translated into four languages. A new collection of essays and stories about fly fishing, ethics, and modern life will appear in spring 1998. Jerry, his wife, and sons Aaron and Nick live in a 125-year-old farmhouse on Old Mission Peninsula, in Grand Traverse Bay. At night they can hear Lake Michigan breaking on the shore and coyotes yelping on the hills to the north.*

LAKE TROUT NIGHTS

JERRY DENNIS

"*The trout appeared shortly after dark. They streamed in and through the channel, glowing white beneath the lamp. At first I could only watch in amazement. Hundreds of lake trout weighing six, eight or ten pounds paraded slowly through the channel, all within fifteen or twenty feet of where we stood above them on the wharf.*"

There were phantoms in the bay that fall. They swam into the shallows at night, attracted to lights on piers and boardwalks, and because they moved without haste and glowed with an eerie paleness against the dark water it was easy to imagine they were the ghosts of lake trout killed in the 1940s and 1950s, when over-fishing, lampreys and alewives ruined the Great Lakes fishery. But by 1970 the lakes had been restored to something like their former greatness, as full of life as anyone could hope, and what looked like phantoms those nights in November turned out to be flesh and blood.

We first heard rumors about them from anglers who said lake trout were being caught at night in the harbor at Leland, on the Lake Michigan shore of the Leelanau Peninsula. But Leland was a thirty-mile drive from our house and there was so much good fishing closer to home that my father and I felt no urgency to go there. We had plenty to distract us: Steelhead were in the rivers, woodcock and grouse were in the poplar coverts, lake-run brown trout and king salmon could be caught from the piers and stream mouths around Traverse City.

But we kept hearing stories about the strange run of lake trout in Leland and finally could not resist the novelty. On a Friday night in late October my father and I loaded our gear in the car and drove over to investigate.

The place was a madhouse. Hundreds of anglers, their rods bristling over the water, lined both sides of the river along the short distance from the dam at Main Street to where it emptied into the harbor. Many of the fishermen had climbed onto the decks of the commercial fishing trawlers and private pleasure boats moored along the edges of the river, ignoring prominent signs forbidding it, and here and there arguments were in progress between boat owners and fishermen. Arguments were in progress as well among fishermen themselves, those whose lines had tangled, or who had lost brief battles with trout because someone cast over their lines or stabbed ineptly with landing nets and panicked the fish, allowing them to get away. The area was bright with streetlights and looked like a gaudy, chaotic, low-budget carnival.

As we walked along the river we were told the lakers were hitting on spawn bags fished on the bottom and on a deadly little jigging lure called, inelegantly, the Swedish Pimple. The lures were supposed to be most effective fished vertically from the bank or from the boats along the river. But though we watched a dozen trout landed, none were hooked in the mouth. Most had been snagged in the belly or side by the sleek jigs.

Nobody seemed to know why the lake trout were there, if they had been coming in like that for years, or if it was a recent phenomenon. Some anglers theorized the lakers had come into the river to feed on the loose roe of spawning salmon and brown trout. Others argued that the lakers had been planted there as fingerlings and were simply returning to their parent stream to spawn. But when female lake trout were caught they were found to carry immature spawn, and biologists insisted that lake trout spawned in late November over rocky shoals in the open lake. The only certainty was that the trout were there, in enormous numbers, and as far as anyone knew (or was telling) they had not been there in previous years.

My father had no interest in joining the fray below the dam, so we took a walk onto a deserted dock in the harbor. At the end of it, beyond the marina attendant's shack and gas pumps, a single neon light on a high pole lit a circle in the water. We had the entire dock to ourselves and could look across the open water of the harbor and see the crowds of people lining the river.

My father reached the end of the dock first, looked down for a moment, then turned quickly and walked back toward me.

"Don't do anything to attract attention," he said. "Stay out here and look casual. I'm going to the car to get the rods."

I walked to the end of the dock and looked down. At first I saw nothing but the startling clarity of the water; in the light of the neon bulb overhead it was blue. Then I saw movement, pale objects drifting past, and I realized I was seeing a pod of six or eight lake trout, so light in color they appeared to glow. They swam slowly past the end of the dock toward the river, turned in a broad circle, and returned the way they had come, as if following an invisible track. Then I saw six more, then twelve. Suddenly there were dozens — hundreds — circling in the open water on the end of the dock.

My father, strolling casually, returned with our rods. We rigged up, aware that fishermen at the mouth of the river were glancing toward us. "This won't last long," Dad said. We threaded small spawn bags on our hooks and weighted the line a foot or two above the hooks with split shot. Taking our time, hoping to give the impression we had no targets, we cast over the cruising trout.

In the clear water the balls of orange roe glowed as they sank. It was impossible to tell if the lake trout noticed them. The fish seemed to swim past without looking at anything, certainly without the appearance of hunting or feeding. We held our rods lightly, certain we would have strikes. When nothing happened, we reeled and cast again.

My father waited to cast until he saw trout coming, then lobbed his bait so it would descend directly in front of them. He had removed a large split shot and replaced it with a tiny one just heavy enough to make it possible to cast. The tiny orange ball sank slowly. A trout approached, swimming with methodical, lazy undulations. There was a slight, barely perceptible change in its motion, as if it had stumbled, and a brief flash of white. The flash of white was the inside of the trout's mouth, revealed as it opened to engulf the bait. My father struck back with his rod.

The trout fought deep, lunging and rolling. Only when it had been brought near the surface did it make anything like a run, enough to force my father's spinning reel to give up some line. By the time we netted it, a fine eight-pound fish, half a dozen other fishermen had reached the dock and more were on the way.

"Are they out there?"

"Jesus, yes, look at 'em."

There was no pretense involved. Swedish Pimples splashed the surface and were retrieved with vicious jerks. Nobody hooked a thing. The trout disappeared. In a few moments, so did we.

Not long after our night in Leland, lake trout were discovered cruising along the breakwall at Clinch Park in Traverse City. The remainder of that fall the rails of the breakwall were lined every night with fishermen standing shoulder-to-shoulder casting sleek jigs into the deep water on the bay side of the wall. You could always see how productive the previous night's fishing had been by going down to the breakwall in the morning. If there was time on the way to school my friends and I pulled into the parking lot behind the zoo and walked out on the broad walkway capping the breakwall. Monofilament hung in snarls from the power lines between the pole lamps along the wall, and discarded lure packages and bait containers were scattered on the cement walkway. Wherever a trout had died the spot was marked with a plate-sized pool of drying blood and slime. Gulls hopped around the blood or hovered just overhead in the wind.

Doug, Russ and I had fished there a few times, lured by the chance to catch big trout on light line. But the scene always appalled us. We were not being righteous — we had, after all, just spent a good part of the autumn snagging salmon from the Boardman River — but there was something so blatant and ugly in the behavior of the people crowding the rails of the breakwall that we found ourselves driven away. Most of the lines cast from the breakwall were tipped with snagging lures of one sort or another, and most of the anglers activated them using the same gung-ho heave and real tactic that was so effective in snagging salmon. When we heard the cry, "Fish on!" — and crying out was necessary to clear nearby lines quickly enough to avoid getting hopelessly tangled and starting small wars — we watched snagged lake trout netted quickly by businesslike fishermen who tossed the fish onto the concrete, unhooked the evidence, and clubbed the fish to death so they would not flop back over the edge into the water.

We heard rumors that a few of the lakers were being taken on spawn bags at the mouth of the Boardman River. The crowd was thinner there, but we stood waist-deep in our waders in the painfully cold water one night and cast hundreds of times without a strike. We finally gave it up — gave up on lake trout entirely. We went back to fishing the river and the forgotten corners of the bay for steelhead, brown trout and salmon.

One night Doug and Russ went exploring in a marina a mile up the bay from Clinch Park. We had caught a few trout and salmon from similar spots, and liked to check them now and then for stragglers. This marina, one of several on West Bay, was in a small, man-made harbor big enough for a pair of mooring docks and several dozen boats. Most of the boats had been hauled from the water and stored. The place was empty and dark.

At the entrance to the little harbor was a deep, narrow channel dredged between a spit of land and a wharf. The wharf extended along the front of a warehouse used for storing boats in winter, and was lit at its end, at the narrowest portion of the channel, by a pole lamp that cast a dome of light on the water. Doug and Russ wandered over to the light and looked down.

They called me about midnight, waking my parents and instigating a minor panic in the household. Doug was so excited he could hardly be understood. But I got the message. Lake trout. Hundreds of them.

We were there before dark the following evening. Doug and Russ had each taken their limit of five lakers the night before and were confident. When I saw nothing in the water I began to doubt them.

"They'll come, just be patient," Russ said.

The trout appeared shortly after dark. They streamed in and through the channel, glowing white beneath the lamp and, like the fish in Leland Harbor, they moved so slowly and mindlessly they appeared to be hypnotized. At first I could only watch in amazement, stunned by their numbers. Hundreds of lake trout weighing six, eight or ten pounds paraded slowly through the channel, some deep, some barely below the surface, all within fifteen or twenty feet of where we stood above them on the wharf.

Doug and Russ had worked out a technique the night before. They attached tiny spawn bags containing only three or four salmon eggs each to small hooks and flipped them without sinkers into the channel. With no weight on the line they could cast the bait scarcely fifteen feet, but it was far enough to reach the cruising trout. In the blue light from the lamp we could see the spawn as it sank. Trout cruised past in weird somnolence. Every third or fourth cast a sudden, yawning flash of white would appear in the deep water — the inside of a trout's mouth as it opened to take the spawn — and one of us would set the hook.

Lakers are not fierce battlers, and these fought even less fiercely than most, as if their minds were somewhere else. Few made long runs or dramatic struggles. Most fought a dogged, distracted battle, swimming to the bottom of the channel or rising to the surface and rolling over and over until they were spiderwebbed in line. We worked them close to the dock and netted them, or more often laid on our bellies and unhooked them with pliers without lifting the trout from the water. We learned quickly not to put our fingers in their mouths: Those catlike teeth were sharp.

After an hour or two no more trout passed through the channel. By then we had caught out limit and had released many others. We walked along the dock toward the interior of the marina and came upon a strong scene. In the corner of the harbor, about the size of an Olympic swimming pool, bounded on three sides by docks and, again, lit by an overhead lamp, hundreds of lake trout swam in a tight, clockwise circle. They were crowded from the surface down to a depth of perhaps eight feet, and swam as if transfixed or drugged in a continuous, unhurried procession around the little bay. Each seemed intent on following the path of the fish ahead of it. Zombie trout. It was possible they were practicing some bizarre spawning rite, yet, as with the fish at Leland, the spawn and milt of the fish we dressed out would prove to be immature. The circling lakers were more reluctant to strike than they had been in the channel, although we continued to hook occasional strays. We tried spinners, spoons and plugs, but, except for occasional — and accidental — foul hooks, the lures were ineffective. Sometimes the trout shied away from the flashing lures; usually they simply ignored them.

We came back, night after night, expecting at any time to find other fishermen had discovered the place and its trout. Within a few nights we were so confident of success we no longer bothered keeping any fish. If our mothers announced that the freezer was empty and the family hungry for baked lake trout it would always be a simple matter to go that night to the marina and catch a brace of five-pounders for the table. We became catch-and-release advocates, not from lofty motives, but because netting, untangling and unhooking the trout took more time than reaching down to the water to pry the hooks free. Each of us, after all, was interested primarily in catching more fish than the others. If there had been some variety in the trout — occasional twenty-pounders, for instance — we might have competed for trophies. But the size varied little. We caught a few twelve-pounders, but the rest, with monotonous consistency, weighed five to ten pounds. The only mark of our skill was in numbers hooked and released.

The weather, which had been pleasant through the end of October, turned ugly in November. A cold front moved in and we fished in snowstorms, the hard, brittle snow blown in from the lake by wind harsh enough to cut through our clothing. It became so cold that landing and unhooking a fish was an ordeal. But we did not have to suffer long. The trout disappeared. One night we noticed fewer in the marina; the next night there were fewer yet. In another day or two we saw none. It was just as well. Those were school nights. We had been going to class on five or six hours of sleep and the pace was wearing us down.

We vowed to keep the marina a secret among us three. We swore on it. We clasped hands and promised we would pluck out our own eyes if we ever told another person about the lake trout. But, of course, that vow did not extend to our families. We had been fishing for years with our fathers; we owed every-thing we knew to them. The last few nights at the marina our fathers and brothers joined us, so there were seven or eight of us instead of three.

Maybe three high-school boys fishing on a quiet wharf at night could fail to attract notice, but eight people could not. Somebody saw us. Or maybe our younger brothers, who had their own circles of fishing buddies who hit the local creeks on bicycles, did what any of us would have done and shared the spot with their friends.

The next year the trout returned in the middle of October. We were waiting. But it was different. The first night three or four strangers showed up on the dock. The next night, eight. The third night, a dozen. The trout appeared but in fewer numbers, and they were skittish. Some nights they began filing through the channel and were met with so many clumsily cast lures that they turned and disappeared back into the deep water. Our fathers abandoned the place, but we stayed out of a sense of territorial imperative. We were outraged when a group of older boys, seniors in high school, showed up one night with surf rods and twenty-pound-test line and began snagging the trout as they showed up in the channel.

"They'll hit spawn," I said. I, the budding diplomat. My friends backed me up with emphatic nods.

The largest of the intruders looked at me with disgust. "Oh, will they, fuckhead?"

"Yes. You don't have to snag them."

"What if I want to snag them?"

"Then you're spoiling the fishing for everybody else."

He reached me in two strides, grabbed me by the collar, and swung me out until I was leaning over the water.

"How would you like to go swimming, asshole?"

"I wouldn't like that."

"How would you like to drown?"

"I wouldn't like that either."

"Then shut your fucking mouth."

He swung me back over the dock. His friends were laughing; mine were fishing a discreet fifty feet away. Snagged trout were flopping on the dock. Several men who had been trying without success to catch the lakers with large spawn bags and heavy bell sinkers had changed over to snag hooks. My friends and I were crowded out, forced to fish in an empty and unproductive corner of the marina. Eventually we went home.

In the years to come, lake trout in the Great Lakes, after rebounding spectacularly from the disastrous infestation of sea lampreys in the 1950s, were in trouble again, threatened by commercial fishing and resurging lamprey populations. Fisheries biologists were concerned that there seemed to be almost no natural reproduction, and that the fish were not growing large. The Department of Natural Resources shortened the season, making it legal to fish for Lake Michigan lake trout only from May through August, eliminating the fall and winter fisheries.

The breakwall at Clinch Park is empty now on autumn nights, and there are no bloodstains on the concrete. The wharf and storage buildings at the little marina where Doug, Russ and I fished have been cleared and replaced with an office building, and there are ranks of condominiums on the spit of land across the channel. The entire area is fenced against trespassing.

But no matter. The best times don't last — they can't. We had stumbled upon a marvelous, abundant mystery, and we came away convinced that there is more to the world than ordinary daylight reveals. I've wondered many times if the lake trout still make their strange, unexplained runs under the lights, but I've never gone back to see.

Winter

"*Like first ice,*

there is something special

about the first serious

snowfall of the season ...

A fresh snow, seen through

the windows of a warm

house, transmits excitement

into that house.

Something new is afoot."

RON RAU

From "Sage Lake
and Time Passing"

BERRIEN THORN

Berrien Thorn grew up on a small farm in Silver Hollow in the Catskills with "a draft horse, a cow, some corn, and chickens in the back." He now lives in a small cabin in Suttons Bay, Michigan. He plays the ukulele, banjo, harp and other instruments and frequently performs at jazz festivals and other events and venues. Berrien took up writing several years ago, and for about six years had a regular column in the Traverse City Record-Eagle, *where the first version of the accompanying selection first appeared.*

●

THE FOLK ART OF WINTER

BERRIEN THORN

"*Winter fills the woods with folk artists stalking deer. I hang around the storytelling of the guys who plow my street, bank tellers and grocery baggers. Big shots and small potatoes; all will be equal in this bleak heart of winter.*"

Last night I stood on my back porch, rocking and humming aimlessly, watching the weather. The sky was a cerulean luminosity above the houses. There was a heaviness to the earth that seemed to eat the light. Above the rooftops an ashen cloud floated from the west like a closing curtain of lead.

This morning, I awaken and sit at the typewriter. Weightlessly, the cat leaps and settles on my lap. I look out the kitchen window. A light rain falls, slowly misting into tiny hailstones, peppering my cabin roof. The limits of my world have become a study in black and gray. Across the street, the tree trunks rise from the snow, stained black poles holding up their rooftop of evergreen branches. Diffused sunlight reflects through thick clouds on the slick, black road. Blacker than the road, a squirrel, nut in mouth, ripples on his tiptoes, flowing from pause to pause across the road to the park. My dog, Uncle Willie, pads over and lays his chin on my knee. I scratch his ear.

Suddenly, the clouds break, and a harsh daylight floods the moodiness with detail. The masses acquire sharp shadows and textures. A shock of changing leaves edging the upper corner of my kitchen window fills with a backlit orange fluorescence. The leaves tremble, hung like killed kites.

This year, what the local tourist industry calls our "color season" has lingered, and winter has taken its time rolling in. It still feels like the beginning of winter, a time when everything drops its face and pulls inside to sleep until awakened by the warmth of spring. It is also a time when everything acquires a special urgency, not unlike the desire to make wills and testaments. The functions of gathering sustenance against the approaching snows balance with thoughts of "How will I make it?"

Now I lay me down to sleep in the arms of the infinite snows. I pray the Lord I put aside enough this summer to keep my dog and me warm and fed.

Winter here in the Northwoods is the hardest season for transplants from warmer climes or form the weather-controlled worlds of Eastern cities. People talk about jet lag and culture shock on trips to Africa, but folks don't know how far we live from civilization until the frosting of snow obliterates the Earth and lead seeps into the sky for weeks at a time. The windows rattle in their frames. I wonder about the potential for a rise in the suicide rate when I read the accident reports of strangers driven into immovable objects after a couple of weeks of sunless gray.

This chill time is punctuated by family celebrations of Thanksgiving and Christmas and New Year's — holidays that compound loneliness for the lonely to the fractured level. Bars acquire a darker, hypnotic warmth, a womblike ambience. Some people are simply not designed for solitude. If you can't take your own company, you can get lost in the bottle and the bottle society. A lot of us do.

Oddly enough, for us long-termers, winter is the best time of all. The ordinary local feeds on winter like a white rice that you eat between tastes of exotic food in a Chinese restaurant. It is an empty space that enhances the experience of summer, a poignancy and bitter sweetness that can linger and drive us out the door and into town to buy pineapples. It is compulsory simplicity. There is no fancy dancing downtown, and no two-week ticket to Arizona that will carry the soul out.

Winter fills the woods with folk artists stalking deer. I hang around the storytelling of the guys who plow my street, bank tellers and grocery baggers. Big shots and small potatoes; all will be equal in this bleak heart of winter. We will tell stories about wild animals — not just the ones people shoot for meat, but the odd bird or a couple of deer skating out on the ice of the bay.

I am not a hunter, but I am a stalker of detail. As a dedicated people watcher, I look forward to the array of characters displayed: farmers and plumbers out for the euchre tournament Sunday afternoon at Dick's Pour House. The woodcutter with elongated physicality will hold the little cards in his long hands and fan them. Sue the bartender will home-make cherry crisps.

Other days there will be an adventure to the Laundromat, or maybe a walk to pick up my mail and sing island music at Cappuccino's cafe. Along the way, I will be practicing my peripheral vision, sharpening my peripheral ear.

This year, when the lakes finally freeze solid, I plan to sit on the frozen surface in a tiny, insulated tin hut and learn the basics of sturgeon with my fishing buddy, Dale. We will tell jokes and stories as we watch that hole in the icy aqua. Down at Eddie's, the workingman's sporting club will be limbering up for darts and pool. The retirees will be lining up for 40-ouncers of Blatz beer at Boone's. There will be lessons in the history of smoking corn silk behind the barn, of sipping apple jack, of watches and dogs. There will be the slow practical jokes that can take three months to collide. Paybacks are hell.

Under the moving edge of a looming cloud of unknowing, I put those Hawaiian shirts away and get out the flannel. We won't be seeing any blue shirts. Everybody will be wearing red plaid.

I check the bindings on my snowshoes and pull the rowing machine out of the basement. I plop it in front of the 1940s Trans-Oceanic radio. I have already stored up on books like a good literary squirrel. I have tried to pick ones that are hard to crack.

In August, while beach bumming, and yard-saling, I bought a huge, cream-white Wurlitzer accordion for fifty dollars. It is a classic. I pull it from its case and set it on the kitchen table. Can I play? Not a bit. That is why I bought it. I'll have time. I can learn. Winters, as we say around here, are long.

JACK DRISCOLL

Jack Driscoll lives with his wife Lois in a house overlooking the Little Betsie River and surrounded by a several-hundred-acre wetland aviary, nesting grounds for mallards and wood ducks. Originally from Massachusetts, Jack was hired in 1957 to help establish a creative writing major at the Interlochen Center for the Arts, and he has lived in northern Michigan ever since. He jokes about having been referred to in a review of his first book as a "Michigan snow poet," but admits that it is this place that most identifies him as a writer. Jack is the author of four books of poems, a novel, and the award-winning collection of short stories, Wanting Only to Be Heard, *where the accompanying story appeared. He has received the PEN/Nelson Algren Fiction Award and seven PEN Syndicated Short Fiction Project awards. His stories have been read frequently on National Public Radio's "The Sound of Writing," and have received both Pushcart and Best American Short Story citations. His novel* Skylight *has been adapted as a screenplay.*

❦

From *Wanting Only to Be Heard*, University of Massachusetts Press, 1992. Reprinted by permission.

WANTING ONLY TO BE HEARD

JACK DRISCOLL

"I thought there would be some talk, a final go-over of the details, maybe even a last-minute pardon from this craziness if my father would unexpectedly burst in. But it was Timmy, back again and out of breath, who said, 'All set,' and Judge simply reached back without hesitation, snapped on the flashlight, then pushed the mask with both hands to his face for better suction and stepped under."

Ashelby Judge was an odd name for a kid growing up in northern Michigan, so we just called him by his last name, Judge. Everyone did. In a way he was always holding court, pronouncing sentences: Kevin Moriarty was a first-class cockroach, Jake Reardon a homo from the word "go." He had once called me a dicksqueeze, but later took it back, gladly, he said, having indicted me prematurely. I was okay, he said, I really was, that being the final verdict.

Judge was not easy sometimes, but I liked him. I liked his impatience with boredom and the way he gathered all the pertinent information in the end, the evidence to prove or discredit a story. He always proceeded step by step, building an airtight case for whatever he was defending or attacking, whatever he was attempting to pin down. It wouldn't have surprised me, forty years later, to read he'd been appointed to the Supreme Court. Judge Ashelby Judge. Or, for the sake of a joke, Judge Judge. I liked famous names that repeated, or almost did, names like Robin Roberts or Ricky Ricardo, or even slant combos like Jack Johnson. The duplication had a friendly ring, a sense of conviction and rectitude, the feeling that they really knew who they were and liked it and would never entirely grow up, grow old.

It was a Friday night, no wind for a change, and we were fishing smelt, three of us inside my father's shanty, when Judge told me and Timmy Murphy about the claustrophobic Irish setter who, after being locked all afternoon in a fishing hut on Torch Lake, jumped right through the spearing hole just after dark and, ten or twelve feet under the ice, swam toward the faint, opalescent glow of another shanty almost fifty yards away (someone later measured it) and came bursting up there from the muck like some monster awakened, the water swelling, convulsing up over the wooden floor. That one simile, "like some monster," was the only embellishment, Judge's single artistic touch.

He was not a natural storyteller who tested his listeners by saying, "imagine this," or "pretend that," or "just think if," and on and on, suspending their willingness to imprint the local tales into myth. He despised the "what then, what next" demands made on every story. Which was what Timmy was doing, all excited and ahead of himself as usual.

"What'd the guy do? Holy shit, I bet he croaked right there. I can't believe it, a dog under the ice. That's great!"

Judge, calculatedly slow and flat, said the guy was plenty scared, who wouldn't be, but not berserk scared the way you might expect. He was old, Judge said — a simple observation of fact, like what day it was or how cold. He never speculated that age buffered the body's reaction to shock or trauma, but I translated it that way anyhow, without thinking.

"Who cares?" Timmy asked. "Twenty, fifty-seven, a hundred-and-two years old. It doesn't matter."

But it did, the way it mattered that the dog was an Irish setter and male and was abandoned by his owner who loved him but hadn't gotten any fish, and instead of a quick trip to the 7-Eleven for a six-pack of Stroh's, he drank away the afternoon, alone in a bar that said just that in red neon, *BAR*, just outside Bellaire, forgetting the dog, and playing, over and over on the free jukebox, Patsy Cline's "Walking After Midnight." Which was about the time he left the bar, broke and drunk, and halfway home remembered the dog and right there, on 137, opened his window full for the few seconds it took him to slow down and power slide into the other lane, the pickup fishtailing back up the gradual incline beneath the stars, the hook of the moon.

And it mattered that he honked his horn a couple of times on the lake's edge, his shanty invisible somewhere beyond the white perimeter of his high beams. That was the real story, that sadness, and the way the guy, on both knees, fiddled with the combination lock until his fingers went numb, the whole time talking to the dog who wasn't even there. When he finally opened the door and lit the lantern, the white flame hissing in the mantle, he stepped back outside and screamed the dog's name a single time across the emptiness.

Judge said you could measure a story by its private disclosures, by how far a person came forward to confess a part of himself, asking forgiveness. The dramatics meant nothing, those exaggerations that served only to engage our obvious and temporary fascinations. And he continued, refining the art of meticulous detachment from such a rare and bizarre event, saying he didn't care what the Irish setter looked like emerging — a giant muskie or sturgeon or a red freshwater seal.

"The fact is," he repeated, "it was a hundred-pound dog. That's it, cut and dried!"

I thought maybe the "cut and dried" part was a pun, and I smiled until Timmy, really miffed, said, "You take away all the magic. You make everything too real, too damn ordinary." But Timmy was at least partly wrong. There was something principled about facts, something stark and real that required nothing but themselves to survive. Maybe that's why I liked "Dragnet" so much, the claim that it was a true story, that the sentence handed down after the last TV commercial was really being served.

I thought of that while leaving the shanty to check the tip-ups set for browns behind us in the dark. My father let me and my buddies use the shanty on weeknights while he worked at the Fisk. Usually he'd drop us off at the state park and we'd take turns dragging the sled with the minnow bucket and spud and the gallon can of stove gas straight toward the village of fifty or sixty tiny structures in a cluster set over deep water.

It was easy to find my father's shanty because it was separated a little ways from the others, and because of the spoked hubcap from a Cadillac Eldorado he'd nailed to the door. His house sign, he called it. Other guys had other things, and it was fun to traipse around at night out there, just looking around, the world glaciated, frozen so tight you could feel your breath clinging to the fine hairs on your face. The name of each owner and the town he was from was painted on every shanty — that was the law — some from as far south as Clare, though those were the ones that were not used very much.

Sometimes, as you passed, you could hear talking from inside, or good laughter, or country music on the radio, and when your returned to the heat of your own hut, maybe you'd be humming a certain song, surprised by how happy you were, how peaceful, knowing that you belonged. I figured that was why my father decided to fish again after all these years, why he spent most of every weekend out here, calm and without worries.

That wasn't the feeling, however, when I stepped back inside and Timmy and Judge were both just staring into the rectangular hole, staring at the blue rubber-band bobbers and saying nothing. The smelt pail was still empty and half the minnows in the other bucket had turned belly up. My father would have said no big deal, that the smelt would go for the dead bait just as good if they were feeding, but either Judge or Timmy, having already given up, had entered a big 0, a goose egg, in the calendar square for February 12.

On the good nights you loaded up fast, constant action, and on the homemade speed reels you could bring in two or three smelt at a time, every few minutes without a break. Just three nights earlier my father had recorded 268, and that was by himself. That's how it happened, streaky and unpredictable, and you simply had to like being out there, maybe sharing a Pall Mall around or talking girls if that's what mystery happened to be biting. But on this night of the Irish setter story, everyone had gone closemouthed.

"No flags," I said, latching the door and hanging the gaff on the hook above the stove. This was Judge's first time ice fishing, and I knew he was bored, knew it even better when he said to Timmy, "Why not?" responding to whether a person (forget the dog) could survive the thirty-three-degree water long enough to swim from this shanty to the one closest by, the one that said *M. Kulanda, Kalkaska, MI*, the largest one on the ice. I'd never seen anybody there, not once.

"Houdini stayed under twenty minutes," Judge said, "under the Detroit River. No wetsuit. Nothing but a pair of pants."

"What was he doing there? A trick?" Timmy asked.

"An escape," Judge corrected, and although Timmy argued, "Trick, escape, whatever he did … ," I understood the difference, the dangerous mishandling of a single word so that a story softened, collapsed like a fragile set of lungs.

"Houdini said later he sucked the air pockets, bubbles trapped between the water and ice, and with the current, followed his dead mother's voice until he emerged, a quarter-mile downriver."

Judge was still staring into the thick, dark water while he talked, until Timmy, excited, just like at first with the Irish setter story, said, "You're shitting me!"

Judge, looking up finally, straight-faced and serious, said, "I shit you not," as if under oath, and they both went silent as if the naked truth of Houdini and the Irish setter were tempting them to find out.

It started simple as that, and next thing I knew we were pacing off the distance between the shanties. About thirty yards. I had once stayed underwater in the bathtub for as long as I could, just sliding back holding my nose. I counted a minute and forty-four seconds, long seconds — one one-thousand, two one-thousand, three one-thousand, the face cloth kind of floating back and forth across my stomach. And sneaking into the Camp Ketch-A-Tonk swimgrounds one night last summer, I breast-stroked real close to the sandy bottom, from the Great Raft all the way up to shore. My father did it, too, swimming behind me, and without coming up for air he turned around and swam halfway back. I was scared, the way you get when someone's been down a long time, maybe just monkeying around, but scaring you just the same.

I remembered whispering, "Come up, please come up," and he did, beyond the blue lifeline, gracefully rolling onto his back in a single motion and kicking, eyes closed I imagined, straight out toward whatever secret had surfaced in his memory. That's how it is with the mind, always buoyant, bobbing up and down on that complex sea of recollection.

Judge knocked on the Kulanda's door, but nobody was there. "Nobody has been," Timmy said, trying to take charge. "Look around. No footprints anywhere." And I noticed there were no bloodstains from trout or pike tossed into the snow, no frozen minnows. Nothing.

The shanty was unlocked, a lousy idea, my father always lectured every time he'd see a door blown open, slapping backwards hard against its hinges. He said that only invited trouble, people snooping around, poking their heads in where they didn't belong, which was exactly what we were doing, and I didn't like it and said, "Come on, you guys, let's go. Let's get out of here." But when Timmy stepped inside with the lantern, the hut was nearly empty, unused, the kind that just got left sitting there until the ice softened toward spring, and one morning it would be gone forever. Who knows, maybe the owner died or got sick or one Sunday started watching the Pistons on TV with his son-in-law and thought, "Screw the fishing," and that was that for the whole season.

Timmy said, "The guy's got a couch in here," and when he sat down he was staring at a calendar hanging on the opposite wall. It was the kind of calendar I first saw in a gas station in Germfask when my father's station wagon broke down. We were there a good part of the afternoon while the garage owner phoned around until he finally located a water pump at the junkyard in Greighton. The owner's kid drove over to pick it up, and while our fathers small-talked engines and horsepower and cubic inches, I snuck into the men's room three or four times to examine, close up, this woman who was showing me everything, her lips parted just enough to show the pink edge of her tongue. The last time I stepped out my father was waiting by the door and he told me, "Pee out back. I don't want you in there anymore." And that was the feeling I had again in Kulanda's abandoned shanty, of wanting to be there and not, both at the same time. Timmy lowered the lantern to the ice, right under the calendar where the fishing hole should have been, really lighting up the glossy nude, and he said, acting the big shot for his lucky find, "I'd swim anywhere if I could surface between those legs."

But it was Judge who decided to really do it, and when my father dropped us off again the next night, we brought along with fishing gear, a book on Houdini and a *National Geographic* that showed people in swimsuits running toward the Atlantic Ocean from a snowy beach, in Rhode Island, I think. And Judge talked on and on about some Mr. Maslowski who chopped a large round hole in the ice of his man-made pond, and letting the same red towel drop behind him, he'd hold his hands flat to the sides of his thighs, and each morning, without hesitation, he'd step right through over his head.

"For his rheumatism," Judge said. "He worshiped what he called 'certitude,' the ancient and natural cure taking place under the world."

Judge had done his homework, covering the Polar Bear Club and U.S. Navy ice divers, the whole time spouting off dates and temperatures and distances, building his case until I believed there was hardly any danger after the initial shock of entering, and he said, staring at me, "You'll be my key witness." And to Timmy, "Who knows what you'll see."

Of course, we wanted to see everything: the entry, the look of his eyes behind the mask the instant he surfaced in Kulanda's shanty. But most of all we wanted desperately to watch him moving under the ice, so later that week Judge waterproofed a flashlight with candle wax and electrician's tape, and tested it by lowering the light about twenty feet under the ice. Then Timmy turned off the Coleman lantern and we just stared, all three of us in complete darkness, at that dim glimmer wavering back and forth below us, slow motion, soporific. Judge was the first to speak, his unquestionable right now, presiding and authoritative, factitious as always, but Timmy was making no objections anymore. Judge said, "It works," and we just nodded, accomplices who had learned to listen closely, to rehearse every detail at night in our dreams. "We'll fasten the light to my back," Judge said, "and you guys can walk right above me."

Although we didn't actually fish anymore that week, we'd make up numbers and jot them down each night on my father's calendar, keeping the records current: 114, 226, and — a slow night, Timmy's entry — 27. "Just to keep things honest," he said, and we laughed, sitting and clowning around and smoking Pall Malls in what now seemed more like a fort, a refuge — not from the gusting wind, but from the predictable, ordinary things we might have done late after school, like playing ping-pong in Timmy's basement, or being home alone tinkering with science projects, or making up a story for English — something sensational and dangerous and totally unbelievable. And whenever my father asked about the fishing I'd tell him Judge and Timmy were splitting up the smelt, taking them home. "Good," he said, as though it were the proper courtesy, the way to make and keep good friends.

If Judge had moments of panic, he never let on, not even on the night of his dive, the Saturday my father decided to work overtime. He dropped us at the state park as usual and asked, "You got a ride back?" — and Timmy said, "Yep, my father's picking us up," which was true, but he was coming later than usual. He wouldn't be here until eleven. I don't know why we wanted the extra time, I really don't. Maybe to change our minds, or to deny, as Judge would have been the first to point out, that redemption had anything to do with danger, with the spectacular moments in a life. But that didn't happen.

We felt transformed, faithful to the careful preparation of an entire week, and when we started across the ice toward the village, we believed those two shanties were ours, and ours to swim between if we wanted, the way you might swim deep under a cliff in order to come up in a secret cave. After the first time, it would be easy. And we felt all set, having already stashed an extra heater and lantern, an army blanket, and towels in Kulanda's. And we'd hung a thermometer on the same nail that held what Judge was calling Timmy's porno queen, but I'd seen him peeking from the couch at those hard nipples, too, or at the red mercury rising slowly between her breasts after we'd fired the heater up.

Right now chips of ice were bouncing off her paper flesh as Timmy started to spud the hole, Judge's exit, and Judge and I left him there and headed for the other hut. But Judge stopped halfway and said, "No hurry," and we stood there, watching the lights of houses blink on the far side of the lake. I felt calm as the lights vanished and appeared again, floating, I thought, behind a cold vapor of darkness. And I could hear Timmy in Kulanda's shanty, a strange thud, as though coming from a great distance, and already we'd begun walking even farther away.

By the time Timmy got to my father's hut he was breathing heavily, but he laughed real hard at Judge just sitting there in his white boxers, his flashlight already taped to his back like a dorsal fin. "All you need now are scales," Timmy said, taking off his gloves and coat, and Judge, reaching into his knapsack, said, "This will have to do," and pulled out a tub of ball-bearing grease.

"Cover me real good," he said, scooping the first brown gob himself with his fingers and sculpting it up and down one arm.

Then he stood there, arms out, and me and Timmy did the rest, each a skinny side, and Judge, still joking around, said, "Save a little for my dick," and Timmy said, "A little is all you'll need," as I knelt and reached my greasy hand into the freezing water to see if this translucent coating really helped, and for that second I was terrified of falling in, the rectangular hole seeming so much like a grave, calm and so carefully ladled out. And without them seeing me, I crossed myself, as my father had taught me to do every, every time before entering strange water.

When I stood up, Timmy, having taken charge of things in Kulanda's shanty, had left again, and Judge was wiping his hands clean on a rag. Then he knotted the white clothesline around his waist, knotted it a couple of times, nothing fancy, but I knew by the way he tugged it wasn't coming free. Still, I wanted something thicker, stronger, a new length of rope, a boat line maybe. Judge said he just needed something to follow back if he got lost or in trouble. It didn't need to be strong.

The other end was already tied off around the single roof brace, the rest of the clothesline coiled in wide loops on the floor. Nobody needed to be there to watch or feed it out. It would uncoil smoothly, trailing behind him, a long umbilical cord. Judge, the literalist, would have hated the metaphor, as he would have hated me telling him he looked a little like the creature in "The Creature from the Black Lagoon," standing there. But he did, primordial and weedy-green in the bright light of the lantern, breathing hard now, hyperventilating for whatever extra oxygen he could squeeze into his lungs.

I thought there would be some talk, a final go-over of the details, maybe even a last-minute pardon from this craziness if my father would unexpectedly burst in. But it was Timmy, back again and out of breath, who said, "All set," and Judge simply reached back without hesitation, snapped on the flashlight, then pushed the mask with both hands to his face for better suction and stepped under. I wasn't even sure it happened — he disappeared that fast, without a single word or even a human splash, as though all that body grease had dissolved his bones, his skull, the entire weight of him so that only a ghost drifted under the ice, a vague iridescence.

When we got outside, Judge was moving in the right direction. All winter the winds had blown the snow from the ice, so we could see the blurry light down there, and Timmy had one of his own which he kept blinking on and off to let Judge know we were right there, right above him, ready to guide him home. The moon was up, too, and suddenly the distance to Kulanda's shanty did not seem so far, not with Judge already halfway there and Timmy, all wound up and hooting, "He's got it made, he's got it now!"

It was right then Judge's light conked out, and we both stopped, as if Judge would surface there. Neither of us wanted to move, afraid, I think, that we would step on him in the dark and send him deeper, and when we started running for Kulanda's, I circled wide, way behind where Judge would be, hoping he wouldn't hear the slapping panic of our boots, the fear inside us struggling desperately to break free.

Timmy pumped and pumped the lantern until I thought the glass globe would explode. Then he held it just inches above the black water, and he seemed to be staring at the nude, staring all the way through her as if counting each vertebra, the soft curves of her back, and I knew Judge was not coming up. I didn't have to tell Timmy to stay. He was crying now. He was all done, and I think if Judge had surfaced right then, Timmy would have just dropped the lantern and walked away and would never have spoken of this again.

I slipped and fell hard, almost knocking myself out, and in the moment of dizziness, face down on the ice, I imagined Judge staring back, just ten inches away, his black hair wavering in moonlight, his eyes wide open behind his mask. And I imagined him pointing and pointing and I got up and ran, sweating now, into my father's shanty. I believed the rope twitched or pulsed when I picked it up, something like a nibble, but when I yanked back there was nothing there, just the loose arc of slack, and I remembered my father always shouting from the stern of the boat, "Reel hard, keep reeling," when I thought I'd lost a big one, and this time the weight was there, solid and unforgiving. It was the same heavy feeling of a snag that begins to move just when you're sure it will bust your line, and I knew that bulk dragged backwards was enough to snap any line with a nick or fray, and to hurry was to lose it all.

I kept it coming, hand over hand, Judge's body drifting sideways, then back again, always rising slowly from the deep water.

I shouted for Timmy four or five times, tilting my head backwards and toward the door, but he did not come. And it was during one of those shouts that the flashlight on Judge's back
appeared in the center of the hole, then the whole back hunched
in a deadman's float. I could not get him up, my arms weak and
shaking, and I hauled back one last time and dropped the rope
and grabbed, all in the same motion, his thick black hair with
both my hands, his face finally lifting out of the water.

His mask was gone and I just held him like that for a long
time, one arm under his chin, the lantern dimming. I was
stretched on my belly, our cheeks touching, and I had never felt
anything so cold, so silent. I knew mouth-to-mouth resuscita-
tion would do Judge no good in this position, his lungs full of
water, so maybe I was really kissing him, not trying to reclaim
a heartbeat, but to confess, as Judge said, a part of myself, and
to ask forgiveness. I did not know how long I could hold him
there, though I promised over and over I would never let him
slide back to that bottom, alone among those tentacles of
weeds. I closed my eyes, and in what must have been a kind of
shock or sleep, I drifted into a strange current of emptiness, a
white, vaporous light, the absolute and lovely beginning of
nothing.

I did not see the two ice fishermen hoist Judge from the hole,
and I did not remember being carried to Kulanda's shanty or
being wrapped in the army blanket on the couch. I awakened
alone there, still dizzy but very warm. I was wearing Judge's
sweatshirt, the one we had waiting for him when he came up. I
did not take it off or even move very much, and I could hear my
father's voice just outside the door, though it sounded distant,
too, and dull, the blunt echo of a voice approaching. I thought,
if he entered, the flood of his words would drown me for good.
But only silence followed him in. I did not look up and I did not
cry when he touched my head, or when he turned away to face
the wall. There would be no sermonizing, not interrogation from
him or from anyone else. Not that night anyway. And I noticed,
eye-level across from me, that the nude was gone, removed like
evidence we didn't want found. The cigarette butts on the floor
had disappeared, too. And it sounded strange to hear someone
knock on the door. My father did not say, "Come in," but a man
did, an ambulance driver, and he bent down on one knee and

said, "How do you feel now?" I didn't know, but I said, "Good," and I wanted more than anything else in the world for the three of us just to stay there, maybe all night, making sure the hole did not freeze over.

————————————

Next morning, as we walked together toward the shanties, my father said, "Tell them everything exactly like it happened. There's only one story." What he meant was that the options narrowed and narrowed when the ending was already known.

"They won't keep us long," my father said. "We'll get back home." I thought he might add, "for the Pistons-Celtics game," but he didn't.

It was Sunday morning and sunny, and up ahead, off to the left, I saw a red flag go up from the ice, then someone running toward the tip-up, shaking his gloves off. I watched him set the hook, and after a few seconds, with his left hand, move the gaff a little bit away from the hole. "Probably a pike," my father said, and I was glad he did, so natural, without the conviction of disguise.

There were not all that many people gathered at the shanty, not the way I thought it would be with a lot of photographers and sheriff's department deputies. Timmy was already there. I could see his green hat and his arms flailing like an exhausted swimmer, and for that split second I imagined he was yelling, "Help, help me," and I started to run, not toward him, but the other way, back toward the car. My father caught me from behind, caught me first by the collar, then wrapped both his arms around me and turned me back slowly to face Timmy and whatever version he was carving of the story. My father just held me there and released the pressure gradually and then, after a couple of minutes, let me go.

His shanty had been moved back and two divers were adjusting their masks at the side of the hole. I did not know what they were searching for, what more they could possibly find. But they jumped through, one after the other as Judge had, but with black wetsuits and yellow tanks and searchlights sealed with more than candle wax and electrician's tape. The sheriff met us and shook my hand and my father's hand and said Judge's parents were not there and wouldn't be. Then he said, "We've called Marv Kulanda," as though he knew him personally. "He's on his way."

I was okay after that. They kept me and Timmy separated, though we caught each other's eye a couple of times. The two fishermen who pulled Judge out kept nodding a lot, and once they pointed at me, both of them did, then shrugged. And they finally left, to fish and talk, I guess, since they walked that way into the village of shanties. I knew the stories wouldn't be the same, but not the same in a way that didn't matter to the law.

The sheriff asked me about approximate times: How long before Timmy ran for help, how long I held Judge partially out of the water — all questions I couldn't answer — and that seemed to be all right. But before he let me go, he said, "Whose idea was this?" It was the first time he spoke without detachment, accusatory now, and I did not deny that it was me, though it wasn't, my father the whole time shaking his head, shaking it back and forth, no, no, insisting that could never be.

Before the first diver was helped out of the hole, he tossed Judge's mask a few feet onto the ice, and then, behind it, crumpled into a pulpy ball, what I knew was the calendar nude. I didn't know why that frightened me so much, except that it was a detail I had consciously left out, perhaps to protect Timmy's secret need to destroy the crime of her nakedness, one of the reasons we stayed there and smoked cigarettes and talked big in front of her, already outlining the plans of our story. When the sheriff unwadded the nude she fell apart, and he just shook the wet pieces from his hands. In his investigation for details, she meant nothing — a piece of newspaper, a bag, anything that might have floated by.

We left and my father said, "It's over," and I knew he'd protect me from whatever came next. Behind us I could hear them nailing my father's shanty closed, and I could see, angling beyond us from the shore, a single man, half stepping and half sliding across the ice. I knew that was Kulanda, who should have locked his hut, who was wishing at that very moment that we had broken in. And beyond him, running between the avenues of shanties, a single dog, tall and thin and red like an Irish setter. But maybe not. Maybe he was something else, barking like that, wanting only to be heard.

JIM HARRISON

Jim Harrison, novelist and poet, lives on a farm near Lake Leelanau in northern Michigan. His writings include collections of novellas titled Legends of the Fall *and* The Woman Lit by Fireflies, *and novels* Wolf, A Good Day to Die, Farmer, Warlock, Sundog, *and* Dalva. *The accompanying selection comes from his essay collection,* Just Before Dark.

From *Just Before Dark*, by Jim Harrison, Clark City Press, 1991. Reprinted by permission.

ICE FISHING,
THE MORONIC SPORT

JIM HARRISON

"*In this locale, winter begins in October and runs unremittingly until the end of March. My friends in warmer climes won't believe we had sixteen and a half feet of snow this year. After a while you no longer believe there's any earth left under the snow. The ground is a fib. A healthy adult with an interest in the outdoors has to do something during these five months.*"

"There are strange things done 'neath the midnight sun."

Bob Service

We're not actually *that* far north. Yes, a small church in the Upper Peninsula had a Blessing of the Snowmobiles, and not a trace of irony was noticed. But the sense of the Arctic does pull on us; days shorten, men mumble, the euchre games at the tavern grow extended and violent. There is much talk in December and January of just when the bay will freeze over. It is the west arm of the Grand Traverse Bay they are talking about, a very grand bay indeed, containing some five by thirty miles of Lake Michigan's water.

The east arm (they are separated by the forefinger of Old Mission Peninsula) usually freezes first, but the lake trout there, for unknown reasons, run smaller. Some years the bay doesn't freeze over, but this is rare. And some years an oil tanker is brought in at an inopportune time, say if there is a steady offshore wind and a warming trend, and the ice breaks up and blows out of the bay. Until February 14, the date on which the ice is usually safe, sportsmen must be content to fish on smaller lakes for perch or crappies, or some of them take up the ancient art of pike spearing. But these activities locally are only considered as warm-ups. On inland lakes, many consider these forms of ice fishing adequate and cases are made for chugging bluegills with corn borers, a small obnoxious worm found in cornstalks. Houghton Lake, a resort area drawing much of its traffic from Hamtramck and other posh Detroit suburbs, throws a gala every winter known as Tip-Up Town, the "tip-up" referring, of course, to the crude rig positioned above the hole in the ice.

Years ago, when I was a temporary prisoner on Long Island and dreamed of a return to trout country, I thought of those hallowed winter nights that resemble Christmas cards, with large jeweled flakes of snow falling softly on humble farm animals and peasant faces upturned in wonderment and looking not a little bit like my relatives. But reality is a different pudding. BRAAOOW-ILL is what we have, my transcription of what is called a snowmobile "safari." Safari is when a dozen or so machines strike out in the night cross-country for another tavern. Let's have it once more: BRAAOOWILL, as if a dozen burly chain saws were mating under a single tympanum owl.

Walking out on any large expanse of ice has always been dramatic to me. After not many steps I tend to stumble involuntarily, as if I were an exhausted survivor of the Byrd expedition. I frankly expect seals or polar bears, perhaps a wolf loping along the farther shore. But if I fall and roll over I can see maybe a 1969 Camaro passing on the road or a guy and gal in his-and-her purple satin overall suits just cattin' around on their throaty Skidoo. This brings me swiftly back to reality.

Here are a few reality facts from the Great North: Our unemployment rate this year is sixteen percent, giving many some much unwanted time off; snowmobiles, mobile homes and motels each outnumber the total population in 1977; most of my friends are unemployed and if I did have any money they would try to borrow it! I am led, though, by many people I meet to believe that they are mainly worried about the Communist Threat and how the "radicals are tearing apart the country." They tell me that they "worked for what they got" and "nobody gave them nothing." In periods of high unemployment the Great Depression again becomes a ruling fact of life. Yet many people up here strike me as more populist than conservative, and there is the kind of generalized suspicion of Big Government that one finds in non-urban Arizona. They are angry at Nixon for selling them that 1952 Buick, but they hated Johnson, who is still blamed for everything but the tight-money policy, which is especially hard on a resort area, the only other large local industry being a state insane asylum.

Oh boy! I have been invited to go ice fishing by two of my friends, Richard Plamondon, who is a bartender, and Pat Paton, a carpenter and machinist and block layer. As I dress before dawn, I feel somehow patriotic wearing Air Force surplus arctic balloon boots and bib overalls over other trousers and thermal underwear and various sweaters and a goosedown vest and an outsized quilted coat from when I weighed 225 pounds. Eighteen articles of clothing in all, and when I got out of my car I found I could scarcely walk. I fell on the slippery ice with padded impunity, a big helpless doll of a trout slayer. The early morning air was bluish with cold, and as I waddled along I thought of the promised steak to come in the afternoon and the whiskey I would use to wash it down. But there I was being asked to spud some holes in the ice. One cannot refuse. Chores are shared. Pat and Richard were organizing the chuggers and tipups. Everyone spuds their own hole, a rule of the Big Ice. I felt the spud was too heavy after only a few chops. I wanted the ice to be very thick for my safety but thin for the spudding.

It became apparent that we could have fished from the security of a railroad car. Over a foot thick, and I was wheezing and steaming and my shoulder ached. I knew then why construction workers liked the sport: They were able to spud the holes. Anyway, Richard tested the depth: 170 feet. A lot of dark down there. I peered in the hole and saw the reflection of a moon face, my own. Richard set a tipup for me and told me to spud another hole to chug in. I couldn't believe it. I thought, whatever happened to the tradition of the gun bearer who in this case might be put to work, or some sallow, nasty teenager might be brought along for a pittance. But I spudded on. Finally I attached a

Swedish pimple (surely the most elegant name for a bait) to a line, dropped it to the bottom, raised it five feet as instructed by Pat and Richard, who watched my motions critically, and began chugging. Sort of ghastly. No question about it. I had become a Chugger. A brutish act, and it was so cold except for my toasty feet in their big white warmonger boots.

Within an hour I had eaten both my sandwiches, roast beef with thick slices of onion. I had also begun drinking my apple wine. After the second bottle I felt quite happy. I was probably cold but I couldn't feel it. The ice had become a mattress against which I snuggled prone, still chugging. No nibbles. Then Richard's tip-up flag went up and we ran over to the hole. He let the spool run freely for a minute to make sure the fish swallowed the minnow, somewhat similar to the way you hook a sail or a marlin. But not too similar. Pat contended that the fish was large, as only a large fish made a long run. I watched the red plastic spool steadily unwind until Richard picked it up and lightly reefed the line. Then he began to slowly draw it in hand over hand as if he were retrieving an anchor or a used kite. I was jealous. Why didn't my flag go up? I wasn't "living right," as they say.

Richard was gaining steadily on the fish. He announced laconically that it wasn't large. We stood peering down the twelve-inch hole until, shockingly, a trout popped out with the tail of a minnow sticking out of its mouth. Then, horrors! It flopped on the ice and gave off a prolonged BELCH!, a sort of berserk flatulence. I was deeply shocked.

"That pressure sure gets to them," Pat said sagely.

"You're not just a ____," replied Richard.

The point was that the fish had been pulled up precipitously from 170 feet and the variance in pressure was explosive in a minor sense, somewhat like the gas released by a semi-impacted bucking bronco at a rodeo. The trout weighed about three pounds, a good eating size. His eyes bulged and quivered in utter defeat, the ultimate tummyache and bends. I went back to my chugging hole after breaking up the thin ice that had gathered in the cold around my tip-up. I wanted to catch a fish and bring it home so that my daughter wouldn't peer over the top of her Wonder Woman comic and say, "You didn't catch any," and my wife wouldn't ponder, "Did he go to a bar and play pool or did he really go fishing?" To no avail did I chug until I got tennis elbow. I grew bored and cold and began playfully throwing chunks of ice at Pat and Richard. They were not amused.

We finally quit by mid-afternoon and drove to a restaurant where the waitress giggled extravagantly over my balloon boots.

"Are your feet *that* big?" she asked.

"I'm an American Ice Fisherman, bring me a drink," I shouted wittily. The jukebox was playing a merry polka.

When she brought the drinks she rolled her eyes again at my feet. I told her then that I was a veteran of many polar expeditions and had tracked the wily seal to his air-conditioned lair. She asked if seal meat was good and I said yes if they take the ball off their noses har har har. Richard and Pat were sullen as the pretty waitress wasn't interested in them but in my feet. *Tuff,* I said. So it goes, this sport of the north, fit mostly for the hardy unemployed, those who dare thin ice with their snowmobiles and often plunge (eight last year) to a gurgly death amidst the very fishes they sought with pimples and corn borers, red worms and dead smelt (two for a quarter).

A few days later I got a call from Richard saying that a group of locals were going out the next morning and I could meet them on Route 22 about 300 yards south of Chervenko's Rung & Bung Works (coopers to the fruit orchard trade). I was several hours late due to sloth and invented errands. I spotted them with my binoculars a mile or so out on the ice. But farther up the bay a Coast Guard icebreaker was leading a tanker with a rather eerie succession of resounding crashes, like hearing a battle from a distance. The ships were well beyond the fishermen, but I decided that the ice looked a trifle soft. Definitely unsafe. Perhaps I would go home and treat myself to an extended nap.

I began to think of ice fishing in the old days. It is, after all, no modern invention. I have a Currier and Ives print of some Pilgrim types hauling shad from the ice. In the 1930s great cities of ice shanties were erected on northern lakes. Even electricity was available. Recently I was in Minnesota, a state that along with Wisconsin can readily be confused with Michigan, chauvinists notwithstanding. In St. Paul, an old timer told me many yarns. He said that entire cottages especially built for the purpose on skids are pulled onto the ice by diesel tractors.

From the comfort of kitchen, bedroom and living room the fabled walleye is fished for. Imagine your own living room with a big hole in the floor. You're lolling in an easy chair fishing through the hole, with a couple of linker walleyes on the floor beside you. Maybe you have the TV on, and Jack Nicklaus is grinning his Ohio grin on an eighteenth green somewhere. You will cook the walleyes for dinner. They taste better than any fish I've eaten, better than mountain cutthroat, Dover sole, swordfish, lake trout or pompano or lungfish. Perhaps Myrna in her tattersall negligee is bringing you a cold one or just plain Mom is across the room knitting. It is imperative for obvious reasons to have your cottage dragged off the ice before it thaws. I might add that the walleye got its name from its particularly weird stare, but then you don't have to eat the eyes.

In my own "old days" we knew none of these sybaritic pleasures. I suspect my father would have thought if comfort were involved it wasn't sporting. So we would get up before dawn, drive out through the snowdrifts along a logging road and fish all day long in the bitterest cold for a mess of bluegills and perch. Nothing sentimental here. It appeared fun because it was supposed to be fun. Kids are doggish, and if you say, "Come kids, let's pick the dump," they will jump at the chance.

Earlier in January I sat with Richard for three days in his shanty on Lake Leelanau looking down through a hole at a foot-long sucker minnow dangling from a line. The shanty is kept totally dark. The hole in the ice for spearing is usually about three feet square. The visibility is amazing — a window on the freshwater netherworld, which, though the life doesn't compete with the multitudinous saltwater variety, is nonetheless a lot better than staying home and waiting for winter to go away. Anyway, the sucker minnow was supposed to attract the great northern pike, or Mister Big Teeth as he is known in some quarters.

When the imaginary pike drifted into our rectangle of vision for a sucker supper, the spear would be thrown at him. The spear was somewhat larger and certainly more cumbersome than the tuna harpoons used off Gloucester and Block Island. Poor pike. But only one appeared in the three days and we were caught unawares, and when Richard lunged with the spear the pike was driven against the bottom and squiggled out between the spear tines. So much for pike spearing, which is in danger of being outlawed. But it was pleasant sitting there in the dark shanty, warm with a propane stove and copious supplies of food and drink.

We would occasionally chug for perch with small minnows while we watched our decoy. In addition to the meat of the fish, perch roe lightly fried in butter is delicious. I suspect that it is healthy, too, though I have no evidence. But some I know who eat it are huge, a trifle fat and can drink fifty glasses of draft beer in an evening. It's never boring in an ice shanty. You talk idly while your head sweats and your feet freeze. There is all the husky camaraderie of the locker room. A sample:

"Do you know that girl in Suttons Bay? You know the one I mean."

"Yup."

"Well I would ___ ____ ____."

"She's built like a rain barrel."

"Pass the wine."

I would like to make an elementary contention here about expediency and sport. In this locale, winter begins in October and runs unremittingly until the end of March. My friends in warmer climes won't believe we had sixteen and a half feet of snow this year. After a while you no longer believe there's any earth left under the snow. The ground is a fib. It was still possible to fish on the part of the bay nearest Traverse City in early April. In fact, a large school of young coho salmon running between two and three pounds were discovered in the shoal water near the power plant. A healthy adult with an interest in the outdoors has to do something during these five months. The snow is almost immediately too deep for rabbit hunting — the beagles flounder on their short legs. Even an instinctively arch and lazy whiner like myself doesn't want to spend the winter looking out the window dreaming of Cozumel, Cabeza de Vaca, Belize. And you worry too much: a night when it is below zero and the wind off Lake Michigan is at forty knots and the car is buried in snow, and you count and time the weird thunks and squealings from the furnace, which inevitably breaks down. The weather seems to lose its threat when you spend time out in it, and if you're not geared temperamentally to skiing or snowmobiling, you're left with nothing to do but fish.

The true force behind ice fishing is that it is better than no fishing at all. *In extremis,* an addictive fisherman will shoot carp with a bow and arrow, set up trotlines for carp and suckers, spear dogfish on Pig Trotter Creek, chum nurse sharks within rifle range. He will surround the crudest equipment with a mystique and will maintain to the uninitiated that there's no sport quite like fishing rainbows with bobber and marshmallows.

And ice fishing has its strenuous converts. Pat told me that a year ago in April, just before the ice broke up, he was chugging out on the bay when a Coast Guard helicopter came over low and motioned him off the ice. He stayed until he got three fish and the helicopter returned. Then he noticed that the ice beneath his feet was sinking a bit. He grabbed his fish and ran and the ice for a mile around began wavering and rippling and heaving. The groans made in this situation convince one that there are prehistoric monsters under the ice trying to get out. It is chilling.

One day I drove up along the water through Pshawbetown, a small enclave of Chippewa and Ottawa Indians who are much worse for the wear. Naturally at one time they owned all the land around here. Now there is little or no running water, few indoor toilets, a ghetto shabbiness if it weren't for the fact that there is space to roam. Most of them are kept busy in the winter cutting wood for their stoves. An uninsulated shack can use an astounding amount of wood. I glassed a small cluster of fishermen about a mile out. In the tavern the night before someone anonymous (I must protect my sources) had claimed he had taken seventeen lake trout with a combined weight of over one hundred pounds in just a few hours. This is well over the legal limit, but there is simply too much ice for the game warden, Reino Narva, to cover adequately. Concern is minimal, however, as the lake trout population is approaching the vastness of earlier in the century through concerted plantings, lamprey control and stringent but perhaps unfair regulation of commercial fishing.

I cut across the peninsula to Leland, a beautiful little harbor town. People here are upset over the government's acquiring 70,000 acres of local land for a National Seashore. Of slightly less concern is Bill Carlson's attempt to regain some of the commercial fishing taken away by the Department of Natural Resources.

An additional severe irritant is the state and federal DDT regulation: Most varieties of Great Lakes fish have close to ten parts to the million, which is above the legal limit for shipping. I eat all the fish anyway because I am young and fat and reckless and love the forms of danger connected with eating. I feel sad, though, when I watch the magnificent steelhead leaping against the dam in Leland; all subtly poisoned, though expensive equipment is needed to determine that fact. They still *look* like steelhead. The breakwater is mountainously covered with ice, but still some waves break over the ice, pushed by our third gale of the season.

Bill Carlson is a fourth-generation fisherman. The nets around his shack remind me of Cape Ann. But far out beyond Cape Ann the swordfish are gobbling mercury below waves dotted, according to Heyerdahl, with eraser-sized gobbets of oil. And then above them a storm petrel or sooty shearwater or plain old herring gull wheels in ordinary gyres carrying a special freight of poison. There is a certain boredom in anger.

I was down on Good Harbor Bay when the ice was breaking up. The bay is about five miles wide and the equal of any tourist-photo bay I know of, though ungraced by Noel Coward and suchlike who go to Montego. A few days before I had walked out two miles on the ice to see Richard and his father Dick and Bruce Price. I followed Bruce's footprints as he weighs nearly 300 and I wanted to feel safe. I stepped over a two-foot-wide crack and peeked for a moment down into the dark clear water. They hadn't had any luck. And Richard was angry. He had dropped a twelve-dollar augur while spudding a hole, and there it would rest permanently a hundred feet below us.

I said that I had stepped over a crack and they said the crack hadn't been there in the morning. But there was no offshore wind that would drive the ice out toward South Manitou Island. I felt edgy and got the creeps as if Lon Chaney were under the bed, turning into a man-wolf hybrid. I nearly tiptoed back to the car, listening for any rumbles or giant sighs that would announce my death by cold water. POET DROWNS, the local paper would read. Or probably MAN DROWNS, as there is a prevalent notion in the upper Midwest that poets are invariably "dead people."

Back on shore a man was whistling hopelessly at his Labrador, who was busy sniffing around the juniper bushes that abut the shore. Dogs. I had recently apologized to a neighbor about my male Airedale Hud "covering" his own dog, but he said it was okay because his dog was a male, too. Nature! Then the Labrador came over and sniffed my leg, smelling my penned bitch Justine. He looked at me soulfully, and I quickly removed my leg to the safety of the car.

I drove to the tavern in the evening, and Richard said he had called the Traverse City Chamber of Commerce, and asked about a petition that would attempt to keep the oil freighters out of the harbor during the prime fishing months of February and March. An unnamed party suggested that the malcontents should be out looking for work. Bumpkin vigilante action has been talked about — say a string of snowmobiles in a freighter's path. Count me out. The ice fisherman is low on the economic totem ratings for logical reasons. One can equip oneself for five bucks. And ice fishermen aren't big spenders in the tourist operations. A five-dollar frozen steak is for Detroiters.

I got up at 5 a.m. to go steelhead fishing, but when I got there my rod guides kept icing up and the line wouldn't move freely. But a week before I had stood on the discouragingly thick ice and cast my fly, a mylar dace, and lost it to a floating iceberg. Oh well. Last year I had broken a rod trying to cast strongly in the bitter cold. Will real spring never come? I said to myself, echoing the poets of yore. I meditated on the difference between a fly rod and a chugging paddle, which resembles a fraternity (or sorority) paddle with no initials carved on it. Pulling a fish in hand over hand has an atavistic glee to it; the fish imparts directly to the senses his electric struggle far below. Meat on the table! The provider! The "little woman" will be right proud of her jolly indigent hubby. Pull that lunker out on the ice and cover him with snow to prevent the effects of dehydration and fish sunburn.

I wandered around the creek estuary until I tore a foot-long hole in my waders. The water pouring in was horribly cold. I walked up the shore to an empty cabin, and a thermometer on the porch read twenty-four degrees. How stupid. I built a small fire out of driftwood and warmed my foot, watching some buffleheads circle above. From out in the bay, the birds were barely visible. I could hear the tremendous cry of two mating loons. I was frankly tired of cold weather and imagined that the loons were also tired of running into icebergs, and the steelhead were tired of dozing in the cold water with their brains asleep to the spawning run.

———————————————

Now the ice is gone and the snowdrift on the hill across the road shrinks daily. I have had two fair weeks of steelhead fishing and am gathering my equipment for a trip to Key West. Fantasies of a record tarpon are rife, though as unlikely as a record starlet. I feel somewhat benign about the preposterous winter I have endured. A crocus has appeared in vulgar purple glory. I will avoid hammerheads and moray eels and rattlesnakes and other imagined dangers, and go through more winters not unlike this one, where the depleted imagination narrows to a singular point. Fish. Anywhere and almost anytime. Even when trees split open from cold and the target is a bowling-ball-sized hole in a lid of ice.

MICHAEL DELP

Michael Delp lives in Interlochen, Michigan, and is an instructor at the Interlochen Arts Academy. He fancies himself "a brook trout expert, muddler minnow afficionado, backwoods hooligan, river rat and steelhead roustabout." He believes in the sacrament of fly fishing and the healing power of branch water mixed with Jack Daniels, and one day hopes to live "in a shack on the North Branch made entirely of deadfallen cedar sweepers." He is the author of the poetry and essay book Under the Influence of Water *and, more recently,* The Coast of Nowhere: Meditations on Rivers, Lakes and Streams *(Wayne State University Press), in which this selection appears.*

Reprinted from *The Coast of Nowhere: Meditations on Rivers, Lakes and Streams*, 1997, by Michael Delp, by permission of Wayne State University Press.

FISHING THE WINTER RIVER

MICHAEL DELP

"*Fishing the winter river seems more meditative. With no intrusion from the human
world, the mind has a way of opening up, even
though the cold is knocking at the door of the
warmest parts of your interior.*"

Thirty-one degrees and wet snow. Marginal skiing weather.
Anyone with the intention of trout fishing is probably in a southern latitude, New Zealand maybe, helicopter fishing for sea-run
rainbows. Better yet, they're fishing for bonefish and permit
somewhere on a tidal flat off Exuma. Or, the lucky ones have
landed writing jobs like going bass fishing in the Congo with
Margaux Hemingway, or fishing stripers with a bevy of Victoria's
Secret models off the Nantuckett coast.

At any rate, anyone at the latitude I'm at right now with an
ounce of sense is watching some kind of exotic flyfishing on cable
TV, perhaps tiny dry flies on the Big Horn, or giant grasshoppers
in Venezuela. Me? I'm about to step into the Au Sable River, fully
layered and outfitted, protected by several skins of cotton,
Synchilla and neoprene. My first thought at the car when I open
the door and the cold air hits me is just the same as yours: This is
madness.

And it is. There are no tracks down to the river. Not any
human tracks, anyway. The woods have that stillness they hold
all winter: In this relatively warm winter, air sound is muffled
enough so that when you speak a word, perhaps your own name,
it hangs only inches from your mouth, then dies quickly. In colder weather I have heard traffic from M-72, three miles away,
sounding as if it were on top of me.

My second thought isn't of the weighted nymphs I'll use or how heavy a tippet to use for a perfect dead drift. I think of June. Late June and this same stretch of water alive with Brown Drakes. I've fished where I'm standing so many times I know I could fish it blind. I fished a score of Sunday mornings up under the sweeping arms of cedars, streamers before dawn. I aimed for the dark pools, the browns looking for one more brook trout before the sun cracked the tree line. And one particular day in mid-August, when it was almost a hundred degrees and no air, I left a friend's cabin, sweating profusely in the twenty steps down to the river, then cast lackadaisically to no fish until I put a grasshopper up under a hanging cedar, dropping it just at the mouth of a small feeder creek. What followed was fifteen minutes of thrashing around in the heat with an eighteen-inch rainbow. Dead luck. Dead hot.

But today, of course, I feel the cold even in my teeth. I feel like something dressed not for this world but for a Martian night, moving stiffly like a kid bundled up for an hour of snowman making. At the end of my line, the nymph hangs from the slightest tippet, almost unworldly in this world of absolute clarity. The river is as clear as ... well ... as ice. And I imagine to myself that this isn't water I am fishing but some form of liquid ice, or the inside of a child's Christmas snow scene. I'm in the crystal ball and the snow is falling like feathers.

Perhaps because of the way the light slants this time of year, or perhaps because of the particular pensive slant of my imagination, I drift between the literal world of the river in front of me and the other world of the river I have in my head. On the winter river, as I see it today, everything looks clearer, somehow close. I remind myself that what I'm walking on is really the till of the glacier. An odd thought that I'm fishing in the belly wash of the last gasp of the Ice Age.

I remind myself, looking up toward the white ridge along the river, that the rocks at my feet slipped slowly out of the glacier and may not have moved far for the last ten thousand years. I slow my pace and lift a few pebbles from the bottom, knowing that sometime in the dead cold of February I'll take them out, lay them on the desk and sort and re-sort, put them in my mouth and taste: glacier, hint of iron. I'll roll them in my fingers like dice, let them fall again and again, reading the pattern, looking for an omen, a prophecy, reading them like braille.

With the stones absorbing body heat in my pocket, I cast a summer cast, or a late fall cast, thinking again of the time I floated through here in a riverboat with the lightning dancing overhead, and suddenly I remember to slow down. December fishing rhythm is slower, steadier, more measured, a way of keeping yourself warm as well as a method of delivering a fly. Fishing the winter river seems more meditative. With no intrusion from the human world, the mind has a way of opening up, even though the cold is knocking at the door of the warmest parts of your interior. So, meditative and cold, as if I were in some Japanese print, I move slowly, like the ice moves downriver.

The water I'm moving through is as haunted as any I know. For over twenty years I've left parts of myself here, first as a resident and now as a visitor. In fact, just downstream there's a stump I call the quarter hole. Once in a moment of absolute boredom when a Hendrickson hatch didn't happen I slipped a quarter into the deeply decayed structure of an old cedar. Now, I do it every time I pass through, the quarters giving off a soft glint, a silver matte patina etched by the daily abuse of the weather.

Back in the real world, the snow makes the river clearer in my head, the water mirroring a gray sky. I think of the river, the sky, the other river I carry inside me and tend carefully in my imagination: a dream river where all loss and despair disappear, a dream river where all the rivers of my life merge into one, while back on this river everything seems to have gone into this perfect grayness, and I become lost in the gray of the river. If I could, I would trade my life, right here, right now, for a life on the river, let myself dissolve out into the snow I see up ahead as the river literally vanishes downstream.

"Where'd he go?" someone might ask at the bar.

"Just disappeared once."

Into the cold. Into the gray. Into the dream river.

So I move slowly downstream, half imagining, half dreaming the nymph at the bottom of pools, suspended like something frozen in ice. I think of its tiny humped body washing in currents I can't see, the wing case only slightly bulging, if at all. And then I think of the magnitude of fishing: this river, all this water and a single dark nymph swimming across the pool in front of me. And I think of the fish, just beginning to settle into a winter of slower metabolism, their tiny brains hazing over with the onset of

months and months of snow, wind and sleet, the constant freeze
and the occasional thaw, the sun mostly a thin, ghostly disc in the
sky. It's the fish I think of late at night all winter, how they hover,
barely moving for hours, pacing themselves, their bodies rippling
against the slow crush of icy water.

Right now, getting colder, I mull over my casting options as I
stand above a pool where, in July, I catch fish on the surface.
Instead, I know they're deep, sulking, turning slowly every so
often to take a winter nymph. If you were down there with them,
watching their eyes, their fins, you would know that they move
ever so slowly, economizing, hunkered down in the dark
December water, almost oblivious to any form of casting. The list
of procedures is short: a cast back upstream for a dead-drift, the
Crosfield pull or the Liesenring-Lift technique, none of which I
am even remotely familiar with on the loose from the study and
the books, adrift here in the gray dream. I opt for a fourth move:
the swimming nymph swing, though I doubt anything, fish or
nymph, is capable of swimming in this weather.

I cast and drift, cast and drift, letting the dark nymph swim
ever so slowly, wading past places I knew, places I know are more
important to me than my own backyard. Just below Pine Road I
head into the stretch of water where I used to spend almost every
summer night. I smell the winter river now, the fresh scent of
snow, the odor of cedar and iron and swamp gas. And I smell, as
I did three springs ago, the acrid smell of fire. Up the bank I can
still see the blackened trunks of trees, the swaths left by the rage
of forest fire. For an instant, wading between the charred banks,
I think I see the ghost dogs of friends, killed by smoke and flames,
rise up out of the snow, their bodies whole, black again. I want
them to leap into the river, but they drift over me and land on the
other charred shore.

I stop fishing, try to start again, work and fight with the idea
of the dogs coming back to life in my head, and then feel my
heart sink, cold and heavy. I give in and then head for the car.
Walking back along the high bank past the water I had just
fished, I realize that I had come up empty. No strikes. No fish.
Nothing but chapped hands, throbbing knees, the cold deep
inside me now. Somehow that was the way it was supposed to
be: destined when I left Interlochen, the leather book of weighted nymphs in the warmth of a fishing vest, my head awash with

the smell of my wife's skin, the warm touch of a daughter's good-bye kiss, and the humid, wondrous odor of my golden retriever. The warmth of home.

I remind myself of the great joy of fishing, even in the cold, even when your hands freeze around the butt of a rod and you have to suck on the line guides to free them up, the small dots of ice drifting in your mouth, almost like small nymphs of pure ice. Suddenly, I am struck by opposing forces of desire: I want to go home and I want to stay on the river. I want to hole up and build a small fire, warm my hands and face enough to want to get back into the water. In the last light of a perfect December afternoon, I want to slip back into the river, fish just one more bend. I want to feel the slight touch of a delicate trout mouth, its jaws turning a nymph over and over. And then I want to disappear, live like a dog along the river so that I can come home and say that I have given myself over to the water, to the elements, that I have rolled the stones and come up feral and, above all, that I have wintered over.

From somewhere above me I want the ghosts of the fire dogs to come back, their coats black and glistening in the healing water of the river. I want them to slide up to me in the current and make them whole again. I want the jackpine to turn green and I want to look down the river once more and see the iris beds in full bloom, the damselflies moving like small, dark clouds. I want to walk back to the warm smells of my house after wintering on this river, my face scarred and lined by snowstorms, the nymphs still warm in their sheepskin cases, my life coming back after being lost in months of gray to warm my bones.

BOB BUTZ

Bob Butz lives in Traverse City, Michigan, with his wife Nancy and Harper, a black Labrador retriever. He hunts with a longbow and prefers hardwood arrow shafts over cedar. A native of Pennsylvania, he is now on the editorial staff at The Retreiver Journal *and* The Pointing Dog Journal. *He guns for woodcock and grouse with a side-by-side, hunts diver ducks from a layout boat in November, and fly fishes for steelhead and salmon with bright green and yellow streamers of his own design. He is working on a collection of bowhunting essays and stories, of which the accompanying selection is a part. He has written short stories and poems, and his writing on fly fishing, wingshooting and bowhunting has appeared in numerous publications.*

🍃

FOLLOWING THE FOX

BOB BUTZ

"That feeling was coming over me again, so much that when I crested the hill I fully expected to see the fox standing there. And so he was, crouched on the wall and staring at something way out over the valley."

Maybe you never had this feeling before — a feeling that told you something wonderful was about to happen. For me, it's a subtle tingling, pinprick kind of thing inside my head at the base of my skull. Call it instinct or intuition, the truth is that most of the time when I have this sensation it turns out to be nothing. But once in a while something out of the ordinary happens, enough so that, although I haven't learned to really trust this thing, I've at least learned to respect it and give it a chance.

I had that feeling this morning when I came upon those fox tracks there along the fencerow in the snow. They were red fox tracks, which you could tell simply by the size of them, perfect little ovals with edges so clean and sharp that you would swear they would lay your finger open if you reached down and touched them.

The tracks followed the fence across the field to the hillside where the Christmas trees were planted in neat little rows. It was a place I intended to go all along, as it was just about the best place in the world to sneak up on deer when the weather turned cold.

But I picked up and followed the fox tracks, and in following the fox I felt a sudden rush of knowing, as if I was being propelled along by feeling. I could almost see the fox moving along the fence line, nosing the wind every once in a while, and checking back over his shoulder before disappearing into the trees.

The fox had probably come here during the early morning to hunt for the rabbits and mice that lived in and around the boughs of the pine and spruce trees. No doubt he would stay, too, after having found a nice quiet place out of the wind to lounge away the afternoon.

I had seen fox in this cover before, once this year while stalking deer. And so I had an idea where this one would go: up, up to the top of the hill, where the land was cut by an old stone wall. I had missed a big red fox here the year before. He was curled up on the top of the long wall, his bushy tail swept over his nose. My arrow clattered and splintered on the rocks below him, and just like that he was gone, just as quietly and quickly as if he had never been there.

I found some strange comfort in telling myself this could very well be the same fox — that big, orange male with the long black legs and too much white on his tail. And, in fact, the tracks I was following told me this fox was a male, for three paw prints and a yellow stain marked the snow at the head of the wall. The smell there was heavy and sweet. I breathed it once, twice, then slipped an arrow from my quiver and fixed it on the string.

There were those low, stubby Christmas trees on either side of the wall, and the snow there was different from what was down below. It was packed hard, so hard that the fox's feet no longer marked it. I lost the tracks there, but kept walking and found farther on where the fox had dug into the snow for something — surely a mouse, I thought, as there was a bit of gray fur lying there and tiny drops of blood frozen into crimson beads of ice that melted on my finger when I touched them.

Down in a shallow depression in the field, I cut the tracks again. They were in the snow on the leeward side of the wall and later up on top of the wall itself. That feeling was coming over me again, so much that when I crested the hill I fully expected to see the fox standing there. And so he was, crouched on the wall and staring at something way out over the valley.

He was a brilliant, warm color of orange, a splash of fire on the snow. And perhaps I focused too much on killing him as I think now that the same instinct that led me here had washed over him, too. For a moment I looked hard at the fur on his shoulder where the wind bristled it ever so slightly. The string leapt from my fingers and the fox without looking from his perch on the wall. And in a flash of color and light he was off through the trees and snow, vanished in the valley below.

The only sounds for some time after were the wind and the lonely, hollow cawing of a crow. Both of these hung in the air, like some strange language that I stood there listening to, trying very hard to understand.

RON RAU

Ron Rau, a resident of Stanwood, Michigan, developed his love for the outdoors during summer visits to his parents' cabin on Sage Lake in Ogemaw County, about a hundred miles north of Flint. His 1983 book, Sage Lake Road, *was based on his experiences there and included the accompanying story.* Sage Lake Road *was listed by* Esquire *magazine as one of the finest outdoor books of all time. Ron's stories have appeared in* Sports Illustrated, National Wildlife, Gray's Sporting Journal *and other magazines. He remains an avid hunter and fisherman and has spent several summers commercial fishing off Alaska.*

●

SAGE LAKE AND TIME PASSING

RON RAU

"It would be difficult to say which has had the greater impact on the northern Michigan woodlands — the snowmobile or the television set. The boys, my son and my nephew, are enraptured by both. I spend a great deal of time each winter trying to separate them from the evils of what I call snomovision."

Look. At the far end of the lake. There are people at the Bluegill Hole. Some are standing, some are sitting, some walking around, but they all seem tiny and remote on the expanse of the ice-covered lake. I wonder if the fish are biting, if there are dozens of hand-sized bluegills scattered on the ice around the fishing holes.

Already there are two shanties on the young ice. Look closer and you can see a fire burning on the lake. Kids probably. One of them is running toward the First Island for more fuel. An adult wouldn't run like that. Not on *this* ice.

Moving into the wind on the snowmobile peels my eyelids back and makes my eyes water. I look sideways at the Third Island as we pass it. The trees are bare, the land is brown and bare and frozen and ready for the snow cover. The snow is late this year, but the lake has frozen over. Three crisp, clear, starlit nights have covered the lake with two to three inches of ice.

Good thing, too, because the boys will be up to the lake in three days. Not having snow for the Christmas holidays is bad enough, but if there were no ice on the lake …

"Three inches of ice holds a team of horses," my father still says whenever it reaches that thickness. Then it is safe for the horsepower and weight of a snowmobile. My father can remember when horses hauled blocks of ice, cut from the lake by men with a crosscut saw. Insulated under a blanket of straw, the ice kept until summer and went into cottage iceboxes. That was, of course, before electricity came to the lake. It would be grand to see horses hauling ice sleds across the lake again, but not today. Without the snow cover, the surface is glare ice, smooth and slippery, dangerous even for two-legged primates.

Our snowmobile (we are riding double) fishtails and threatens to spin out, so my father backs off the throttle. Still, we make it to the Bluegill Hole in about four-and-a-half minutes. I've timed it. Approaching the Second Island, I look down through the glasslike ice and the green weedbed and light brown sand passing beneath us. It is wonderful to be around lakes when they first freeze over. There are now more than twenty cabins on this island, one occupied year-round. When our family first came to Sage Lake, nearly thirty years ago, there were only two shacks on the island. When my father first found the lake, nearly fifty years ago, there were none.

I remember the two shacks. Now the twenty or so A-frame, H-frame, duplex, triplex, uniplex ranch-style, suburb-style homes on the island, all with television antennas, offend me. They have made me old before my time. They cause me to say things to the boys like, "Before those cabins were there … "

I sometimes have a hard time keeping pace with Heraclitus. He seems to be on a roll these days.

Between the Second and First islands, the aquatic vegetation passes quickly below us. I can imagine that we are standing still and the lake bottom is moving. Soon this becomes confusing. I like the glare ice. Snow will come soon enough. It always does in northern Michigan, count on it. The dense green weedbed is suddenly yanked from beneath us and we are sliding over a clear, watery grayness — the drop-off. The word still retains a sense of childhood danger from swimming, as in, "Don't you dare go near the drop-off." It is right there with the word "cramps." And polio.

We stop a hundred yards from the Bluegill Hole and the small crowd of people. This is an act of courtesy on our part so as not to frighten the fish, and also an act of antisocial behavior, because we would rather find fish away from the crowd. There are more people than it seemed from a distance, but that isn't unexpected. It's the week between Christmas and New Year's, the week of "first ice," and a frozen lake has this magnetic pull.

My father takes the ice spud and walks toward the island. He turns right, backs up, looks at the trees, walks forward again a few paces, and stops. "Right here," he says, jabbing the steel blade into the ice. Sharp slivers explode on impact and skid, tinkling, across the smooth surface. The air is clean and odorless, a reflective complement of the new ice.

"Out a little farther," I say, uncertain of our lineups — the birch tree on the island against the yellow house on the opposite shore as far out as the point of land to the south.

"Nah, right here," he says. And he spuds the ice, littering its smoothness with wet chips.

I look at the crowd of people. The fishermen are congregated in the area the size of a large city lot. They are above the Bluegill Hole, but it seems to me they are a bit too near the cove. I watch them for activity — pulling in lines, baiting hooks, changing fishing holes, the quick jerk of a missed strike. Most of the fishermen are hunkered over the holes, sitting on a wide range of things that pass for stools — buckets, sleds, snowmobiles, folding chairs, homemade tackle boxes with ice runners. I am looking for a large old man wearing a plaid red and black mackinaw.

We just call him the Old Man. I think his name is Carl something. He lives a mile from the lake, alone, and is, by common admission, the best fisherman the lake knows, winter or summer. He spits tobacco juice on the ice around his fishing holes, a dead giveaway. He also leaves the hulls of goldenrod stems, gathered locally, from which he has extracted the small, lemon-yellow larvae with coal-black heads. It is good, cheap bait, pleasant to gather; however, it is soft. From the tobacco juice and goldenrod hulls, you can tell which holes he has been fishing. Find one, walk about ten paces east, and you'll find the frozen remains of small bluegills and perch. Like many people in the area, he believes it isn't good to have so many small bluegills in Sage Lake. They all become "stunted." Maybe they're right, but the lake has a healthy proportion of large bluegill. I return my small bluegills to the lake but I leave the nuisance perch on the ice because I am convinced there are too many of these.

Away from the others, though not very far, I see the heavy mackinaw. And the round head covered by the shiny leather of a World War II U.S. Army Air Force cap. The earflaps are always up. His ears are always red, like two large tomato slices. The old man has made it through another summer, an extremely hot one. I'm glad.

I haven't spoken more than a couple hundred words to him in nearly thirty years, although I see him on the ice three or four times each winter. He doesn't speak to anybody for very long. Once, when I was about twelve, I asked if he was having any luck. "I don't call fishing luck, boy," was the answer. Two years later I asked if they were biting. "So-so," he said. Mostly we just nod at each other or maybe raise a hand. I wonder if my hair might not be too long.

Sometimes we find them away from the Bluegill Hole, but only in two or three places, and those within a hundred yards of the crowd. In summer there are very few places where you can drop a line and not catch bluegill, but in winter they are all at the south end. I know. I have spent hours, days, looking elsewhere on the lake for a secret Bluegill Hole. My father has just about given up the search, conceding that "they just go south for the winter." It is one of the great winter mysteries of the lake and I spend time trying to solve it. One day, in thin young ice, I chopped fifty well-scattered holes and found only miniature perch. I hurried down to the Bluegill Hole that evening in the waning light in time to catch a nice mess of 'gills. I had the place to myself then, but that wasn't the point.

My father has his line in the water and is watching the cork bobber. He lifts the bobber from the water, jiggles it, and drops it into the water again. It rests motionless for a moment and then dips suddenly. He sets the hook and brails in about twenty feet of nearly invisible monofilament line, until a squirming three-inch perch slithers from the hole. He removes his gloves, works the tiny hook free and tosses the fish aside. The perch skitters across the ice, flops briefly, straightens out and is quickly welded to the smooth lake surface as fish wetness turns to glazed ice. With difficulty, because the line is so hard to see and gets caught on ice chips, he works the line back into the hole and mutters something about too many little perch in the lake. The bobber no sooner touches the water than he has another perch. Two or three more of these, without a bluegill, will have him digging another hole.

I walk away with the spud and chop a hole of my own. I love that ice spud. My father made it himself out of a four-foot section of galvanized pipe that he welded to a wedge of hardened steel.

He did this at the Buick Motor Division down in Flint where, unknown to them, General Motors has produced a lot of ice fishing spuds along with automobiles.

I wonder if you can even buy an ice spud anymore. They have been nearly replaced by large augers, which look like giant powered corkscrews. They cut a perfectly round hole, as though someone had heated up a metal dish with a welding torch and then set it on the ice. The first augers were hand-operated and then, of course, someone rigged up a two-cycle motor.

The power augers are one of the new noises on the lake in wintertime. From a distance they sound like chain saws, another relatively new winter noise. Everyone in the north country now owns a chain saw. And a snowmobile or six.

I wonder what the Old Man thinks of all this new stuff out on the ice. I know what I think of it. Mostly, I don't like it, even if we did cross the lake in under five minutes. A half-hour walk would have been fine with me, but it would have offended my father, who relishes the fact that we are transported so quickly. I am the anomaly, resisting change. He is, after all, the one who remembers the horses.

We fish away from the crowd and find only small perch. We move closer, infiltrating the crowd, and see a few bluegill scattered on the ice. We fish, unsuccessfully, until sunset, then pick up our gear, load it onto the snowmobile and race home across red-streaked ice. I'm still wondering about all this new stuff out on the ice. And at home. We will, thanks to the snowmobile, arrive in time for the six o'clock news. Television is sort of new to the lake, too.

The boys, my son and my nephew, are enraptured by both. I spend a great deal of time each winter trying to separate them from the evils of what I call snomovision. It is the posture associated with these activities that I object to. Both are done sitting down.

It would be difficult to say which has had the greater impact on the northern Michigan woodlands — the snowmobile or the television set. They appeared very nearly at the same time. WNEM-TV of Saginaw was the first to penetrate the Lake Huron side of the state after erecting a 1,060-foot tower in 1956. Earlier, WPBN-TV of Traverse City and WWTV of Cadillac had started beaming signals into the woods on the Lake Michigan side. Full network viewing came with the addition of a station in Alpena and Cheboygan, creating a solid belt of mindless distraction across the northwoods. And the migration began. Not only did people go north for winter holidays, many decided to retire north as well. Businesses that normally closed for the winter months found it profitable to remain open. The influx of population created a winter economy where before there had been none. To the omniscient observer, it might seem that television had replaced religion as the opiate of the people.

The impact of snomovision at the Bluegill Hole soon became apparent. Instead of ten or twelve men and boys in wool mackinaws and hunting pants, there were twenty-five or thirty people, half of them wearing shiny nylon, multiemblemed, space-age snowmobile outfits. Water sloshed in the fishing holes with the passing of every snowmobile "safari." Oldtimers, eager for a new excuse, claimed that this spooked the fish, and cast disgruntled looks at the "weekenders."

"Water skiers in summer and these people in the winter. They're probably the same people."

"They can mess with our fun, but we can't bother theirs."

"I wish they had a Rose Bowl every day. Ever notice how quiet it is out here New Year's Day?"

Still, we catch our bluegills. They are greedy and numerous and tasty, and I notice how the Old Man doesn't even look up at the passing of a group of snowmobilers. He's busy baiting his hook or watching the bobber intently for another strike. Always jiggling, always teasing the fish.

My grandmother claimed until her dying day that the very first Sputnik altered forever the Michigan winter. With all respect to grandmother, it may not have been Sputnik itself but the technology boom it spawned, which in time produced an arsenal of anti-winter weaponry that only makes a Michigan winter *seem* easier. Space-age fibers, for example, used in the insulation of both people and homes.

At any rate, a northern Michigan winter is much less formidable than those I spent in the pre-Sputnik, pre-expressway, pre-snowmobile days. Certainly there is more to do indoors than there used to be. Especially for kids. For electronic entertainment, we as kids had a small table radio; we had to hold a hand on it to make it come in loud enough so that everyone in the room could hear.

These days, in the northwoods, the kids who come up for a holiday have a full complement of Saturday morning TV cartoons to entertain them. The Bluegill Hole, which is where I want to take the boys, simply is no match for the Road Runner or Pink Panther or the variety of monsters and super-people they are into. And then there is Fran Tarkenton (of all people) in a commercial inserted slyly between monsters and cartoons, urging them to play electronic football when the cartoons are over. They can sit in a chair and play football with their thumbs.

To the boys, having a good time at the lake is watching TV and riding the snowmobile. Like any well-meaning, confused adult, I am welded into the past and know what is best for them.

We have rules. One concerns electronic football. I've imposed a daylight curfew on that activity. One morning just after Christmas I heard them *beep-beeping* and arguing in a back bedroom. I burst in like an angry Vince Lombardi.

"All right, you guys. I caught you. You know that rule. You can play that game at night but not during the day."

"Well, what are we supposed to do?" Just the question you want to hear three days after Christmas.

"Let's go ice fishing," I said.

"We went yesterday. They're not biting. All we catch are those stupid little perch."

"Maybe today the bluegills are biting," I suggested.

"Why don't you go out and find them and then come back and get us?" Jake said.

I wisely abstained from a long and hopeless lecture on "earning" the fish.

"OK," I said. "No fishing. But let's go outside and do something."

"What?"

"You guys think of something."

"SNOWMOBILING!" they shouted.

For the tenth time I explained that Grandpa thought the glare ice was too hard on the snowmobile runners and didn't want to run the machines — except to the Bluegill Hole, of course — until we got snow. Despite the obvious bribe, the Bluegill Hole still didn't appeal to them.

"Think of something else," I said.

They couldn't, and neither could I. The big problem was the unexpected lack of snow for Christmas.

"OK. Look," I said finally. "Let's just get the soccer ball and kick it around on the bare ice."

And like three modern-day Abner Doubledays, we invented the game of hoccer. Or sockey. All you need is a frozen lake, a soccer ball and four old automobile tires that served as boat bumpers in the summer.

You put two tires at either end as goals, however long you want the playing field to be, and go from there. The rules sort of develop by themselves. But you have to have hard, smooth glare ice to really appreciate the game. Snow on ice slows and stabilizes the game too much. Playing on glare ice is not unlike climbing a playground slide wearing roller skates. You take four steps before you begin to move. Usually backwards.

It was Jake and Darren on one side and Walter Mitty on the other. Mitty, for the first hour or so, was, ahem, outstanding. He used both cunning and style to lure the kids out of position and then boomed fifty-foot kicks between the tire goal posts. He developed a shot — you had to watch closely for the opportunity — through the tiniest of openings between the two defenders. Because of the slipperiness, you could attempt this shot twenty feet away from the defenders and watch gleefully as they helplessly tried to scramble toward the ball on the icy surface. The best way to block a shot was to go all out in the classic goalie maneuver, throwing a leg out and sliding across the ice on your bottom. Mitty won the first two games easily, 10-2 and 10-4.

Then the kids discovered teamwork. They learned to approach my goal from either side, luring me out of position, and then actually *passing* the ball to each other. Still, I won the third game, 10-6. They were getting stronger and wiser, and I was getting tired, but I discovered a sneaky method of getting a much-needed timeout. I deliberately kicked the ball hard and wide of the goal and watched it skitter a few hundred feet along the lake shore, one of the kids in hot pursuit. I then collapsed across the tires and caught my breath. Refreshed, I pulled out the last game, a 10-9 cliffhanger.

I went to bed early that night, exhausted but doubly victorious. Not only had I beaten the boys four games to none, but I had also thoroughly beaten snomovision for one day. The kids had spent most of the day outside on the lake, as they should have.

The next morning I was awakened early and abruptly by two fired-up ex-snomovision fanatics.

"Come on. Get up, dad."

"Yeah, get up, Uncle Ronnie. We want to play hoccer."

"Sockey."

"No, it's hoccer."

"Sockey."

"Hoccer."

"It's sockey, isn't it, dad?"

"Mmmmmmmm. Why don't you guys go watch television."

But I got up, and the entire day, with a couple of hours off for lunch, we spent playing on the frozen lake. The boys began beating me, but the games were all close. We played until darkness again. Once more I had beaten snomovision, but the price was high. I limped off to bed shortly after the evening news.

"Dad, it snowed."

That was my wake-up call the next morning. The words were pudding to my ears. Sockey or hoccer or whatever it was, was finished.

Like first ice, there is something special about the first serious snowfall of the season. It is both an ending and a beginning. The lawn, that same thick lawn which under the summer sun is a haven for crickets, ants, earthworms, fireflies, frogs, grasshoppers, gophers and mosquitoes — the summer lawn vibrant and alive with thousands of crawly things — is now a frozen white sterile desert. Something indeed has ended. But the whiteness and cleanness of the new snow, untracked and unsoiled, a soft white inviting carpet returned like an old friend, says to children and some adults, too: Dress warmly and come play. A fresh snow, seen through the windows of a warm house, transmits excitement into that house. Something new is afoot.

The kids were dressed early and outside waiting for grandpa and, yes, the first bona fide snowmobile ride of the winter. Even grandpa hurried through breakfast. The snowmobile fired up noisily, almost obscenely, warming and waking up like a metallic yellow and black bear roused from its den, smoking, fuming, sputtering, but soon running smoothly. Even then, we had to shout over it to be heard.

I have never looked at a snowmobile through the eyes of a child, and perhaps this explains my antagonism. They are alien to my childhood memories of the lake, and therefore distasteful. To the boys, reared in this space age, a snowmobile is as natural as snow. They hopped on behind my father, and the machine, growling and popping, took them down the short incline to the lake and across it faster than any team of horses. I listened until they were out of earshot. Then the sounds of other machines succeeded theirs, and I was left standing in the soft morning snow, the gentle flakes still coming down, the wind very still, but morning calmness obliterated by the hornets' nest out on the lake. Nobody ever wrote, "I hear those snowmobiles go jing-jing-jing-a-ling on ... " Before going inside for coffee and the morning Detroit Free Press, I counted sixteen machines on the lake.

The boys' ride lasted until lunchtime, almost three hours. They returned exhilarated, their cheeks rosy with winter health, telling of races with other machines, of jumping a small hill many times, of climbing a very large and steep hill and almost "spinning out" near the top. They made snowmobile noises to emphasize their stories. They were wound up with unspent energy — they had, after all, been sitting on their butts for three hours.

Snomovision had won Round 1 for the day. But I thought I could win Round 2 for the good ol' days.

"I've got an idea," I said.

"What?" said one.

"What?" said the other.

"What what what?" I mocked them.

"What what what what what?" They were jumping up and down now.

"It's a game we used to play called Track 'Em Up," I said.

"How do you play?"

"Well, we have just what we need, a fresh snow. All we do is go over to one of the islands. I start running and you guys count to a hundred and then you try to track me in the snow. All you have to do is see me."

It sounded good to them, though I did have to include a snowmobile ride to the island as a bribe. And I knew what was in their minds. After humoring me through my silly game, they would try to get me to take them for another marathon ride.

We covered what should have been a five-minute walk in about fifteen seconds. I shut the thing off. They began counting and I ran off into the woods. They were up to fifty before I was gone from sight.

The Third Island, just across the lake from my folks' place, is uninhabited. There are the remains of one cabin, once occupied by an eccentric artist from Detroit. I ran directly to it and saw by tracks in the snow that a group of snowmobilers had already visited. With a stick I wrote THIS WAY in the snow and drew a long arrow after it so the boys wouldn't be confused by the other tracks.

I jogged for five minutes around the periphery of the island, nearly back to the snowmobile, and then cut inland, crossing my earlier tracks and those of the boys. I was now tracking them, as they tracked me. They would need to come completely around before discovering this and I could spy on them from behind.

Eventually, I got close enough to hear them congratulate themselves for deciphering a maneuver in which I had backtracked and then leaped to one side, down an embankment. I was also within hearing when they came across the meeting of our trails.

"Hey! He's following us." Excitement, anticipation. Snomovision was on the ropes, bleeding from the nose. Jake figured it out.

"You follow the tracks back the way we came and I'll follow them this way," he said to Darren.

They had me. With the leaves and foliage gone, the island was too small to hide on for long. I surrendered.

"Hey, that was fun," said Darren. "Let's do it again."

"OK," I said. "But we'll have to go to another island. This one is all tracked up."

"Yippee! Another snowmobile ride."

"Yahoo!"

We noised to the near end of the First Island in about three-and-a-half minutes. I already had a plan.

"This time count to two hundred," I said.

The First Island is the largest and has virgin pine on it creating a thick canopy overhead. There was only a dusting of snow on the ground, on the brown needles, just enough so that the boys would have trouble tracking me. I jogged the length of the island, occasionally running on bare ground to confuse them and slow them down. I needed a little time for this maneuver.

I ran close to the trunk of the huge pine I had in mind, ran off the edge of the island into the brown bulrushes along the lake, and stopped. A hundred yards away, out on the lake, was the Bluegill Hole with eight or ten fishermen bent over their fishing holes. Predictable as a park statue, the Old Man was there.

Stepping backward, I retraced my steps so that it appeared I had run into the bulrushes and suddenly disappeared. I backtracked to the pine and hoisted myself off the ground into the lower, thick-limbed branches above me, branches whorled like wagon spokes, one for each year. I began climbing the large branches of the early 1900s.

The lower branches were sturdy and even-spaced and I climbed easily through the teens and into the 1920s, a time when Ernest Hemingway fished and hunted in northern Michigan. Then into the 1930s when my father first came to Sage Lake and rented a cabin with kerosene lanterns because electricity was still miles away. I climbed through the 1940s up into the '50s, when I first saw the lake. The climbing grew harder and more uncertain but I made it into the '60s, the era of snomovision, and stopped well before the '70s, the era my son and nephew know. Beyond, the branches were small, thick and treacherous, and I could go no higher. The view from that height was both exhilarating and depressing. There were now so many cabins around the lake.

The boys were closing in on me. I could hear them coming through the woods, breaking branches and quizzing each other as to where I would be. In a few years, the lake would be theirs to use as they wished.

🍃

Also from
The Cabin Bookshelf

*These fine books are available
at your favorite bookstore.*

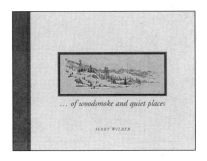

... of Woodsmoke
and Quiet Places

J E R R Y   W I L B E R

Jerry Wilber presents a full year's worth of daily
reflections on the outdoors, and on life in the
mythical North Country town of Lost Lake.
Wilber's insights amuse and inspire, and along the
way provide hints on how to be a better hunter,
citizen, angler, camper, canoeist, cook, parent,
spouse, friend.

Notes From Little Lakes

MEL ELLIS

Mel Ellis describes how he and his wife and their five daughters (The Rebels) turned a tract of pasture-land into a haven for trees, flowers and wildlife. In the lore of nature and the environment, Little Lakes is as familiar and as important as Aldo Leopold's Sand County.

The Land, Always the Land

MEL ELLIS

Never have the sights, sounds and moods of the seasons been captured more vividly than in this collection of Mel Ellis' writings. Ellis leads us through the year, month by month, drawing us into a world we often miss amid the swirl of daily life. After reading this book, you will see the world anew on your trips to the countryside and in your daily travels across town.